THE NEW UNTOUCHABLES

How America Sanctions Police Violence

John DeSantis

The Noble Press, Inc.

CHICAGO

Printed in the United States of America

Library of Congress Cataloguing-in-Publication Data

DeSantis, John.
    The New Untouchables : how America sanctions police violence/
John DeSantis.
        p.   cm.
    Includes bibliographical references and index.
    ISBN 1-879360-31-4 : $22.95
    1. Police—United States—Complaints against—Case studies.
    2. Civil rights—United States—Case studies.   I. Title.
363.2'3'0973—dc20   94-18643
                                                          CIP

Noble Press books are available in bulk at discount prices.
Single copies are available prepaid direct from the publisher.

The Noble Press, Inc.
213 W. Institute Place, Suite 508
Chicago, Illinois 60610
(312) 642-1168

*For my beloved niece, Jacqueline Elizabeth Bottie, in hopes that
she might have a better world to grow up in.*

CONTENTS

ACKNOWLEDGMENTS

Many individuals and organizations have contributed to this work directly or indirectly, in the way of assistance, cooperation, data, encouragement, and support in various combinations. However, I wish to make it clear that my acknowledgment of such a contribution, or inclusion of material from any specific organization, in no way indicates that the individual or organization concerned shares any or all of the views expressed in this book.

Research drawn from the resources of the Police Executive Research Forum, the International Association of Chiefs of Police, the Medgar Evers Center for Law and Social Justice, the National Association for the Advancement of Colored People, and the National Institutes for Justice was instrumental to some chapters.

Attorneys Colin Moore and Santo Alessi, Julia Bryant at John Jay College of Criminal Justice, and Christie Hicks of the Graduate School and University Center of the City University of New York provided invaluable assistance, as did Sgt. Barry Fletcher of the New Orleans Police Department and the entire staff of the office of the Deputy Commissioner of Public Information, New York City Police Department. Special thanks are also due to Dr. Michael Baden of the New York State Police; Ellen Borakove of the office of Chief Medical Examiner of the

City of New York; Dr. Kalil Jiraki of the Wayne County, Michigan Medical Examiner's office; Lt. Thomas Sbordone and Det. Sonia Burgos of the New York City Housing Authority Police Department; the staff of the House of Representatives Committee on the Judiciary; the United States Department of Justice; the New York State Office of Criminal Justice Services; and Norman Siegel, Executive Director of the New York Civil Liberties Union.

By permitting me to continue my free-lance work as a reporter in New York City, Skip Martin, the New York bureau chief of United Press International, allowed me to be in the places I needed to be in order to cover breaking news as it related to this book. Some of my colleagues—by their example, sharing of views, and thorough but fair criticism—have also been of help, especially Eric Shawn of WNYW-TV.

The New York State Commission on Criminal Justice and the Use of Force, although disbanded, left as its legacy a thorough study of the police brutality problem that I drew upon heavily for some chapters. Jerome Skolnick and James Fyfe are the authors of *Above The Law*, which provided excellent background material that I used in the latter stages of this book's development.

There are personal thanks owed to a number of people, including Curtis Hollis, William Glasser, Charles Loetzerich, Lisa Shawn, David Schwartz, John Henry Delventhal, and Constantine Gavalas, for reasons known well to all of them. Larry and Gil Beinhart in Woodstock, Dick Gardner of WKNY in Kingston, and Jerry Gross of Gross Associates have been especially supportive of my efforts.

For those cases that I did not personally cover, I relied on accounts published in the *New York Times* and other newspapers and magazines. Some historic background information was gleaned from the New York City Police Museum and the *World Book Encyclopedia*.

Gratitude is owed to the many police officers I interviewed, or who permitted me to observe their work first-hand, including Lt. Ralph Pascullo of the New York City Housing Authority Police Rescue Unit.

Finally, thanks are due to my agent, Mrs. Bobbe Siegel, who has provided a steady guiding hand to my career. Douglas Seibold, my editor at Noble Press, has great patience; he served to flag my spirits when they needed it most and must be commended for his vision for this project, thus allowing it to see the light of day.

AUTHOR'S FOREWORD

DURING THE WINTER AND spring of 1991 I was completing work on my first book, *For The Color Of His Skin*, about the shooting death of an innocent black teenager whose only crime was being of the wrong complexion in the wrong New York City neighborhood on the wrong summer evening in 1989. Proper perspective and focus would best be maintained, I believed, by completing the work in an environment removed from the anger and pathos within which I had been immersed while covering the case. So I rented a small cabin in a secluded hollow deep in New York State's Catskill mountain region.

The cabin and its bucolic environs were nothing less than a writer's paradise; the near-impossibility of adequate television reception without prohibitively expensive equipment was a lagniappe that aided concentration and focus. It was also why I missed two of the most-seen television events of that year. The first was the Gulf War, which I followed through radio reports and newspapers. The second was the videotaped beating of Rodney King (Los Angeles resident, "parolee," "motorist," or "ex-con"—take your pick of adjectives) by members of the Los Angeles police department. As an indirect result of this latter incident, more Americans lost their lives within the state of California than were killed on foreign sands during Desert Storm.

Not having seen the tape myself, I found the heated reaction reported in print and on radio—in a sense—difficult to fathom. I was only too well aware that during the first eight months of 1989 a total of thirty-nine individuals had *lost their lives* in New York City during incidents in which excessive police force was alleged to be the cause of death. During the first two months of Mayor David Dinkins's administration (January–February 1990), more than ten people had been shot by police officers—some under questionable circumstances. As the King furor escalated, I felt offense that pleas from families of the previously battered—and dead—for special prosecutors and federal intervention into their cases had gone virtually ignored. At least Rodney King lived to testify about his ordeal.

I was not so naive as to be ignorant of the reason why King's case garnered so much attention. The injustices of Jim Crow had not, after all, become etched into the national consciousness until the travails suffered by Dr. King's marchers had flickered on the old family Philco. The horrors of war had not bled onto the living rooms of American homes before Vietnam. Prior to the first telecast of the Rodney King videotape, claims that African-Americans in our major cities were sometimes treated with a harshness befitting the Oxford or Selma of two score years past were often dismissed out of hand. Those claims, most often made by community leaders who were considered suspect by the establishment, suddenly took on a frightening credibility—but only because the incident was videotaped.

In the King case, neither the initial incident, nor the eventual acquittal of the officers involved, nor the rioting that followed surprised me or anyone else who had spent any amount of time in the inner city with at least one eye and ear open.

The movie *The Untouchables* (based on the old television series) starred Kevin Costner as a squeaky-clean Elliot Ness, relentless in his pursuit of the evil Al Capone but hell-bent on doing so within the law. Ness's agents were given their nickname because, it was said, they were indeed "untouchable"—incorruptible by the lure of mob money.

The title of this work was chosen because in many of our cities, good-faith prosecution of law enforcement officers whose actions result in death or injury to people they are sworn to protect is—even in the post-Rodney King age—minimal at best, making them "untouchable" by the laws they are sworn to uphold. Prosecutors with the power to secure indictments against criminally negligent or culpable officers are all too willing to be hamstrung by the incestuous relationship that exists between their offices and law enforcement; they too are equally "untouchable"—above criticism even in cases where gross police misconduct has been proven to some degree of certainty. Voters continue to return many of these prosecutors to office year after election year.

"The New Untouchables" also refers to a developing subcaste in American society. The mentally ill who roam our streets without proper treatment in the wake of "deinstitutionalization," the petty criminals who live lives, in the words of an old Bob Dylan song, "chained and cheated by pursuit," are all entitled to the same rights enjoyed by the most dangerous criminals. Yet they often are subjected to abuses not even visited upon the truly sociopathic products of our worst neighborhoods. No matter their crimes, they all are entitled to due process of law. The police officer acting as judge, jury, and executioner cannot be tolerated in a society that calls itself free, particularly when the worst crime that officer's victim has committed is the offense of being poor and emotionally distressed, or just exhibiting "contempt of cop."

While I hope to educate the reader as to how these kinds of

cases reveal aspects of systemic abuse, I am not motivated by any desire to cast aspersion upon those men and women who responsibly discharge their duties as police officers. They too are victims of the "few bad apples" in the big blue barrel. When community tensions are aggravated by improperly adjudicated instances of police abuse, resulting in predictable acts of civilian violence, it is the police themselves who are placed at greater risk. A system that seeks political expediency and the minimizing of municipal liability at the expense of justice and truth often does so at the expense of individual officers as well. They are left to fend for themselves in controversial cases, denied the opportunity to defend themselves in an open court of law, and thus forever relegated to live in the shadow of a misconduct allegation. It is this bureaucratic attitude that has done the most to shape the "code of silence" so often written and spoken of in the wake of the King debacle.

It is a foregone conclusion that without the videotape of the Rodney King beating, his complaint would have been just one more unsubstantiated allegation of police brutality by a person of questionable credibility. It's just as likely that federal prosecution of the police officers involved was an anomaly prompted more by the rioting following their acquittals in state court than by any sincere desire on the part of the powers-that-be that justice be fairly administered. We must move beyond this mindset if our system is to ever truly be called "just."

The highest government officials declare publicly, "We will not tolerate lawlessness or civil disorder." Yet past failures to recognize patterns of police abuse, and a dismal record on the part of federal authorities when it comes to investigating or prosecuting abusive officers, sends a dangerous message to disenfranchised communities: "If you want justice we shall not give it to you. You shall have to take it at the point of a gun."

We are a self-governing people. Our elected officials and the administrators they appoint are answerable to us, and it is we who must demand fairness and integrity from those who enforce the law in our name. Administering justice for justice's sake should be an active purpose of our government rather than a grudging concession. It is my hope that this book will identify the frustrations felt to this day by individuals and communities still powerless against the systemic tolerance of official misconduct by the police and those who should police them—the prosecutors, the judges, and ultimately, the public at large.

—John DeSantis
Jackson Heights, N.Y., 1994

ONE

DEATH BY ASPHYXIATION:
THE CASE OF KEVIN THORPE

THE GOWANUS-SOUTH BROOK-
lyn area is typical of many inner-city neighborhoods in the
United States. The architecture, streets, schools, and population in general have long suffered from benign indifference—
or outright neglect—from municipal authorities. In the 1980s
crack cocaine began proliferating in urban areas, and with it
came a deadly new underground economy. Gunfire pierced
the night; the actual and perceived risks to police and civilians
posed by the new breed of street-level bootleggers increased
daily. At the same time, programs for the deinstitutionalization of the mentally ill had made the population many police
officers had to deal with more volatile.

By 1989 many of the city's low-income housing projects
had become bastions of crime and terror, located in neighborhoods where aggressive police tactics—part and parcel of
what would be dubbed "the war on drugs"—were utilized to
crack down on street-level drug traffic. These efforts accomplished little in the way of stemming the drug tide, but they
did overstretch the resources of courts, police, and correction
departments. Friction developed between police and the communities they were charged with protecting, and a "them versus us" mentality became prevalent among some officers—not
all, but enough to make a difference. Community activists

1

complained that police discretionary standards relating to the use of force, and police authority in general, had eroded to the point where many law-abiding people feared not only the bad guys, but the cops as well.

Esther Thorpe was one of the law-abiding people, a quiet and soft-spoken woman who had raised four children in Apartment 2-F at 126 Baltic Street in a project called the Gowanus Houses. Her tight-knit family had never experienced any problems with the police. One grandson was a correction officer; a son-in-law had retired as an assistant warden at a correctional facility. In 1989, things were difficult; the previous year had not been a good one for her. In the winter months a beloved sister had died of a heart attack, a crushing blow to a woman for whom family was everything.

All through Mrs. Thorpe's small apartment were photographs of daughters, sons, grandchildren, and other relatives. There were also bright watercolors and crayon drawings hung on the walls and posted on the refrigerator with little magnets.

The artist was her son Kevin, age thirty-two, who suffered from severe developmental disabilities. He attended a special school and still lived at home. Sometimes caring for Kevin was too much for the aging Esther, and other members of the family often helped out. Mary Scott, Kevin's older sister, an administrative assistant at New York's Chemical Bank, believed that Kevin was also autistic, although she is not certain whether such a diagnosis was ever made.

One of Mary Scott's fond memories of Kevin concerned his affection for a dog the family had when they lived in a house on Brooklyn's New York Avenue before moving to public housing. The dog, an all-American named Missy, had a habit of getting underfoot. One night in 1975 Esther Thorpe was cooking when she was tripped by the dog, causing her to spill the hot food. The food landed on Missy, who was badly injured and had to be euthanized.

"Kevin kept walking from room to room, looking everywhere," Mary Scott said. "We didn't realize at first that he was looking for Missy, but eventually we figured out that's what he was doing. After a few weeks, though, he stopped."

Kevin couldn't have told them what he was doing because, outside of a few guttural sounds that the family had come to understand, his condition made talking almost impossible.

"That's all he made was sounds," Mary Scott said. "He could say a word like 'Wilma' (the cartoon character on the Flintstones) but he couldn't say whole sentences. But as long as he had his jelly beans and could watch television and do what he wanted, he was fine."

Kevin never ventured out alone, and was always escorted to the bus that took him to his school. "He didn't know what anything was," Mary Scott said. "I don't think he knew what a police officer was, except from the TV. He never had to put up with anyone teasing him. Except for school he was never out."

Kevin was heavy but not tall, and had a moustache. His favorite pastimes included making dolls out of clothes and other items found around the house.

On July 10, 1989, he had trouble opening the refrigerator door. Because of motor problems associated with his disability, Kevin sometimes found simple tasks difficult to perform, and he would become highly agitated—especially if hungry or thirsty. He had prescribed medications that kept him calm, but he hadn't taken them that day. Esther Thorpe tried to help him, but his agitation continued and so she called her daughter Mary.

"I can't calm him down," she said. "I'm really worried about him."

"She'd never needed to call the police before," Mary Scott

said. "But I suggested that she call because she was there with him by herself. I told her if you call the police they could help."

Esther Thorpe did call the police, and informed a 911 operator that she was having some problems with her son, who was mentally retarded. Kevin calmed down on his own and changed into pajamas, then retired to his room for more television. Esther's granddaughter, fourteen-year-old Maleeka Scott, who lived downstairs, came by to visit and the two engaged in conversation. Esther Thorpe never canceled the 911 call, and some time later there was a knock at the door, in response to which the pajama-clad Kevin padded down the hall from his room. No one ever came to Apartment 2-F except for family and neighbors, and he enjoyed greeting company. Esther beat him to the door, however, and when she opened it there were two uniformed officers in the hallway.

She later claimed that the two officers made no attempt to interview her, but instead addressed Kevin. Although Kevin would usually comply with requests from people he knew, especially family members, he did not listen well to strangers. The officers told him to sit, then told him again, but Kevin's only response was to issue ever-louder sounds of protest.

"He didn't know why he was being told to sit down," Mary Scott said. "He didn't want to sit down, and that's when they tried to make him sit down." She admits that at that point Kevin "may have been resistant."

Maleeka Scott said that an officer forced Kevin to sit in a chair, and a scuffle ensued. Court papers filed by the family offer a chilling narrative: "They found Kevin Thorpe in a subdued and tranquil state of mind . . . police officers rushed into the apartment, grabbed Kevin Thorpe and threw him to the floor, face first, causing him to hit his head against a wall."

Esther Thorpe ran to her bedroom in tears, and the teenaged Maleeka remained in the living room as the officers wrestled Kevin to the ground and handcuffed him. Maleeka called her mother.

"I remember my daughter was crying over the phone and said they had Kevin in handcuffs and one of the cops was leaning on him," Mary Scott said. "I asked to speak to the officer and he assured me that my brother was okay and they were trying to calm him down, so they said."

Inexplicably, although Mary Scott was assured that her brother was "okay," more police arrived at the apartment where the handcuffed Kevin lay on the living room floor, alternately crying, making sounds, and calling out. The apartment door was open and concerned neighbors peered inside, while arriving officers told them to go back to their apartments. No less than ten additional officers entered and, according to Maleeka, at least one kept leaning against Kevin while his head was buried in the carpeting. Another had a nightstick against his back. The end result was that Kevin could not breathe but was unable to tell them so.

The court papers are graphic: " . . . a few minutes later over a dozen police officers swarmed into the room . . . some officers were lying on Kevin's back, some were holding his legs, some were securing his arms with plastic restraints and others were hitting him about the face and head."

"Maleeka called me [again] and she was hysterical," Mary Scott said. "She said, 'I think Kevin's dead, he's not moving,' and I thought this couldn't be true, the officer told me he was okay and my daughter said 'I think you'd better come over now.' So I left my job and they had already taken him away in the ambulance. My mother was in her room, sitting on the bed, dazed, in her nightgown. She hasn't been the same since."

"As a result of the accumulated weight of the police officers on different parts of his body, the supply of oxygen to Kevin's lungs was cut off and Kevin Thorpe died," the court papers stated.

Kevin Thorpe had died on his mother's living room floor, and Esther Thorpe and the rest of her family were devastated. She loved Kevin dearly, and struggled to accommodate his disability, seeing to it that he received proper care and a good home. The call to the police had been motivated by a desire to help her son, not hurt him—and certainly not to kill him.

"I just couldn't believe it happened," Esther Thorpe remembered. "I thought somehow they had maybe made a mistake. How does this happen that a person winds up dead?"

The Thorpe family wanted answers from the authorities, but none were forthcoming, except a media report attributed to police sources stating that Kevin had possibly been high on drugs. This infuriated the family. "I remember them saying that and I called the coroner's office myself," Mary Scott said. "I wanted to know what they had found out. Whatever it was I knew it wasn't going to be that."

"I thought they were supposed to have people in the field who came to the house where people are mentally retarded," she continued. "Kevin was autistic. And I remember thinking, 'Aren't the police supposed to be trained to look at someone and know something is wrong—to get help for him?'"

The answer to Mary Scott's question is an unqualified yes. New York City has one of the finest police emergency service units (ESU) in the United States. Its members contend with the impossible and the improbable on a daily basis, and are often called to assist cops in situations involving emotionally disturbed individuals. The NYPD patrol guide, in fact, has a standing interim order that specifically addresses the issue of the "EDP," or emotionally disturbed person. It is a well-founded and well-formulated policy that calls for isolation of the individual by patrol officers until ESU can arrive at the scene. The emergency service trucks are equipped not only with the experience of these special officers, but special tools as well, including nonlethal force devices and restraints.

With nowhere else to turn the Thorpe family sought legal counsel, and were referred to Colin Moore, a Brooklyn attorney with a reputation for activism in high-profile cases. By the time they had their first meeting with Moore the medical examiner's findings were released.

The New York City medical examiner's office is one of the busiest in the United States. Kevin Thorpe's death was one of 2,938 reported to the agency that month. His autopsy was one of over 8,000 performed that year. The medical examiner plays an important function, even though his office is one that does not usually receive a wealth of publicity.

The mission of the Office of Chief Medical Examiner, established by city code, is to investigate and evaluate the deaths of people who die "from criminal violence, by casualty, by suicide, suddenly when in apparent health, when unattended by a physician, or occurring in a correctional facility or in any suspicious or unusual manner . . . " The office is responsible for determining the cause of death (such as the injury responsible for the fatality) and the manner of death, meaning its classification as homicide, suicide, or natural causes.

Dr. Charles Hirsch had been appointed New York City's chief medical examiner in January 1989. He succeeded Dr. Elliot Gross, a well-credentialed pathologist who left the post under fire in 1987, in part because of alleged improprieties concerning the death of a man named Michael Stewart, who died while in the custody of transit police. An interim chief, Dr. Beverly Leffers, was appointed while the city searched for a replacement for the embattled Gross. It was important to city officials that the new medical examiner be capable and credible, and that public confidence be restored to the office.

Born in 1937, Hirsch, the former medical examiner of nearby Suffolk County, Long Island, had compiled impressive credentials over the course of his career. Among the changes he made upon taking office in New York was a strict reclassification policy, to the chagrin of police officials. *All* deaths caused by the act of another person would, Hirsch determined, be classified as homicides, and that included those where the other party was a police officer.

A word is in order here about terminology. The generic term "homicide," purely stated, means the taking of the life of a living person by another person. It does not in and of itself imply criminal culpability, which must be determined not by doctors but by the criminal justice system. Thus a person who *within his legal rights* shoots and kills an intruder when no other course of action was available has committed a homicide, even though a jury might determine that the homicide was *justified*. In like fashion, if a police officer takes action that he or she is permitted—indeed, effectively licensed—to perform, such as the shooting of a dangerous felon, it is technically a homicide as well.

Prior to the Hirsch administration, deaths in police custody were designated "unclassified." What Hirsch did was reclassify these deaths as homicides.

The premature police pronouncement of drugs being involved in Kevin Thorpe's death had received significant public attention, and in an effort to clear the record Hirsch's office released a statement:

> Our evaluation is based upon information provided by the New York City Police Department, the findings of our own investigators, and the results of the autopsy and toxicological testing. Toxicological testing disclosed therapeutic concentrations of medications (i.e. Mellaril and Benadryl) prescribed by Mr. Thorpe's physicians. He was not under the influence of alcohol, cocaine, narcotics, or other illicit drugs. It is our conclusion that Kevin Thorpe was asphyxiated as the result of chest compression by overlaying during restraint by police officers. It is our further opinion that natural disease neither caused nor contributed to his death.

The issue of people dying in police custody was not new to the Thorpe family's new attorney. Moore knew from experience that a satisfactory explanation of what had happened to Kevin might never be forthcoming. But Moore began laying the groundwork for an investigation conducted by David Walker of the Center for Law and Social Justice (CLSJ) at Medgar Evers College. The CLSJ, a civil and human rights research, advocacy, and litigation institution established by the New York State legislature in 1985, had taken an immediate interest in the Thorpe case.

A record of questionable incidents involving use of force and minorities was already being compiled by the CLSJ. In almost all of these incidents, disciplinary action against accused officers was nearly nonexistent.

The CLSJ had released a report prior to the Thorpe case, that was a critique of police policy and procedures in both excessive force cases and civilian instances of racially motivated crimes. "Ironically," the report stated, "these guidelines have proven more protective of police than of victims and thus have been cosmetically changed, adjusted, and refined in the wake of the continued police slayings of minority civilians with alleged 'mental disorders.'"

Few of these cases were well known to the general public, with the exception of that of Eleanor Bumpers. Bumpers, an emotionally disturbed black woman, was killed in 1984 when police answered a call to assist with her eviction from city-owned housing. Bumpers had thrown lye at police officers, and when the Emergency Service Unit arrived, a veteran police officer named Steven Sullivan opened fire with his service-issued shotgun when the elderly Bumpers lunged at him with a knife. Sullivan was indicted on criminal charges and stood trial in Bronx Supreme Court, but was acquitted of any intentional wrong-doing. Guidelines for dealing with disturbed individuals were supposedly tightened up after the Bumpers

case, however—but so had they been several years earlier,
after an emotionally disturbed teenager sitting on his mother's
living room floor with a pair of scissors in his hand was rid-
dled with bullets when he lunged at six armed police officers
while still holding the scissors.

The excessive force claims made in the CLSJ report, however, were not limited to situations involving emotionally disturbed people like Kevin Thorpe: "The videotaped police beating of Alberto Flores, the 106th Precinct Stun Gun case, the
murder of Mrs. Eleanor Bumpers, and other documented
cases of unjustified brutality and shootings show that highly
publicized cases are, at least, investigated. However, there are
many unpublished incidents that are administratively mis-
handled by the NYPD."

According to the CLSJ's findings, cases that receive little, if
any, media attention are dealt with by the police department
without any outside notification. The CLSJ's own investigators
interviewed complainants in cases where, according to their
findings, what was perceived as clear and unmistakably inappropriate conduct had not only gone unpunished and unaddressed, but actually resulted in sanctions against the *victims*.

The CLSJ did not publish the names of the victims in these
cases in order to protect their privacy. The cases included the
complaint of an Indian physician who was seated in his automobile while a nearby store was being robbed. The perpetrator attempted to commandeer his car, but was unsuccessful
and fled. Shortly thereafter, arriving police officers dragged
the doctor out of his car. When the doctor protested that he
was not a criminal but a victim, they struck him in the face
with a police radio. The doctor was charged with attempted
robbery. According to the CLSJ report, witnesses who verified
his story were pressured to change their account by a lieu-
tenant and a captain. The NYPD's Internal Affairs Unit, after

investigating the physician's ensuing complaint, found it to be "unsubstantiated."

In another 1987 case, a black woman in Brooklyn was standing in front of her house, paying little notice to a police car parked nearby. By the time she realized that an officer in the car (who was also black) was ordering her inside her own house, it was too late. The officer, apparently enraged, allegedly handcuffed the woman who was three months pregnant. As she tried to resist she was beaten, dragged on the ground, and placed in a nightstick chokehold. Her mother, who was drawn to the door by the commotion, and allegedly intervened, was also beaten and then handcuffed. Allegedly, a total of eight people in the woman's family were all beaten. Another family member (besides the woman herself and her mother) was also arrested. No disciplinary action was taken against the officers involved.

The horror stories are not limited to people of color. In December 1987, a twenty-five-year-old white man was stopped by police in front of his home for suspected involvement in an auto theft. As he was being arrested and handcuffed in front of his house, he attempted to escape. Family and neighbors reported that the man was beaten by police before being thrown into a patrol car. The young man's mother subsequently could not locate him for two days, during which police denied knowing of his whereabouts. Police later informed her that her son was confined to a municipal hospital, where she found him lying in a pool of vomit and urine. He was missing teeth, had fifteen stitches in his face, an additional twenty-five in the back of his head, and had suffered a broken ankle and a broken foot.

The man told his unnerved mother that the officers had taken him under a highway not far from his house and stripped him of his clothes—except for his sweatshirt which they pulled up over his head. They then began to beat him with gun butts and bags of some sort. The mother took photographs of her son's abused body, but the pictures were immediately confiscated by the officer whose duty was to guard her son, since he was still in custody. The district attorney's office, according to the CLSJ report, wanted to check the man out of the hospital for his arraignment, but after repeated and vociferous protests from the man's mother they consented to a bedside arraignment by a criminal court judge. Charges were still pending against the young man at the time of the CLSJ report. No disciplinary action was taken against the officers involved.

As a result of researching stories like these, the CLSJ issued recommendations for means by which allegations of police brutality could be better monitored. The suggested guidelines, like others that had resulted from an investigation of police violence requested by the governor's office several years before, were basically ignored.

———

A month went by after the death of Kevin Thorpe, and the police officers involved in his death remained unidentified, despite requests for disclosure of this information by Colin Moore—who assumed that a grand jury would hear evidence on the case, ostensibly for a possible indictment. The media had taken a passing interest as well; the *New York Times* had even run an editorial roundly criticizing the police department's response. But Moore had no reason to believe that this case would be any different from others in which criminal culpability was alleged in a case of death or injury that occurred in police custody. He determined that the case would have to enter the public consciousness, and with the help of the CLSJ's David Walker and an activist minister named Rev. Herbert Daughtry, Moore set out to make that happen.

Black churches have always met a variety of community

needs. After the Civil War and emancipation, it was often ministers who had access to books and other educational resources, and who set up schools for former slaves. Before, churches were often major switching stations on the Underground Railroad. The importance of black churches has continued into the present era; it was the churches that spearheaded the civil rights movement. In more recent times the churches in urban areas have helped give voice to disenfranchised communities. When controversial issues affect African-Americans, the news media often turn to local ministers for reaction.

The outspoken Daughtry's wiry frame and pencil-thin moustache were widely recognized in New York. Like other activist ministers, he had earned his share of media attention, both favorable and unfavorable. He had stood by the side of the Rev. Jesse Jackson, the first viable African-American presidential contender from a major political party, throughout both Jackson's 1984 and 1988 campaigns. In 1989 Daughtry was emerging as a visible supporter of New York's first African-American mayor, David Dinkins.

After meeting with Thorpe's family and Colin Moore, Daughtry organized a press conference. He was well aware of other excessive force claims involving the NYPD, and believed that the Thorpe case was a dramatic example of a deadly pattern.

At first, the issue of race might not seem relevant to such cases. But Daughtry and other activists continued to insist that a different standard applied in cases involving minorities, and that officers were less likely to use deadly force against whites.

The House of the Lord Church is an imposing brick and stone building, which looks old enough to have been standing when cows still grazed in the neighborhood. The August afternoon Daughtry had chosen for his media announcement was hot and dry. As he scanned the collection of reporters seated on folding chairs near the altar, Daughtry prepared to tell them that life in New York had the potential for becoming a lot hotter than the weather.

"New York City is a powderkeg," he intoned that day, in a clear and powerful voice that belied his gaunt appearance. "It will only take the slightest spark to set it off."

The public's response to such messages is often paradoxical, depending most on who has uttered them. During the 1990 trial of two young white men accused of participating in the racially motivated murder of a black teenager (which also occurred in Brooklyn), several public officials were asked by reporters whether acquittals might lead to violence. The general response was that while they hoped disorder would not ensue, it was a distinct possibility. Yet, when an outspoken black minister was asked the same question and responded the same way, his statement became front-page news. Rather than being seen as "predicting" or merely "commenting," ministers and other activists are instead reported as "inciting violence" by making such remarks. Daughtry's pronouncement was part of the text of a letter from which he read aloud, which he and other activists had sent to New York State's governor, Mario Cuomo.

Daughtry went on to explain how many of the city's minority neighborhoods had reached a boiling point of anger, fear, and frustration, because so far thirty-nine people had died while in police custody that year. In some of those cases, he stated, death had come *after* police assistance was requested on behalf of a distressed family member.

"These families asked for help and ended up with a corpse," Daughtry said, pausing for emphasis. He then got to the heart of the matter; a request that a special prosecutor be appointed to investigate the Thorpe case, as well as other police violence situations.

A Brooklyn grand jury heard evidence regarding the

Thorpe case. Their job was to determine whether a crime had been committed. If the grand jury decided to indict any or all of the officers involved, then prosecutors could file formal charges. Esther Thorpe was subpoenaed and testified under questioning from an assistant district attorney. But Maleeka Scott and other witnesses were never called. As Moore had predicted, the grand jury found "no true bill"—that is, they voted that insufficient evidence existed to prove that a crime had taken place.

This situation has proven to be the rule rather than the exception in cases of alleged police abuse of force. Grand jury proceedings are secret; it would be possible, some activists have argued, for prosecutors who did not wish to prosecute police officers (at the risk of alienating the very law enforcement personnel their offices have to work with on a routine basis) to give less than effective presentations during such inquiries. After all, as the old saw says, if a prosecutor can indict a ham sandwich, he can just as easily unindict one.

In the Thorpe case, Daughtry's request for a special state prosecutor went unheeded. In desperation, the Thorpe family petitioned the United States Attorney for the Eastern District of New York—the local arm of the United States Department of Justice—to intervene, claiming that Kevin Thorpe's civil rights had been criminally violated. The Justice Department never interviewed members of the family, nor, to their knowledge, did it interview any other witnesses. No action was ever taken at the federal level.

———

Apologists for police misconduct often paint the attorneys for families who sue the police for money damages in the wake of cases such as this one as money-hungry entrepreneurs eager for publicity and a fat settlement. Yet, as the Thorpe case illustrates, there is no other recourse after all other requests for redress are exhausted. Because of the secrecy attendant to grand jury proceedings, specifics of the Thorpe investigation will never be known. The state refused to intervene, as did the federal government. And so Esther Thorpe, as administratrix of her late son's estate, sued the New York City Police Department and the individual officers involved in state court. As of December 1993, the case was still pending. Mary Scott later said the family's decision to sue was not difficult to reach.

"We sued because of the fact that the police are able to do things like this and they can justify that they were right when they know they weren't," she said. "Nothing happened to the police. Nothing at all. They committed a crime, and I think the only reason we pursued it that way is because nothing happened. We don't want the money. They're getting off scot-free and there has to be some accountability."

Mary Scott is still bitter, as the litigation—which may provide the only substantive answers regarding her brother's death—grinds its way slowly between the millstones of justice. "They tried to cover up what happened," she said. "The police that were there at the time it happened, no one had their names or anything. They said my brother was taking drugs—which wasn't true. Some said they were injured, with scratches from my handcuffed brother. Now how does he accomplish this with handcuffs?"

There are unanswered questions regarding both sides of the case, concerning the family as well as the police. Why did Esther Thorpe permit the police into the apartment at all, if Kevin was already calm? Why had Kevin not taken his medication? And how much resistance did Kevin offer to the police officers who first arrived? The police department will make no statements about the case, which is its policy when the city is named as a defendant in a civil suit. But even if the answers to those questions reflect poorly on the family's civil case, the allegation of a less than dutiful standard of care on the part of the NYPD carries significant weight, especially in light of the NYPD's public misstatements of fact.

If the Thorpe case ever does go to trial, it will have to be decided whether the police, by not following established procedures for dealing with emotionally disturbed persons by "laying on" Kevin Thorpe with unnecessary force, were liable under state law for wrongfully causing his death. The officers in the case have not, as of this writing, been identified by the police department, and the plaintiff's discovery process is still ongoing.

Cases such as the death of Kevin Thorpe pose a grave threat to the effectiveness of local law enforcement efforts and to the safety of working officers. With racial tensions already high in many of our cities, deaths of persons in custody (since they largely number members of minority populations) make people in minority communities more hesitant to call the police for assistance. Anti-police sentiment is fueled, and cooperation in enforcement efforts is damaged.

It is not the mere fact that Kevin Thorpe died during attempts by police to restrain him that gives rise to concern. Rather, it is the dearth of accountability in such a situation, where a life was taken, that creates the problem. Let us assume, for the moment, that Kevin Thorpe had in some way been *responsible* for what happened to him. Perhaps he verbally or physically threatened officers. We might also assume, for the moment, that the death was purely accidental, and that there was nothing the officers could have done to prevent it. But since these facts have never been—and might never be— public record, only suspicion, doubt, and accusations remain. And sometimes unsubstantiated—or even false—accusations can visit incredible harm on communities.

Taking the worst-case scenario, however, the officers, by causing Thorpe's death, committed a crime for which any private citizen would be arrested, held on high bail, and if convicted, imprisoned. The charges at best might be criminally negligent homicide—at worst, manslaughter or perhaps murder.

The Thorpe case never made it out of New York, and had little national significance, just like many other police-abuse-of-force allegations in other jurisdictions. Few victims of alleged unnecessary force by police officers are as innocent, childlike, or in most people's minds, deserving of sympathy as Kevin Thorpe.

———

Admittedly, there has been a dearth of information regarding the Thorpe case coming from the police. The only witnesses free to tell the story are those whose views might certainly be prejudiced.

What is clear, however, is that procedures that could and should have been followed were not, in the initial stages of what became an encounter with a tragic and unfortunate resolution. At the bottom line, Mary Scott's words address at least one reason why we should be concerned: "[Kevin] was a gentle, loving, caring person who never hurt anybody in his life, never would hurt anybody, and didn't deserve what happened to him."

Kevin Thorpe was buried in Brooklyn's Bushwick Cemetery without a headstone. Some family members have made pilgrimages to his grave, but Mary Scott, who first told her mother to call the police for assistance, has not. Since 1989 she has tried to live with the advice she gave her mother.

Excessive use of force by police cannot be tolerated in a society that calls itself free; any allegations that it has occurred must be investigated thoroughly, in the glare of public spotlight. Excessive force is an issue most of us would rather not have to think about, yet it is a fact of life that must nonetheless be addressed by police administrators, the government officials who appoint them, and ultimately the public. At one time such allegations could easily be attributed to zealous activists in search of an issue, easily dismissed out of hand. That was until the spring of 1991.

Mary Scott was among millions of Americans who re-coiled in shock while watching a television newscast that showed tape of a man lying prone on a California sidewalk as nightstick blows rained down on his body.

"I felt it was unnecessary," she said. "He was handcuffed, he was on the ground, and they were beating him. I thought this was another case where the police are in the wrong, and hoped something would be done. But in my brother's case nothing's been done."

Indeed, this situation was a far cry from Kevin Thorpe's case. Before the year was out, the name of the victim of the most publicized police brutality case in United States history would be a household word. This man's name was Rodney King.

TWO

THE WRITING ON THE WALL

Fuck tha police comin' straight from the underground
Young nigga got it bad 'cause I'm brown
And not the other color so police think
They have the authority to kill a minority . . .

— N.W.A.

DOMESTIC DISTURBANCES have always been high on the list of situations that place police officers in jeopardy. A recent FBI study involving line-of-duty police officer slayings places radio calls for domestic disturbances as the third most perilous assignment for police personnel, with crime in progress/arrest situations at the top of the list.

Second on the list are automobile stops. Even though these do not rank as the number-one danger situation, they can cause anxiety and, often, outright fear in individual officers. A traffic stop occurs when an officer has chosen to pull over a vehicle, usually because it can reasonably be expected that some law has been broken, as in the case of a DWI. Between the moment an officer signals an offending vehicle with lights and siren, and the time the driver complies by pulling over to the side of the road, a dozen scenarios can be played through the officer's mind. *Does the driver have a weapon? Is he wanted for*

21

something else, and I'm going to get shot because of a defective tail light? Will I be forced to shoot this person? The possibilities are endless, and although the officer may be considering them only in his or her subconscious, they are still representative of the tremendous toll stress takes on members of the police services.

The FBI cites one report of a twenty-seven-year-old officer with four years on the job who pulled over a pickup truck. He was aware that the driver, a quiet, complacent young man, had been cited six weeks before for numerous violations. The man's truck had been impounded (along with equipment he needed for work), and he had depleted all of his savings to reclaim the vehicle.

The officer had observed the truck making an illegal U-turn and stopped it. He ordered the offending driver into the front seat of the patrol car while he had a dispatcher run a license check. As the officer suspected, the driver's record indicated a still-active suspension, and he asked for a tow truck: the vehicle was going to be impounded one more time.

The officer then ordered the offender out of his patrol car, possibly to search him, but as the officer came around the back of the car the man sped over to his pickup and removed a pistol from its rear bed. The officer attempted to duck behind the patrol car, but it was too late. One bullet smashed through the revolving roof lights and the second through the officer's head, causing his death.

This true story is but a variation on the many appalling possibilities that are part and parcel of car stops, where the unexpected must always be expected.

It is important to keep all of this in mind when evaluating any car-stop situation, but particularly one that results in a pursuit. In many municipalities, car chases are now sometimes terminated by supervisors if it appears that things are getting out of hand. It may well be possible to pick up the offender again, once the plate number has been noted. But a high-speed chase through a residential neighborhood imperils the fleeing driver, the police, and innocent members of the public alike. It is not difficult for an officer to imagine that, if an offender is taking the kind of risks inherent in this sort of chase, something must be gravely wrong. The car could be stolen. The driver might be in possession of drugs or a weapon. The whole car-stop-scenario parade begins anew, but with graver potentialities.

Something else happens when an offender refuses to stop. The public and private authority of the officer is challenged. The adrenaline flow prompted by the chase, the feelings of fear, and the personal affront taken by the officer has, in some situations, led to deadly consequences for the offender. One of these situations will stand out in American history.

———

At approximately 12:40 A.M. on March 3, 1991, a California Highway Patrol unit observed a white Hyundai being driven at excessive speed on a freeway. As the Hyundai headed toward the exit ramp the cruiser followed with its roof lights activated. The driver of the Hyundai continued driving at high speed, in an unmistakable attempt to elude capture. Other police cars and a helicopter soon joined in the chase, which at times reached speeds of eighty miles per hour, but lasted less than ten minutes and ended at the intersection of Florence and Normandie Avenues in South-Central Los Angeles.

The car was occupied by three African-American men. The driver, thirty-eight-year-old Rodney King, was maddeningly slow to respond to police commands that he lie down on the ground with his hands on his head. *U.S. News & World Report* described a highly intoxicated 6'3", 225-pound Rodney King, who:

> Danced a little pitter-patter, waving to the helicopter; he
> threw a kiss and wiggled his butt at a female officer who
> had ordered him, at gunpoint, to lie down; finally he
> heaved four male police officers off his back who tried to
> handcuff him and seemed to shrug it off when police
> stunned him with a taser . . .

While laying on the ground after finally being handcuffed, King was the recipient of numerous nightstick blows and kicks inflicted by police officers, which caused him multiple injuries and bone fractures. What police did not know at the time was that an amateur video photographer named George Holliday had recorded ninety seconds of the ugliest portions of the incident on videotape.

Holliday at first tried to bring the tape to the attention of the LAPD, assuming that they would want to know about a beating inflicted upon a civilian, but there was no interest on their part. They also refused to answer his questions about the condition of the beating victim. Holliday finally brought the tape to a Los Angeles television station; after it was broadcast locally, CNN aired it nationwide and then throughout the world.

Civil rights activists who had long made complaints of systemic police brutality against minorities suddenly felt vindicated. The proof, they said, was certainly there on tape for all to see, and at least in this case their allegations could not be shrugged off as exaggerations or misinterpretations of events. The shocking video provided seemingly irrefutable evidence of a suspect being brutally beaten while laying on the ground, handcuffed.

Public reactions on the part of many officials—including President George Bush—was swift and sharp, although Los Angeles police chief Darryl Gates said words to the effect that the incident was atypical of his officers' behavior.

The officers involved maintained that King had acted so irrationally and posed such a grave threat to their safety that the
use of force depicted on the tape was necessary and justified.
Based on King's actions, which included attempts to get up
while being beaten down, the officers alleged that he was
under the influence of PCP, which is known to cause irrational,
often dangerous behavior and displays of superhuman
strength.

Over twenty police officers responded to the incident at
Florence and Normandie. No supervisors attempted to stop
the beating. King's beating might never have seen the light of
day were it not for the Holliday video; a commission appointed to investigate police use of force in Los Angeles,
headed by Warren Christopher, acknowledged that supposi-
tion publicly in its report. Paul King, Rodney King's brother,
had even attempted to report the beating several days after the
incident, and was rebuffed by officers.

The Christopher Report noted that sixty-three "problem
officers" were the subject of twenty or more reports each of excessive force filed between 1986 and 1990. During that time a
total of eighty-three civil lawsuits filed against the department
resulted in settlements of $15,000 or more. Yet the disciplining
of the officers involved was often minimal or nonexistent. But
then, substantial evidence of the LAPD's less-than-sterling
record on human rights had existed well before the King incident.

From 1986 through 1988, statewide complaints of police
brutality made to a legal referral organization had increased
223 percent; close to half of those reports were made against
members of the LAPD and the Los Angeles Sheriff's Department. Between 1978 and 1982 nearly a score of Los Angeles
civilians died as a result of the LAPD's employment of choke
holds, which are now banned. These included techniques for
cutting off blood flow in the carotid artery as well as respira-

tion. The LAPD under Chief Darryl Gates had not classified chokeholds in the deadly force category, which meant that such holds could be used in any number of situations where officers lives were not in danger.

In 1992 the U.S. House of Representatives Subcommittee on Civil and Constitutional Rights continued hearings that were begun in the wake of the King case. Witnesses included James J. Fyfe, professor of criminal justice at American University in Washington, D.C. Fyfe has had an impressive career that includes a landmark study of police-related shootings in New York, where he served for sixteen years as a police officer and police academy instructor.

"In both its official policies and its street practices regarding use of force, the LAPD has long been the outlaw among big American police departments," Fyfe said in his prepared statement. "The LAPD equated chokeholds—euphemistically, 'carotid control holds'—with wristlocks and other non-lethal police control techniques, and trained officers to use them to subdue motorists guilty of nothing more than loudly protesting traffic tickets."

Johnnie L. Cochran, Jr., a Los Angeles attorney and former prosecutor, cited seventeen choking deaths at the hands of L.A. officers before that same committee, and " . . . a long history of shootings and beatings of minorities with guns and clubs."

Civilian complaints are not always adequate indicators of excessive force patterns by a particular police department. For one thing, such incidents (like crimes in general) tend to be underreported. In some jurisdictions citizens have been actively discouraged from making such complaints at the local level. Even when they are filed, many are often marked unfounded out of hand, or investigated with something less than due diligence. Other complaints of police misconduct may not be rooted in hard fact; an individual might allege excessive force when a police action is thoroughly justified. Additionally (although this would not appear to be the case in Los Angeles) in those departments where protocols for filing complaints are more user-friendly, increased numbers may result. It is difficult to say whether these variables cancel each other out.

Bearing all of this in mind, it is interesting to note that a United States Department of Justice study covering complaints in fiscal year 1990–1991 found that the state of California pulled the nation's highest numbers, with the LAPD contributing significantly. Yet throughout periods of stormy criticism, Chief Gates continued to deny anything was wrong. What appears evident is that the beating of Rodney King was one of the *less* atrocious applications of excessive force on the part of the LAPD, and a case can be made that it was just one episode in a long-standing pattern of sanctioned thuggish behavior by officers.

In December 1987 a man named Stewart Vigil was transported by Los Angeles officers to U.C.L.A. Harbor General Hospital, on the belief that he was mentally ill. As the police car approached the facility, Vigil reportedly became unmanageable and officers forcibly removed him from their vehicle. Reports indicated that he was struck with nightsticks eighty times, "as if he were a piñata, while as many as twelve officers watched." Also, the handcuffed and hog-tied Vigil was reportedly tasered several times during the ordeal, according to witnesses. He was dead when wheeled into the hospital, tasers clutched in his hands.

One year later L.A. officers were involved in what was described before Congress as a "notorious case of lawlessness." Believing that members of a street gang were living in homes at 39th and Dalton streets, a search-and-destroy mission was carried out by the LAPD against those homes. More than seventy officers, including supervisors, beat, terrorized, and humiliated residents and thoroughly destroyed some homes. Lawsuits are still pending.

Anti-police lyrics in popular music, most notably those contained in a song called "Cop Killer" by the rapper Ice T, have been the subject of recent national attention. Such lyrics had been around for years before any major disputes arose, however, in work done by the rap group N.W.A. (Niggaz With Attitude) who came (as their album title stated) "Straight Outta Compton," a community adjoining L.A. That black youth in Los Angeles heavily identified with the rhymes of revolt against oppression should not be surprising. Under Darryl Gates's direction, the LAPD instituted an ostensibly anti-crime, anti-gang frontal assault in 1988 called "Operation Hammer," which resulted in wholesale arrests of tens of thousands of young black men for little or no cause save their race and choice of clothing.

Paul L. Hoffman, legal director of Southern California's ACLU Foundation, testified before Congress on the subject, complaining that the operation resulted in stops, handcuffing, and arrests with no intention on the part of officers to file actual criminal charges, an accusation Hoffman claims is validated by the record.

"In the course of Operation Hammer sweeps in 1990 more than 25,000 youths had been arrested," Hoffman testified. "Yet fewer than 1,500 were ever actually charged with a criminal offense."

In 1990, twenty-six black and Latino teenagers filed a 5.2 million-dollar damage suit against the LAPD citing civil rights violations. The case did not go unnoticed by the national media, and was detailed in a lengthy *Time* article. Yet the allegations caused barely a ripple in the national consciousness.

There should be little wonder why the anti-police rhetoric of so-called "gangsta rap" was first popularized in Southern California when one considers the traumatic effects of police actions like "Operation Hammer" on impressionable youth, actions which might be considered more dangerous than the product of any lyricist's pen. While proponents of record bans and artist boycotts are motivated by fears of life imitating art, it would appear that in fact it's the reverse that is true.

These incidents represent but a glimpse of the Los Angeles that existed before the Rodney King videotape flickered across so many millions of television screens. And it should be noted that in the most egregious cases cited here, no action was taken against police officers. Except for a plethora of civil lawsuits filed against the LAPD, few officials took seriously any suggestions that police conduct was out of hand.

As ACLU attorney Hoffman stated in his testimony regarding "Operation Hammer," it is little wonder that a group of police officers in March 1991 could not only engage in such brutality, but have little fear of recrimination from their colleagues, who stood by and watched the most cherished of American liberties seep into the Los Angeles pavement along with Rodney King's blood. Incidents that received little or no media attention prior to that now celebrated case should have been seen as ominous handwriting on an ominous wall.

Criminal indictments were issued against Sergeant Stacy Koon, and police officers Lawrence Powell, Theodore Briseno, and Timothy Wind, and all pleaded not guilty. Their trial in Los Angeles Superior Court stretched into 1992. The proceedings were moved out of the city on a motion by defense lawyers that the officers would be unable to receive a fair trial there.

The trial was held instead in Simi Valley, north of Los Angeles, a middle-class, mostly white suburban community where Rodney King represents the residents' worst nightmare, and the police are seen as the only protection against people like him—or so critics of the proceedings would later maintain. Reflective of the community, there was not a single African-American among the potential jurors.

King himself did not make a highly sympathetic victim. In March 1991 his legal status was that of parolee—a fact that was not and, indeed, could not have been known by the officers who beat him. From the moment the trial began, attorneys for the officers attempted to paint Rodney King as a threatening man who gave officers on the scene no reason to doubt that they were in danger, thus justifying whatever force—including that shown on the videotape—was used to subdue him. Placing the onus of a crime on the shoulders of the victim is hardly a new tactic for defense attorneys. In the King case, however, there was a slightly different twist, one which echoes the difficulties inherent in bringing criminal charges against law enforcement officers.

Between the moment Rodney King exited his Hyundai at the termination of the pursuit and some unknown point on an ensuing imaginary time line, the police officers at the intersection of Florence and Normandie were authorized, permitted, and, without any question, duty-bound to exercise force if he did not comply with their directives. As with many excessive force incidents, then, an argument can safely be made that the King case began with a *lawful* use of police power. The jury's job would then be to decide when—if at all—the line had been crossed between those actions that the law deems appropriate and necessary, and those taken outside the scope of proper authority.

For prosecutors, the most important single piece of evidence was the videotape made by George Holliday; therefore, this video was the most important obstacle for defense lawyers to overcome. The jury would have to be convinced that the eighty or so seconds of tape were but one aspect of the events of March 2, and the actions of the officers would have to be seen within the context of everything that occurred from the moment the roof lights of the first highway patrol car were flipped on. King himself would not be difficult to discredit.

Our system of criminal justice is predicated upon certain basic tenets that are sometimes misunderstood by the public at large. For one thing, the presumption of innocence within which defendants are cloaked is only donned during the trial. However, only about 10 percent of all felony cases in the United States result in a trial. Most are plea-bargained into lower-grade felonies or misdemeanors as a result of agreements between the defendants and prosecutors. In the overwhelming majority of cases, then, constitutional guarantees of due process are not applicable. It is only when a defendant maintains his or her innocence that the state must bear the burden of proving guilt beyond a reasonable doubt.

The highest-profile criminal cases often result in trials for a variety of reasons. For one thing, the more aware the public is of a case, the more likely a judge might be to impose a stricter sentence. For another, few criminal defendants can afford defense attorneys outright, and overburdened public defenders are often reluctant to push a case to trial unless absolutely necessary. Even defendants who can afford a private lawyer often cannot foot the bill required for a trial. So, those cases the public is most aware of are aberrations rather than the rule. This is why the public is so badly misinformed about our justice system, and why the videotape of Rodney King, although damaging evidence, could not be expected to guarantee a conviction.

The odds, then, are usually stacked slightly in favor of the defendant because of procedural guarantees at trial, although it can be argued that this is offset by the overwhelming resources the state has at its disposal. But in the case of the officers charged with assaulting Rodney King, their status as men authorized to use force helped tip the scale of justice in their favor.

It is widely held that the decision reached by the Simi County jury was rooted in racism and classism. While this theory has circumstantial support, it is also possible that even if the trial had been held in the city of Los Angeles, not all of the indictment counts would have been upheld. What appears certain is that the police officers—unlike *most* criminal defendants—were indeed tried before a true jury of their peers.

Whatever the reason, however, the jurors chose to acquit the officers on all charges. What happened in the aftermath of the jury's decision, announced on April 29, 1992, is only too well known. Sixty people died and property damage reached the billion-dollar mark in what has been described as the worst American rioting in this century, when Los Angeles resembled nothing less than a tattered and scorched war zone.

The rioting began three blocks from Florence and Normandie, where Rodney King first met up with the acquitted officers. The location, as well as the timing, were among several factors that made the L.A. violence atypical of past disorders sparked by police violence situations.

Actual or rumored police misconduct has more often than not been the spark that set off civil disturbances in the past; in that light, had Los Angeles followed historical precedent, the rioting would have occurred a year earlier, when news of the King beating first spread. Jim Galipeau, a police officer with extensive L.A. gang experience who had spoken with some local youths an hour before the city exploded, made this observation to *U.S. News & World Report*: "They didn't care about Rodney King. Guys like King had been beaten up for decades in these neighborhoods ... "

Published on May 31, 1993, over a year after the riots, the *U.S. News* account of the incident is one of the more thoughtful and well-investigated pieces on the tragedy. According to the account, a minor incident at Florence and Halldale avenues shortly before 5:30 P.M. prompted the first encounter between police and the public in the area, followed by a more serious encounter at Florence and Normandie.

"Before five minutes had passed, eighteen cop cars and some thirty-five officers had sped there," the account read. "But the crowd was swelling, too, and eventually, more than 100 residents surrounded the police. The first face-off was about to begin—and it was the LAPD that would blink."

An unpleasant melee erupted in which some rocks and bottles were thrown, and although arrests were made, the officers at the intersection were ordered to retreat. The *U.S. News* account and other accounts of that incident noted the presence of video cameras. The police, alleged to have been fearful of yet another brutality case, used no force at all against the burgeoning crowd and retreated.

The neighborhood around Florence and Normandie is not the typical situs for an urban riot. Many of the area residents are employed, and there are, reportedly, few of the signs of urban decay one might expect to find in a place that was the spawning ground for the violence that spread through the city.

The rioters themselves were, again atypically, white and Latino as well as black. It should be noted here that some of the most serious race riots in U.S. history (the infamous "red summer" of 1919 stands out in particular) were perpetrated not by blacks but whites. Riots in black neighborhoods were largely a product of the 1960s and later decades. In light of the published information available on the riots in L.A., the question of just how much the violence had to do with the beating of Rodney King or the eventual verdict must be raised.

It would be accurate to say, based on all available information, that pre-existing social conditions (along with greed and a predisposition to criminal behavior on the part of some individuals) provided the *motivation* for violence, while the King verdict provided *opportunity* and *circumstance*. The opportunity existed by way of citizens gathered at locations within the city who were of a common mind on the issue of the jury's verdict.

Contrary to popular belief, a riot is rarely an organized wave of lawlessness. Rather, civil disorder is better characterized as a series of individual criminal acts committed in an environment made ripe by the anonymity of a mob—a *bal masque* of violence and crime.

The rioting was not, however, confined to L.A. Violence attributable to the King verdict was reported in many U.S. cities, including Atlanta, Las Vegas, Seattle, Tampa, San Francisco, St. Louis, and Toledo. Even Toronto, Canada was not immune. And even in those cities where violence did not occur, there was protest. Students of Xavier University, a black college in New Orleans, marched up Tulane Avenue chanting in protest on the night of April 29. But no property damage or other forms of violence were reported.

———

Specific redress of grievances—with a proactive eye toward further government action against the officers in the King case—almost certainly could not have entered into the minds of the arsonists, murderers, mayhem artists, and looters. *U.S. News* reported that black-owned businesses were attacked despite signs identifying themselves as such, which indicated either a lack of concern for that fact on the part of rioters, or a profound illiteracy.

Nonetheless, if the past record of the U.S. Justice Department's involvement in civil rights violation cases is any indication, the decision to prosecute the King cops in federal court could only have been motivated by the violence that consumed L.A.

Stacy Koon, Theodore Briseno, Lawrence Powell, and Timothy Wind were indicted in the United States District Court and charged with violation of Rodney King's civil rights. This time, the jury was chosen from a population more representative of the city's demographics.

Among the rife misconceptions after the federal indictments were handed down were those surrounding the issue of "double jeopardy"—that provision in the Bill of Rights that says an individual shall not be twice put in jeopardy of life or limb for the same offense. In fact, the federal indictments in no way involved double jeopardy. The elements of the civil rights violation, even though based on the same evidence as the criminal case, differ from those attendant to the charges in the original trial.

If an individual commits a bank robbery he or she can be charged with the *state* offense of robbery, and/or possession of a weapon, reckless endangerment, or any other provision of the state law. He or she may *also* be charged with the crime of bank robbery as a federal offense, which is an entirely separate crime.

United States District Court Judge John G. Davies, who presided over the federal trial of the King cops, addressed the issue of double jeopardy:

> The federal prosecution . . . did not place those defendants in double jeopardy. Under the doctrine of 'dual sovereignty,' the state and federal governments are free to prosecute violations of their respective laws. (See *Heath v. Alabama*, 106 S.Ct. 433 [1985]). Successive state and federal prosecutions for the same act do not violate the fifth amendment.
>
> Nevertheless, a federal conviction following a state acquittal based on the same underlying conduct does create an unusual circumstance, and significantly burdens the defendants.

While the federal jury deliberated the fate of the officers, there was wide concern over the possibility of more violence if they were acquitted again. As it turned out, only two of the four defendants were convicted. Koon and Powell were convicted of violations of Title 18, Section 242 of the United States Code and have begun serving prison sentences. Briseno and Wind were acquitted. But there was no more violence, not even after Judge Davies displayed what some observers saw as surprising leniency in sentencing. The judge concluded in his fifty-four page sentencing memorandum, "Mr. King's 'serious' bodily injuries were attributable to a lawful use of force, whereas certain bodily injuries of a lesser degree were attributable to Koon's and Powell's unlawful conduct . . . " Addressing the "double jeopardy" question, the judge acknowledged that successive state and federal prosecutions, "though legal, raise a specter of unfairness."

The judge went on to note once again that King contributed to the events that occurred the night he was beaten:

> The evidence at trial supports a finding that Mr. King engaged in illegal conduct prior to and during his arrest. Mr. King was admittedly intoxicated while driving. He exceeded the speed limit at times. Mr. King failed to stop his vehicle, even after he belatedly perceived the flashing police lights and sirens. Perhaps due to his intoxication, Mr. King was slow to comply with police orders to exit his car. In any event, he failed to remain prone to the ground as the police ordered him to do. Rather, Mr. King resisted Officers Briseno, Solano, Powell, and Wind. He attempted to escape from police custody. In doing so, Mr. King, a still unsearched felony suspect, ran in the direction of Mr. Powell. He intended to escape into the unlit recreation area. At this point, the officers' use of the baton commenced . . . Significantly, defendants Koon and Powell, along with the other LAPD, C.H.P., and School District officers at the scene of Mr. King's arrest, were present only by happenstance. Had Mr. King pulled over, and not caused the C.H.P. officers to pursue him for up to eight miles, Koon, Powell and the

other LAPD officers would not have been summoned.
Messrs. Koon and Powell did not seek out a victim; rather,
their very presence at the scene was a consequence of Mr.
King's wrongful conduct.

The judge's words certainly support an earlier conclusion
presented here, which is that the King beating (like many
other police brutality incidents) began as an instance of lawful
force that police are entitled to use. Judge Davies later identified the exact point at which he determined the officers had
crossed the line—at time marker 1:07:28 of the Holliday videotape:

> . . . Mr. King's provocative behavior eventually subsided
> . . . Mr. King was no longer resisting arrest. He posed no ob-
> jective threat, and the defendants had no reasonable percep-
> tion of danger . . . Messrs. Koon and Powell were convicted
> of conduct which began as a legal use of force against a re-
> sistant suspect and subsequently crossed the line to unlaw-
> fulness, all in a matter of seconds, during the course of a dy-
> namic arrest situation. However, the convicted offenses fall
> under the same [sentencing] sections that would apply to a
> jailor, correctional officer, police officer or other state agent
> who intentionally used a dangerous weapon to assault an
> inmate, without legitimate cause to initiate a use of force.
>   The two situations are clearly different. Police officers
> are always armed with 'dangerous weapons' and may legit-
> imately employ those weapons to administer reasonable
> force. Where an officer's initial use of force is provoked and
> lawful, the line between a legal arrest and an unlawful dep-
> rivation of civil rights within the aggravated assault guide-
> lines is relatively thin.

One of the more unusual aspects of the entire federal case
was the fact that such prosecutions are so rarely initiated com-

pared to the numbers of complaints that are made nationwide requesting them.

In summarizing the Rodney King case, it's important to realize that only after a failed prosecution (and resulting civil unrest) did the federal government make any serious attempt to prosecute the alleged perpetrators under existing law. And once that prosecution was completed, the standard under which the convicted defendants were sentenced was admittedly distinct from those employed for other classes of defendants who have violated federal laws.

Are these federal laws, then, inadequately tailored for the prosecution of excessive-force cases? And if they are, then what can be done about it—if indeed federal prosecutions in such cases are desired at all? If the federal government cannot or should not undertake such cases, then what can be done to ensure that state governments diligently prosecute cases of police violence?

Before attempting to answer any of these questions, a better understanding of what is meant by deadly force—and excessive force—must be thoroughly established in the minds of all Americans.

THREE

HISTORY LESSONS AND FLEEING FELONS

*There is a violence that liberates, and a violence that enslaves;
there is a violence that is moral and a violence that is immoral.*
—Benito Mussolini

A POLICE DEPARTMENT'S primary goal is the protection of life and property, and fulfilling that mission often places officers in dangerous situations. If an officer passes a burning building where people are calling for help, he cannot just ask a dispatcher to notify the fire department and then go on as if nothing happened; it is the officer's duty to rescue those people if at all possible. An officer who sees an individual fleeing the scene of a crime is duty-bound to attempt an apprehension. This crisis-intervention aspect of policing is most closely associated with what are called patrol functions.

Police departments perform many services, from crime investigation and detection to the suppression of civil disorder and the giving of speeches aimed at preventing crime. It is the patrol function, however, along with the keeping of public order, that is most strongly identified with police work in the minds of the public. This is why the nightstick and the gun are not only tools, but icons of police work, even at a time when so

many police officers are being trained to use lap-top comput-
ers for gathering crime data.

In the earliest days of the United States there were no police departments. During colonial times, ad hoc posses of
townsmen—vigilante groups—would gather to apprehend
evil-doers. Many villages, towns, and cities had night watch-
men. They carried whistles or rattles to sound the alarm if a
fire or other emergency was spotted, and often were not paid
for their services, but performed them on a voluntary basis.
The militia was responsible for maintaining order, but was
only employed for that purpose in the most extreme situations, as when President George Washington called up 15,000
militiamen to western Pennsylvania in 1894, in order to suppress a rebellion by farmers incensed at the excise tax on alcohol distilled with their own grain. This Whiskey Rebellion, as
it came to be called, was one of the first national police actions
on a wide scale.

The very first modern police force was organized not in
the Americas but in England, in 1829. The British statesman Sir
Robert Peel secured passage of the Metropolitan Police Act,
which authorized a law enforcement body that would differ
markedly from the military in both attitude and dress. The
British soldiers wore red coats. The "Bobbies"—as they were
nicknamed in honor of Peel—wore blue.

On the other side of the Atlantic, the loose network of local
constables and sheriffs that had sprung up had trouble maintaining order in the face of race riots in New York and Boston,
where those who should have been maintaining order sometimes had a hand in the violence themselves. In 1838 the first
full-time, salaried municipal police department in the U.S. was
chartered in Boston, modeled after Sir Robert Peel's experiment. Other American cities followed suit.

Municipal policing got off to some rocky starts. In some
northern cities the sworn officers functioned little better than

vigilantes when rioting broke out, usually over issues of race. One of the bloodiest conflagrations occurred during the New York draft riots in July of 1863, when poor Irish immigrants, incensed that they would be drafted into the Union Army because they couldn't afford the $300 fee with which one could buy a substitute, did battle with police and the militia. Men, women, and children died on the streets of the city, and marauding mobs attacked hapless blacks. Over 1,000 lives were lost.

These earliest municipal police departments were necessitated by northern industrialism and some of its less pleasant consequences. The agrarian south did not have a widespread need for such organizations until after the Civil War, when mob violence afflicted that part of the country during Reconstruction.

A biracial metropolitan police force organized under the Reconstruction government of Louisiana Gov. William Kellog was first put to the test in New Orleans on August 14, 1871. Members of the infamous White League—ancestors of people who are still some of that city's most notable families—had attempted to receive a shipment of arms at the Mississippi River and Canal Street for use in a planned insurrection against Kellog's government. The Metropolitans stood in the front lines of a massive contingent of state militiamen, and were among the first to fall in a fight against the re-establishment of white supremacy. Those who remained standing after the first volleys beat a hasty retreat into the streets of the French Quarter.

By the last decades of the nineteenth century, police departments were firmly established in America's largest cities, although the old form of vigilante justice was still practiced in parts of the west. Gradually, however, more and more police forces were organized across the country.

Americans point to the perception of rampant crime in major cities today as an indication that "things are worse than they've ever been." But particularly in the 1880s, urban centers were plagued by individual acts of crime and violence—essentially, what we would refer to today as street crime. In New York City, gangs of homeless children, many of whom called the Hudson River wharves home, prowled the gaslit streets and preyed upon the gentry, stealing their money and generally wreaking havoc. Waves of immigrant groups made for numerous other difficulties, and police were relied upon to maintain social control and order. Their efforts did not endear them to the residents of the cribs and tenements in the city's more fetid quarters, such as the notorious area on the west side of Manhattan known as Hell's Kitchen. To Irish immigrant youths in that neighborhood, a policeman's wool coat was a sought-after trophy, and more than one unobservant patrolman was knocked unconscious by such prize-seekers. Things got so bad for awhile that police officers refused to patrol west of Tenth Avenue.

The system of due process that provides for the accused to be indicted for serious offenses, and tried by a jury of peers, requires the physical transport of a person to a court of law. Municipal police have long served as the "long arm" of the law in order to accomplish that end. Early police officers also intervened when a crime was being committed, and would remove the offender to the local police station, which oftentimes also served as a courthouse and lock-up.

The invention of the automobile and its adaptation to police use in the early twentieth century had a marked positive effect on policing efforts, making officers far more mobile. But the vise grip held on American cities by political "machines" brought the police as many steps backward as technology brought them forward. One of the most notorious such machines was New York's Tammany Hall, the Democratic organization nourished throughout the nineteenth century by its beneficent gestures toward new immigrants. Political patronage was the key weapon in the Tammany arsenal. Police officers, who owed their jobs to party bosses, and worked under supervisors equally indebted for their promotions, were not above enforcing the law of the machine rather than the law of the state. Passage of the federal Volstead Act in 1920, which criminalized the sale, manufacture, and transportation of alcoholic beverages (initiating what came to be called "Prohibition"), swelled the coffers of criminal organizations and offered new profit opportunities for corrupt police officials.

In addition to outright corruption and graft, other problems stemmed from common police methods of questioning, which came to be known as the "third degree." Torture, intimidation, coercion, food and sleep deprivation, and beatings were routinely administered in some police departments. Some police officials, however, claimed the use of such tactics was always more myth than reality.

A burgeoning reform movement eventually developed in reaction to the enormous consequences of police violence and corruption. In 1931, Douglas Wickersham, a former U.S. Attorney General under William Howard Taft, was tapped by President Herbert Hoover to head a commission that would investigate claims of ineffectiveness and illegal behavior among the crimefighters.

The Wickersham Commission had little trouble identifying accusations as fact. Its findings and recommendations, while no more welcome in the law-enforcement community at that time than similar reports are today, had a measurable effect on police culture. Police department procedures took on a more humane and professional quality. Just as the automobile and two-way radio had affected the profession's technology, the Wickersham Commission and its recommendations influenced—to some degree—its conscience.

Methods of policing improved in the post–World War II years, keeping in step with new technological developments.

A series of U.S. Supreme Court decisions on criminal procedure issues forced police personnel at the local level to pay greater attention to due process rights guaranteed by the federal constitution. Many of these rights were also incorporated into state constitutions, but until the Warren Court judicial "revolution," many were not followed.

Officers on patrol are still the backbone of any police organization. Their presence alone often serves as a deterrent to crime, and the police officer's physical presence is still law enforcement's most important tool. The most advanced detection techniques, from DNA testing to forensic toxicology, are geared toward determining who must be held culpable for a crime that has been committed. However, it is the individual officer who is most vital to the process of apprehending criminals. The electron microscope, the test tube, the laboratory serology protocol, the taser gun—all are extensions of the officer's hands, arms, legs, eyes, and ears; without cops, these complex technical tools would be useless.

Ultimately, when all the lab results are in and all the computer profiles of offenders have been completed, the accumulated evidence will point to an individual who will have to be physically brought to appear before a judge. This is accomplished by the use of various degrees of force.

In the world of physics, force at its simplest can be defined as an influence that, by pushing or pulling against matter, induces motion. In the world of law enforcement, force means compelling an individual to do something against his or her wishes, under the authority of law. Punishments, from paying a fine to serving a prison sentence, are accepted forms of forcible action taken against those who violate the codified rules of the state. In the U.S., authority flows from "we the people" to our elected officials, who write and enact the various laws. The police are charged with bringing individuals alleged to have committed violations before a court to answer for their crimes. This is what is called an arrest. It is not the job of the police to punish individual offenders, but merely to cause them to appear before a judge, who is the representative of the state.

This taking of a person, or the taking of, entrance upon, or searching of property for law enforcement purposes, must be accomplished by police officers who are simultaneously protecting those rights guaranteed to the individual who has been accused. These procedures are what is called due process, and any act by the police outside the scope of their lawful authority can be construed as a due process violation.

The enormous scope of the state's power, through the police, to abridge the liberty of an individual cannot be overemphasized. The state—no matter its particular government philosophy or practice—is without any doubt the most powerful of humankind's institutions. Religious organizations may demand strict compliance to their norms, as can families, with ostracism the most severe penalty for proscribed behavior in either case. But only the state lords over all organizations, cults, clubs, and belief systems by its sheer power to compel individuals to do what they otherwise would not, against their will and desire.

If you belong to a church that mandates the wearing of a red suit and white shirt at services, the priest can certainly deny you admission if you are wearing blue, or even ban you from coming back in the future. But if as punishment for your transgression the priest took you *against your will* to the church basement and kept you there for a week, he could be charged with false imprisonment or any number of related offenses. A father heartbroken by his adult children's failures to abide by his wishes may certainly disinherit them, or even evict them from his home. But he cannot lock them inside his attic for a week without risking recrimination. If he learns that his son murdered his wife he cannot search for the young man and gun him down on the street to make him pay for his crime, because that would be an act of murder. The state, on the other hand, can indeed hold people against their will, or even take a life—but only after a trial has been held and an individual has been found guilty of the alleged offense.

It is, then, understood that many of the actions routinely taken by the police in the name of the state, from ordering a driver to stop a vehicle to executing a search warrant to making an arrest, would in most cases be *criminal acts* if done by a private citizen. If a police officer acts outside the scope of authority by personally inflicting punishment on an offender, for example, this shield of the state does not apply. Since such an act is not state-sanctioned, then there is little difference between that officer and a common criminal. But, since the initial use of force (an arrest, for example) *was* lawful, a determination must be made of when and how the line delineating illegal behavior was crossed.

In addition to the force that police can use to induce a person to be brought into custody, there is even greater latitude given to officers who commit other acts that would normally be considered criminal, because it is understood that officers cannot be effective if they are killed or injured. Since there is a responsibility for the state not only to prosecute offenders but also to protect citizens against injury, the police officer may have to take a life in order to save his own or that of a third person.

Physical force, which involves anything from the use of handcuffs or other restraints to holding or even punching offenders, striking them with nightsticks, or dragging them off from the scene of a demonstration, does not ordinarily involve life-threatening actions. Deadly force, on the other hand, to be used only under specially prescribed circumstances, is calculated to kill not as a form of punishment, but as a means of preventing something worse from occurring. The safety of the public and the police, in such situations, is balanced against the life of the offender, and if the risk against public or police outweighs the individual's right to live, the offender loses.

The onus, then, is on the individual officer in the field to determine how much force is required to accomplish a specific goal. Shoplifters are not apt to find revolver muzzles placed against their heads upon leaving the grocery store. But the shoplifter who attempts to escape and fires shots at a pursuing officer could well expect to be shot at in return. In crime situations it is the offender who most often establishes the rules of engagement. The level of force used by the officer will escalate along with the offender's behavior.

The use of force authorized by law has not, however, always been commensurate with the threat faced by officers—or others. In one case cited by the Police Executive Research Forum, a door-to-door salesman exhibited unusual persistence in the peddling of his wares, and his abrasive tactics escalated to the point of his committing a misdemeanor assault. Kansas, where this incident occurred, is a state where fleeing from a crime—even if it is a misdemeanor—is considered a felony. As civilians pursued the fleeing salesman the police arrived on the scene and joined in the chase, during which one officer discharged his revolver in the direction of the salesman. When interviewed about it later, the officer voiced no regret over the action, which was in all respects lawful, if injudicious. In fact, in the 1950s and 1960s some states and localities authorized use of deadly force—including the use of firearms—to apprehend perpetrators accused of misdemeanor offenses.

In March 1989, the House Subcommittee on Criminal Justice held hearings on police abuse of deadly force. Congressman John Conyers, Jr., the chairman, noted that each year in the United States 100 to 125 law enforcement officers are killed by civilians; however, three times that amount of civilians are killed by police, with members of minority groups making up a disproportionate portion of the dead.

At that time, some large police departments still did not have clear guidelines governing the use of deadly force, although significant reform efforts had been undertaken by such groups as the National Organization of Black Law Enforcement Executives (NOBLE) and the International Association of Chiefs of Police (IACP) in hopes of standardizing policies. The definition of lawful or unlawful force varied from jurisdiction to jurisdiction, as did legal definitions of what constitutes justifiable homicide.

A police-related shooting, or other police-caused death of a suspect, can be justified legally and morally in situations where the individual is armed. But history has shown that when it comes to the police killing unarmed civilians, particularly minorities, such deaths can dramatically exacerbate preexisting community tensions. Recognizing this, the Community Relations Service (CRS) of the U.S. Department of Justice released a "conciliation handbook" in May 1982 for use by police and civilians alike. This handbook described the typical scenario evoking use of deadly force as involving an officer attempting to arrest a minority group member, shooting the person, and only then finding that the person was unarmed. The CRS recognized that further injury to civilians, as well as a risk to the officers involved, can easily result from such situations, making conciliation approaches and strategies a necessity—with an emphasis on proactive measures. The CRS suggested that firearms policies be reviewed regularly by all police departments, and that avenues for citizen input regarding such policies be provided. Recommendations were also made for in-service police sensitivity courses and enhanced screening and psychological testing of officers.

In 1985 the Chicago Police Department approved a "protection of life" policy, which explicitly authorized deadly force in situations where an individual has displayed a serious bent toward violence—ostensibly but not necessarily—in the presence of police. Kansas City and Atlanta had adopted similar policies a decade before.

A standard for police action in the taking of fleeing suspects was set by the United States Supreme Court in early 1985, with its landmark ruling in *Tennessee v. Garner*. Garner, a burglary suspect, had been shot and killed by police as he fled the scene of the crime, even though the officer had no reason to believe Garner was armed. A civil rights action was brought before the court on his behalf.

Up until this time, Tennessee law had permitted police to use deadly force against any *suspected* felon fleeing arrest. Such a method of arrest, the Supreme Court ruled, was a taking or *seizure* under the provisions of the fourth amendment. "The intrusiveness of a seizure by deadly force is unmatched," the court ruled, noting the fourth amendment proviso that searches and seizures must be *reasonable*. This was the argument used by Garner's post-mortem advocates to advance the case. Thus, the use of deadly force in the apprehension of *all* fleeing felony suspects, under the reasonableness standard, was found unconstitutional. "Notwithstanding probable cause to seize a suspect, an officer may not always do so by killing him," the court noted.

Under the *Garner* standard, then, an officer must have probable cause, to believe not only that the suspect is indeed wanted for a felony, but that the suspect poses a significant risk of death or serious physical injury to the officer or others, and that deadly force is necessary to prevent such person's escape.

"A state statute or rule that makes no distinction based on the type of offense or the risk of danger to the community is inherently suspect," the Supreme Court ruled, "because it permits an unnecessarily severe and excessive police response that is out of proportion to the danger to the community . . . [when] the suspect poses no immediate threat to the officer and no threat to others, the harm resulting from failing to apprehend him does not justify the use of deadly force to do so."

The *Garner* ruling significantly affected police standards of conduct, and state legislatures began to abolish so-called "fleeing felon" rules from their books.

State laws, even when they conform with *Garner*, can still have only a limited effect on police standards in the street. It is up to the individual police department to advise officers of what is expected of them in day-to-day conduct.

An officer who believes his life or the lives of others to be in danger cannot reasonably be expected to reflect on niceties of the law at the same time his life may be flashing before his eyes. This is where training and strict procedure enter the picture. It is argued in some circles that departments use their state laws as a minimum standard of conduct.

The IACP formulated a model policy in 1989 that it invites law enforcement agencies to adopt, in order to provide police officers with guidelines for the use of lethal force. The policy statement begins with this preamble:

> This department recognizes and respects the value and special integrity of each human life. In vesting police officers with the lawful authority to use force to protect the public welfare, a careful balancing of all human interests is required. Therefore, it is the policy of this department that police officers shall use only that force that is reasonably necessary to effectively bring an incident under control, while protecting the lives of the officer or another.

Defining deadly force as "any use of force that is likely to cause death or serious bodily harm," the policy authorizes the police officer to fire a weapon in order to protect himself or others from what is reasonably believed to be an immediate threat of death or serious bodily harm (sound familiar?), and/or to prevent the escape of a fleeing felon whom the officer has probable cause to believe will pose a *significant* [emphasis added] threat to human life should escape occur.

Before using a firearm, the IACP policy statement dictates that officers shall identify themselves and when possible state their intent to shoot. Further strictures prohibit warning shots or the firing of weapons at or from a moving vehicle, or under circumstances where innocent persons may be injured.

As much of an improvement as the IACP model might be over various departmental policies in effect across the country (even after *Garner*), it is not without its critics in the law enforcement community. The Commission on Accreditation for Law Enforcement Agencies (CALEA) demands that its member departments enact use-of-force policies with a written directive stating that personnel will use only the force necessary to effect lawful objectives, and that "an officer may use deadly force only when the officer reasonably believes that the action is in defense of human life, including the officer's own life, or in defense of any person in *immediate* [emphasis added] danger of serious physical injury." An additional directive states that the use of deadly force against a fleeing felon must meet the conditions required by that standard. At a November 1990 meeting CALEA adopted the following addendum to the directive:

> A "fleeing felon" should not be presumed to pose an immediate threat to life in the absence of actions that would lead one to believe such is the case, such as a previously demonstrated threat to or wanton disregard for human life.

The key word in the CALEA standard is "immediate" as regards the fleeing felon. The word "significant" is used in a comparable context by the IACP. The Police Executive Research Forum maintains that the IACP guidelines do not meet the more stringent CALEA standard, which it endorses instead.

The IACP and CALEA standards, along with the volume of literature on use of force available to law enforcement professionals, indicate that there exists serious concern at the highest police management levels over how much force is used by officers, and what training methods can be adopted to ensure that use-of-force standards are followed.

But no matter how well formulated the policy or procedure, no matter how stringent the standard employed by a police department, actions speak louder than policy papers. It is the officer in the field who makes the decision to employ lethal force. Once a gun is fired or the chokehold pushed to its ultimate limit, the effect is irreversible. Under the best of circumstances, what this means is that the police officer has avoided the loss of his own life or that of an innocent person. But the taking of a life by a police officer, in the name of the people of the state and municipality that issues his license to kill, can also be construed as a tragedy worthy not only of disapproval, but punishment in the form of a criminal prosecution.

———

On June 9, 1987, a criminal suspect in New York City, Eric Thomas, twenty-five, was being held by two undercover police officers. Thomas was laying on the ground chest-first with his hands behind him, a police officer's knee on his back. Police officer Neil O'Donnell then shot Thomas in the head and killed him. The shooting was found justified by authorities because, according to the officers' own account, Thomas had tried to grab for one of their guns.

In April 1988, thirty-one-year-old Lydia Ferraro, a white New Jersey mother of two, allegedly ran a red light in New

York City, and her vehicle was pursued by police officers through East Harlem, at non-excessive speeds, during which an NYPD sergeant fired at her moving vehicle. After her auto was stopped by a roadblock of police cars, a total of five different police officers fired thirteen shots into her automobile. During this incident, which the Center for Law and Social Justice described as a "massacre," Ferraro was killed, although no weapon of hers was ever found. The Manhattan district attorney's office presented the case to a grand jury, but no indictment was issued against any of the officers, even though forensic evidence indicated that at least one of the bullets that struck her head was fired at a range close enough to leave powder burns on her scalp.

Even assuming that some officer truly thought Lydia Ferraro was reaching for a weapon and posed an imminent threat, or that Eric Thomas's prone form somehow represented a grave hazard, their stories would merely be proof that all the regulations in the world cannot save lives, and cannot thoroughly buffer the police or the public against mistakes and misjudgments.

New standards on police use of force are seen by some critics as a way of "handcuffing the cops." But a prime example of the tragedy that can result when standards are minimal or nonexistent became painfully clear in one Los Angeles case that occurred five years before the *Garner* decision, but which could conceivably occur in any city with inadequate rules on the mere *unholstering* of an officer's gun. As this case will demonstrate, the absence of proper and safe standards can strip the public and the victim of adequate redress under the law after such an event occurs. It can also seriously erode public confidence in the overall mission of the police.

FOUR

DEADLY FORCE AS LETHAL ERROR:
ANATOMY OF A SHOOTING

ON THE NIGHT OF OCTO-
ber 15, 1980, at 10:20 P.M., a woman named Eileen O'Maye was
standing next to her parked car on El Camino Drive in Beverly
Hills, conversing with John Faulstick, a friend. As they talked
a brown 1979 Oldsmobile occupied by two Latino men pulled
alongside; the man in the passenger seat asked O'Maye if she
knew where the Beverly Wilshire Hotel was located. She ignored the man's request. Then, as she continued talking with
Faulstick, the passenger reached out and grabbed the shoulder
strap of her purse. The car screeched down El Camino Drive,
dragging O'Maye 150 feet to the corner of Wilshire Boulevard,
at which point she managed to free herself and fell to the pavement, sustaining numerous abrasions and lacerations. In addition to Faulstick, three other witnesses observed this strong-
arm robbery. No weapons were displayed.

A passing Beverly Hills police officer was flagged down,
and he took a report that described the car as a brown sedan,
possibly an Olds, bearing California license plate "220-WAK."
The description of the passenger and driver were minimal at
best, but the plate appeared valid, registered to David and
Lena Ramirez, 11401 Rincon Street in the San Fernando Valley.

At 12:17 A.M. Beverly Hills police notified the Los Angeles
police of this information, and it was broadcast on all LAPD

radios three minutes later. LAPD Foothill station officers Curtis Edmonds and Kenneth Sinz heard the transmission and drove to 11401 Rincon Street, where they noted an empty parking space in front of the address. They parked their car nearby and awaited the arrival of the suspect vehicle for twenty-seven minutes, and then responded to a radio call directing them to another location; no brown Oldsmobile had been observed as yet.

———

Earlier that day, Kenneth Ramirez left his home on Rincon Street for his job at Lockheed International, in time to begin his 4:00 P.M. shift. His younger brother, Christopher, drove him to the plant in Kenneth's brown Oldsmobile—bearing the license plate "220 WAK"—because the young man would be using the car later that evening.

This was not unusual, and Kenneth did not mind his brother using the car so long as he appeared on time to pick him up from work at midnight. A friend and co-worker, John Herrera, also made the trip to the plant with the Ramirez brothers.

At 12:30 in the morning on the sixteenth, Kenneth Ramirez and Herrera left the plant and started walking to a liquor store, where they were going to meet two other Lockheed employees, Hector Quintana and Victor Villareal. On their way there Christopher Ramirez and a friend, Richard Galvan, pulled up in Galvan's maroon Chevrolet Monte Carlo. Kenneth and John got in and the group went to Galvan's North Hollywood home, where they switched cars; earlier Christopher had left the Oldsmobile there. The Ramirez brothers, with John Herrera, left North Hollywood and stopped at Kenneth's fiancee's house, where they visited for approximately five to ten minutes. After dropping off Herrera the brothers drove to their home on Rincon Street, and the car was parked at the empty curb space.

Hector Quintana and Victor Villareal had continued waiting for Kenneth Ramirez at the liquor store near the plant, unaware that he and Herrera had been picked up by Christopher. After buying some beer they drove to the Ramirez residence, where it was common for the men to get together after work. At approximately 1:00 A.M. Quintana parked his Mustang nearby and the two men exited the car, soon to be joined on the street by Christopher and Kenneth Ramirez. The men stood and talked. A short time later, Kenneth walked into the house.

About that same time Foothill station officers Michael Sullivan and Wendell Rhinehart were monitoring their police radio when the earlier broadcast regarding the wanted Oldsmobile was repeated, including the Rincon Street address. Since they weren't far away the officers decided to take a pass by, and within two minutes they were driving down the block where the Ramirez brothers lived. It was a dark night with an overcast sky and there were no streetlights on that block of Rincon. The high-beam lights of the prowl car were on as the officers crept by the location at around five miles per hour.

Quintana, Villareal, and Christopher Ramirez were still standing in the street in front of the house when they were noticed by officers Sullivan and Rhinehart. Neither of the officers, however, noticed the Oldsmobile or the house with its address. When the car reached the end of the block it made a U-turn and continued slowly back down the street in the opposite direction.

At the same time the police car was making the U-turn, Kenneth Ramirez came back out to the street and entered the parked Oldsmobile. During the time it took the police car to get close to his house he had finished whatever business he was about, and exited the vehicle with the keys in his hand. It was at that time that the officers noticed the Oldsmobile. At the same time they saw Kenneth locking the door and removing the key from the lock.

Sullivan turned to Rhinehart and said "That's the car."

Rhinehart had just then focused his attention on Hector, Victor, and Christopher, and observed Kenneth walking away from the Oldsmobile and north on Rincon Street, toward the police car; he also noticed—and realized the significance of—the Oldsmobile's license plate.

Sullivan stopped the police car four feet east of a parked 1976 Oldsmobile, and twenty-six feet north of Ramirez's car. Rhinehart immediately started out of the vehicle with a flashlight in his left hand as Kenneth continued walking toward the cruiser. When Kenneth reached the right front tire of the cruiser Rhinehart withdrew his service revolver; within one second the gun discharged once. Kenneth fell to the pavement, and Sullivan later recalled that Rhinehart exclaimed, "Oh shit!"

Sullivan called for assistance and ran toward Hector, Victor, and Christopher, ordering them to turn away from the street.

Rhinehart stood next to Kenneth Ramirez's lifeless form and wept.

Foothill station Sgt. Denis Pelch arrived on the scene within fifteen to twenty seconds of the call for assistance and was briefed on the incident. Rhinehart said he was all right and requested an ambulance. Meanwhile David and Lisa Ramirez, Kenneth's father and sister, had come out of the house. Shocked at what they saw, they ran toward Kenneth but were kept away by Rhinehart.

Because there was blood on Kenneth's shirt, the officers thought that Kenneth had been shot in the chest. But when Rhinehart reportedly attempted first aid and cut away Kenneth's shirt with a knife supplied by Sgt. Pelch, no wound was found. Kenneth's head was moved away from the front tire of the car and it was then that a wound was observed above his left eyebrow.

Kenneth Ramirez was pronounced dead by a Los Angeles Fire Department Rescue Unit at 1:24 A.M.

———

The next day, October 17, Christopher Ramirez was arrested for the Beverly Hills robbery. The investigation revealed that there was no way Kenneth Ramirez could have been involved, since it was well established that he had been working at Lockheed during the time it occurred.

Deputy Medical Examiner Lawrence Cogan, M.D., performed an autopsy on Kenneth Ramirez and ascribed the cause of death to a single gunshot wound to the head, with evidence that supported the finding that the weapon was discharged from a distance rather than close-up—there was no sooting or stippling noted on the skin around the wound.

An investigation by the Los Angeles County District Attorney's office continued, and all witnesses were interviewed. Investigators attempted to interview Rhinehart, who was reported to have been distraught after the shooting. But the officer declined interview requests, as he was constitutionally permitted.

He did, however, give an oral statement to investigators from the LAPD, and said that he and Sullivan had driven to the Rincon Street address because of the radio report, made the U-turn, and observed three males standing near the suspect Oldsmobile. He recalled seeing a male Latino walk away from the Oldsmobile directly toward the radio car, and that after Sullivan braked the auto he, Rhinehart, exited by pushing the door open with his foot. He had a flashlight in his left hand, which he intended to shine in the face of the approaching man.

As Ramirez passed through the beam of the radio car headlights Rhinehart believed he was one of the Beverly Hills robbers and withdrew his pistol from its holster with his right hand. His left foot was still in the car and the right on the pavement, and, he claimed, as the gun reached waist level it accidentally discharged.

It should be noted that the gun, a double action .38 Smith & Wesson revolver with a four-inch barrel, was tested and found free from defect, and that ten pounds of pressure is required to pull the trigger. It should also be noted that although Rhinehart said his gun discharged from waist level, the medical examiner found that the single wound to Ramirez was "front to back, slightly *downward* [emphasis added] and slightly left to right."

The D.A.'s office first had to determine whether intent existed on the part of officer Rhinehart to take the life of Ramirez. Investigators used the instruction given to juries by judges in cases where intent is an issue, which finds intent to be evinced by: "(1) A statement of his intent made by the person committing the act or (2) by the circumstances attending the act, the manner in which it is done and by the means used . . . "

No statement of intent could be discerned; therefore, the circumstances were the key to making any determination that Rhinehart's act was intentional.

There was no indication of any dispute or harsh words between Rhinehart and Ramirez, and the only words any of the witnesses ascribed to the officer were those of his exclamation after the shot was fired ("Oh shit"). All of the statements given by Rhinehart were, in fact, corroborated by the witnesses, and a determination was made that the shooting was unintentional.

The California Penal Code, however, still required a finding of whether, although unintentional, the shooting was *ex-*

cusable. For Rhinehart's conduct to be excusable, his drawing of the revolver upon exiting the police car had to be found as a lawful act taken with "usual and ordinary caution."

The D.A. found that Rhinehart and Sullivan had every reason to be on Rincon Street at the time of the shooting because of the widely broadcast alarm for the Oldsmobile. Indeed, another police car had already been to that location during the prior shift. General as the description of the robber (a male latino) may have been, the D.A. also found that, given the presence of the Oldsmobile at that address, Ramirez could reasonably be regarded as a possible suspect, warranting at the very least further investigation. The determination was that at the time he exited the patrol car, Rhinehart was engaged in a lawful act.

This brings the analysis to the question of whether Rhinehart's withdrawal of his weapon from its holster was legal. The L.A.P.D. officer's training manual in use at the time provided as follows:

> An officer's firearm is not to be drawn arbitrarily. However, when an officer has reason to believe that danger exists, the weapon may be drawn. For example, officers respond to a silent burglary alarm at a warehouse. They observe that the front door of the warehouse has been pried open and the decision is made to search the warehouse for perpetrators. For their own safety, the officers may have their weapons drawn while searching the building.
>
> In another situation, officers respond to a "shots fired" investigation. At the scene, a witness advises the officers that the suspect is in a particular backyard. The officers may draw their service revolvers while searching the backyard.
>
> The apprehension which some officers experience in a stress-filled situation may be sufficient itself to warrant an officer drawing a weapon. As a general rule, though, officers do not draw their weapons without a reasonable belief

that it is necessary and in no case would a mere feeling of apprehension justify firing the weapon.

In the case of the Ramirez shooting, due to the circumstances, the darkness of the street, and the close proximity of four possibly suspect individuals on the street, the district attorney's office then found that Rhinehart's drawing of the weapon was justified.

The next legal step down the ladder was involuntary manslaughter. In its report, the district attorney's office cited Penal Code section 192, which defines involuntary manslaughter as a homicide occurring " . . . in the commission of a lawful act which might produce death in an unlawful manner without due caution and circumspection." Three California Supreme Court decisions were also cited.

People v. Penny (1955), defined the phrase "without due caution and circumspection" as "conduct which is such a departure from what would be the conduct of an ordinarily careful or prudent man . . . as to be incompatible with a proper regard for human life, or in other words, a disregard for human life, or in other words, a disregard for human life or an indifference to consequences."

In *Somers v. Superior Court* (1973), a police officer shot an innocent person whom he suspected of being a robbery suspect. The court held that in order to find the defendant guilty of involuntary manslaughter, something more than ordinary negligence is needed, noting that "the defendant must have acted in an aggravated, culpable, gross, or reckless manner . . . "

The most typical of the manslaughter cases cited was *People v. Walls* (1966), in which the defendant was demonstrating his fast draw to his niece when the gun went off, killing her. He was convicted of involuntary manslaughter.

"The appellate court," the D.A.'s office noted, "had little

trouble finding that Walls acted so recklessly as to be incompatible with a proper regard for human life."

The Ramirez case offered few parallels to such a "true" manslaughter case, according to the D.A., and thus such disregard and recklessness were not found.

The final possibility for any finding of wrong-doing on the part of Officer Rhinehart concerned the issue of negligence.

"The only conceivable basis for a claim of negligence . . . could be predicated upon Rhinehart's position half out of the patrol car when he drew his weapon," the D.A.'s report read.

A 1915 California case, *People v. Sidwell*, was cited, in which the defendant, a deputy sheriff, was listening at the door of a hotel room and heard what he believed to be gambling activities. He took his gun out and as he was breaking the door open it discharged, killing one of the occupants. The court ruled against Sidwell:

> The handling of a loaded firearm in a public street or in a building or other place where a number of persons are assembled or are passing to and fro is always attended with more or less danger, even where some degree of care is exercised in the handling of such weapon. But how much more danger must there be in the handling of such weapon by a person at a time when his mind is occupied by another matter of paramount concern to him. His mind could not at any time be upon the weapon to such a degree as to enable him to handle it with the care and caution with which ordinarily he would probably handle it.

The district attorney's office noted that in *Sidwell* the defendant was not acting in response to a dangerous situation, but rather embarked on his own plan to kick a door in while holding his weapon at the same time. Rhinehart's drawing of the weapon, the D.A. concluded, was in response to Ramirez's approach. The conclusion contained the following statement:

> The totality of circumstances created the apparent necessity
> for Rhinehart to draw his weapon when he did and under
> such circumstances it cannot be said that Rhinehart acted
> with disregard for human life . . . Based on our review of all
> available evidence, we find that the tragic and unfortunate
> death of Kenneth Ramirez was the result of accident with-
> out criminal negligence and must, therefore, be deemed
> under the law to be excusable homicide.

———

Why, one might ask, should anyone be interested at all in prosecuting Officer Rhinehart? He was apparently acting in good faith, was obviously distraught by the incident, and there was certainly no evidence of intent.

At the time of this incident, though, there was serious friction between the Latino community in Los Angeles and the LAPD It is precisely in situations such as this (here the suspect was not only unarmed but also innocent of any wrongdoing) that rumor and fear charge the atmosphere.

The issue that became prominent in the D.A.'s treatment of the Ramirez tragedy was whether a due standard of care was employed by Officer Rhinehart. Why was this the case? Any prosecutor enjoys wide discretion in deciding whether to take on a particular case. Indeed, a conscientious district attorney must take into account the defenses available to a defendant, and how adequately the presumption of the accused's innocence on *any* charge can be attacked by the state.

Certainly, it would be rare for a *civilian* unholstering a weapon out of fear or apprehension to be accorded the same amount of latitude the D.A.'s report granted Rhinehart. Yet the prosecution summary of the case takes on the tone of a defense memorandum, citing a case from sixty-five years prior as the basis for a finding of no negligence—and in a negative vein at that. There are some clear parallels between *Sidwell* and the actions taken by Rhinehart, yet they are immediately discounted by the very office whose job is to prosecute offenders, even when the circumstances surrounding a particular situation are, perhaps, accidental.

In the Beverly Hills robbery of Eileen O'Maye, no mention of a weapon was ever made by either the victim or any of the police personnel who broadcast the alarm over police radio. As Ramirez approached the police car there was no suspicion that he was reaching for a weapon or that he had one visible, or anywhere on his person. The problem, however, may be more in the LAPD guidelines in use at the time, which as excerpted above give an officer great discretion—even condoning, in heavily couched language, the unholstering of the gun.

A standard for safe handling of firearms in New York City is worded as follows:

> [Officers] are justified in removing firearms from holsters and/or gun mounts and pointing the firearm if: 1) there is a justification to use a firearm against a person or animal; 2) the member reasonably believes that a person or a situation poses or may pose an immediate threat of death or serious physical injury either to himself or another person.

The Houston, Texas, Police Department issued revised standards of conduct for officers which included a provision that read, "Police officers shall not draw or display their firearms unless there is a threat or probable cause to believe there is a threat to life, or for inspection."

Examining the "totality of circumstances" in the Ramirez case gives pause as to whether Officer Rhinehart's action would have been considered proper in that jurisdiction.

The methods by which accidental discharges of police firearms are documented varies according to jurisdiction. New York City keeps some of the most wide-ranging data. A 1990 study there revealed that three out of sixty-two total accidental *discharges* (whether or not injury resulted) occurred during holstering or unholstering, with one additional discharge occurring while a gun was unholstered as the officer was sitting in a chair.

The most common cause of accidental discharge was a perpetrator hitting at an officer's hand or grabbing a weapon, which occurred sixteen times that year. Discharges resulting from struggles with a perpetrator came in second with seven incidents.

Even trained law enforcement officers can sometimes make thoroughly careless mistakes. One incident in the New York study involved an officer placing a gun in an oven for safekeeping, then forgetting about it and turning the oven on. This was not a unique circumstance. The following year in New York an officer placed a gun in an oven and forgot about it. When the appropriate temperature was later reached, six shots were reportedly discharged.

Perpetrators aren't the only parties (in addition to the officers themselves) to cause a weapon to discharge. In one cited case an officer was trying to re-holster his gun while struggling with a suspect. The complainant, while trying to strike the suspect, struck the gun instead and caused it to fire.

Assuming that Rhinehart's shooting of Ramirez was indeed accidental, despite the ten pounds of pressure needed to discharge the double-action weapon, there are still a few unpleasant possibilities involved in this case. The hammer of the gun could have been cocked (something Rhinehart may or may not have mentioned to police investigators); if that was the case, we are faced with an instance of severe negligence on Rhinehart's part. Such an action would have endangered not only innocent bystanders and any suspects, but also the officer and his partner. If the hammer *was* locked, then Rhinehart might well have intentionally pulled the trigger because, very simply, he panicked. But we shall never know.

In fact, the entire D.A.'s report on the Ramirez case, while thoughtful and thorough, is absent any trace of the one thing that makes our criminal justice system function with any degree of effectiveness: that is, its adversary nature.

Officer Rhinehart's refusal to speak with the district attorney's office, an exercise of his fifth amendment right against self-incrimination, is something that should not be considered as an indication that he had done wrong. Yet in a case like this, the perception by the community that the officer had something to hide could be enough to spark a riot, if other combustible factors are also at play. That possibility is considered only because society will act more often out of self-interest than a desire for true justice.

The brief and highly selective history presented here on the use of deadly force by the police has included cases where, although errors in judgment occurred, officers were pursuing a specific goal of law enforcement when deadly force was employed—as in the Ramirez case.

For instance, the officer whose gunshots precipitated the *Garner* decision acted within the scope of the law as authorized at the time. Even the Ramirez case, though tragic, was at worst due to a moment of panic on the part of the officer, and in any event occurred before the tightening of many firearms handling standards—five years before *Garner*. The point of its inclusion here is not to vilify the officer involved, but to serve up an important point that goes far beyond the Ramirez incident in scope.

But what happens when a firm allegation can be sustained that the officer, rather than acting in good faith, *intended* to use force beyond the scope of authority? Are such cases, when the infliction of pain, injury, or worse are intentional, handled with any greater care than that of the Ramirez shooting?

The Rodney King case cannot be used as a model to sustain such allegations one way or the other. The officers most directly responsible for that incident, though not convicted in state court, *were* still indicted (if only because of the videotape). What makes the King case so frightening, of course, is that King's death *could* have occurred as a result of his beating. In examining patterns of police behavior, the use of all kinds of excessive force must be examined, and not just in those instances that result in death. The living can still speak and tell their stories—even if nobody much chooses to listen.

FIVE

CRESCENT CITY BLUES AND DEMON RUM

THE FRENCH QUARTER OF New Orleans is a sixty-six-square-block Disneyland for drunks and history buffs, a never-never land of historic antebellum buildings graced by world-famous iron-lace balconies, located on the banks of the mighty Mississippi, where paddle-wheelers still ply the river's rough current on daily cruises. Narrow Vieux Carre streets are benignly haunted by the ghosts of creole aristocrats and Jean Lafitte's pirate crew, while spirits of a far different nature pour non-stop, twenty-four hours a day on Bourbon Street—named for the royal French family of that name, not the booze.

It is difficult for tourists, who rarely stray north of Canal nor south of Esplanade, to realize that they are visiting a real American city with problems not unlike those of most other urban centers. Residents of the Ninth Ward, the Treme, Uptown, and Algiers (the only portion of the city proper on the river's west bank) are more accustomed to hearing gunshots and sirens in the night than the sounds of jazz.

Racial tension is not as apparent in the Crescent City as in many other American cities, in part because of its unique history as the only Southern city where people of color enjoyed free status prior to the Civil War. Marie Laveau, the Voodoo Queen, was a free mulatto woman who had access to some of the finest white and mixed-blood creole homes during the mid-nineteenth century. After the Civil War, Reconstruction government officials did not have to look far to find qualified, well-educated blacks to place in office as a snub to the conquered local Confederates. But racial tension exists nonetheless, and is aggravated by the perception prevalent in the city's minority populations that the lives and well-being of the free-spending, predominantly white tourists are sometimes handled with greater care than their own.

New Orleans is also a city where blacks are in the majority—close to 80 percent of the population. But unlike some other cities, the percentage of black police officers there is more in keeping with the population demographics. A study of minority police representation in major cities showed the New Orleans minority index at 0.63. A city comes closer to proportional demographic racial representation in its police force as it approaches 1.0, the "perfect" score. New Orleans's 0.63 figure is not the highest; Washington, D.C., is actually overrepresented, at 1.03; New York, with .40, has the lowest figure of any major city on the scale.

Community-based recruitment efforts have assisted the New Orleans Police Department in its integration, and although on the surface it would seem that residents enjoy an unusual rapport with their law enforcement officers, there are considerable problems.

New Orleans has, according to a recent survey, the highest number of brutality complaints against its officers of any city in the United States. But statistics are not the most reliable indicators of the truth. The high number of complaints against the N.O.P.D., for example, could be due to the ease with which citizens are able to make complaints, according to Sgt. Barry Fletcher, an N.O.P.D. spokesman. And in the most recent years, city officials have worked hard to address the brutality issue. But serious problems still remain.

———

The mule-drawn carriages that clip-clop and rattle through the French Quarter's narrow streets are a source of delight to many tourists, and the bane of animal-rights activists. Harry Sommers, an African-American Vietnam veteran, has been driving these buggies for nearly fifteen years on the narrow Vieux Carre streets. He neither drinks nor smokes and is a certified tour guide, who points out historic sites while relating anecdotes about the Ursuline Nuns, Andrew Jackson, and the House of the Rising Sun. Awestruck tourists provide a chorus of oohs and aahs beneath Harry's deep, rich baritone.

The busiest time of year for Harry Sommers and most of the other people who earn their living in tourist dollars is Mardi Gras, that magical time prior to Ash Wednesday when party seekers from all over the world flock to participate in the greatest free show on earth. On Mardi Gras itself—Fat Tuesday—the company Harry works for doesn't take the mules out on the streets.

"They'd be tryin' everything," he said of the unruly crowds. "Be tryin' to fuck these mules here if you let 'em."

It was the day before Fat Tuesday—Lundi Gras, February 6, 1989—when Harry Sommers learned that being a working man and a life-long Louisiana resident couldn't immunize him from mistreatment at the hands of the people his tax dollars paid to protect him.

"I had these people on my buggy," he said while stroking the neck of his new mule, Bernice. "All white people. And it's real crowded out here. Nice folks, havin' a good time."

Harry said that a man broke from the crowd of bystanders across from Jackson Square, at Washington Battery Park, and tried to climb on his buggy.

"I had women and kids on there," Harry related. "I don't

know what this cat is tryin' to do, so I start tryin' to get him off."

Having a drunk madman on his buggy in bumper-to-bumper carnival traffic when he already had a full load and was also trying to control a frightened animal at the same time was harrowing. Harry reached for a wagon wheel spoke on the floor of the buggy and began swinging. The man fought back and the two ended up on the ground, at which point the man identified himself as a police officer. Harry saw the familiar shield—the crescent and star that is the New Orleans police insignia—and before he knew what was happening, on-duty officers in uniform were involved.

"They beat me senseless," Harry said. The damages included broken ribs and internal injuries. Harry was arrested. His supervisor brought the driverless mule and buggy back to the barn, and Harry wasn't physically able to work again for over a year.

The criminal charges against him were found meritless. But Harry's anger remained. Determined that somebody should pay for what happened to him, he has pursued his case in United States District Court for the Eastern District of Louisiana. It is still pending. As is the custom in most cities, officials could not comment on the case because of the active litigation.

In 1990 an incident occurred in the Crescent City that residents still talk about as proof of the fearsome nature of the local officers. A black man, Adolph Archie, had shot a white officer and was in turn shot by other pursuing officers as he fled. As he was being apprehended, Archie—already suffering from the gunshot wound—was kicked, punched, and then taken, barely conscious, to a hospital. There he was kept on the ramp in the police car until word of the officer's condition could be learned. When word reached the officers holding Archie that the white officer Archie shot had died, they did not bring Archie into the emergency room for treatment. Instead they took him to a stationhouse. Less than an hour later he was returned to the hospital with more broken bones, abrasions, contusions, and other injuries. A few hours later, Archie was dead.

A cover-up ensued. The truth was only brought to light after independent doctors examined Archie's medical records. Eventually, a successful criminal prosecution by the civil rights division of the United States Justice Department was brought, and there were high-level changes of personnel in the medical examiner's office, as well as a police department housecleaning. The Archie case brought police brutality in New Orleans out of the closet.

———

Legitimate pain-compliance techniques ranging from thumb and wristlocks to chokeholds are used freely in New Orleans, especially on the Bourbon Street honky-tonk strip, where almost anything goes. It is there that some of the more vociferous complainants about police violence can be found, especially among out-of-towners who have never had much contact with the police before, or have never been so highly intoxicated in a public place. On some nights thousands of people mill around the street, which closes to traffic after eight every night. They swill drinks from plastic and paper cups, singing and dancing and soaking up the atmosphere.

One night in 1993 a trio of mounted officers observing the strip, as they often do, from the corner of Bourbon and Toulouse streets, across from the Old Opera House nightclub and directly in front of the Best Western Inn on Bourbon. The night air was heavy and sweet, without being too warm, and by 10:00 P.M. the crowd was growing. Four young women, among the dozens who had done the same thing in the space of two hours, stopped to pet the horses and make small talk with the cops.

Suddenly one of the horses spooked backwards, frightening the girls. A passing young man, drink in hand, had slapped the horse in the face. In a flash the officer directed his steed toward the offender, grabbed him by the collar, and dragged him back to the corner of Toulouse. Other officers in the area saw the trouble afoot and had run to the scene; they took the miscreant into their custody. As he sat on the ground, already handcuffed, he protested, "I didn't do nothin' man."

A mounted sergeant's horse stepped to within inches of where the young man sat, surprising him, since the New Orleans police horses are shod with rubber, their approach is silent. The sergeant looked down at the arrestee with daggers in his eyes.

"If that was my hawse you hit," he said "you'd be bloody."

A short time later a radio car arrived and picked up the offender, and the crowd that had gathered dispersed into the larger throng. At Bourbon and Toulouse it was business as usual, as a brass band backed up an opera-house singer wailing "Mustang Sally."

"We don't mind if they think we're tough," a young cop said in an interview a few days later. He was working a "detail"—a paid private security assignment that he is permitted to perform in uniform. "But we ain't out to hurt nobody."

He said that low starting pay is a blow to the morale of officers, and that if he didn't work details he couldn't make ends meet. (This was during the same year that New Orleans officers, complaining of mandatory cuts in overtime, staged a nine-day sickout.)

"We got these drunks out here, and some of them get real bad," he said. "They come from all over, some of them from places where they can't drink at all, let alone what you can do here. And then they have too much and they act like assholes.

Sometimes they'll want to fight you and figure you're just part of the party and you're not gonna lock and they're wrong."

The officer said that there are some cops—not many but some—who have a reputation for being harder on suspects than they need to be, and admitted that even when complaints were made, other officers didn't try to make the investigative process any easier. This blue wall of silence exists in New Orleans, he said, because the city doesn't back the cops up.

"Somebody, especially a minority, does something and you get involved in a problem, they say you beat them up or whatever and the city's all over you. They throw you to the wolves." The self-insured city of New Orleans, he said, dreads lawsuits. "The city'll do whatever it can to clear its own name, and lay it on you and then you get sued. So how I'm gonna co-operate with an investigation of some other cop? It could be me next time. You take a guy been out here all his life for a little bit of money, does a good job, and then one thing happens and he's gonna lose everything. Lots of times it's a mistake. Somebody loses it. But we're dealing with the real world out there, not television. I make a mistake because I think if I don't I'm gonna die, I got no choice."

On another end of Bourbon Street the sounds of jazz blasted out through the open door of the Famous Door night-club, and a barker wearing a derby strutted up to a quartet of middle-aged women, twirling his parasol, enticing them inside. A hatless uniformed sergeant stood in the middle of the street, arms, thick as tree trunks, akimbo.

"We get complaints," the sergeant said. "But you've got to look at where they're coming from. You *say* something some-body doesn't like and they got you up on charges. Sometimes you try to make someone do something and they don't and it's trouble, so you have to start out strong and prevent that. Me, I'm good to you until you show me different. You want to be an asshole it's not going to make any difference to me. I don't even have to process you. I'll just cuff you and call for a car. Simple."

The officers themselves do not have to follow low-level arrests through the system. The Orleans Parish Sheriff's Department (Louisiana has parishes instead of counties, owing to its Roman Catholic roots) runs the lockup where suspects are taken after arrest, and the arresting officer does not have to appear in court until an appearance date is given to the defendant—if one is given at all. One benefit of this system is that the officers and defendants spend very little face time post-arrest, minimizing acrimony.

———

The ordeal of Harry Sommers and, most certainly, the Archie case made the warning of the mounted N.O.P.D. sergeant—"you'd be bloody"—sound like a gentle reminder to someone that they ought to mind their manners. But despite its track record, the Big Easy may be turning into a kinder, gentler city after all.

In chapter three, mention was made of the 1871 Battle of Liberty Place at the foot of Canal Street. The branch of the White League that attempted this insurrection against the Reconstruction government was made up mostly of young men from the St. Charles Avenue silk-stocking district. Many belonged to families that had lost considerable fortunes as a result of the Civil War and its aftermath. In their view they were, under the post-war government, needlessly oppressed. Oppressed or not, they weren't accomplished street fighters, and their rebellion was unsuccessful. Modern-day blacks found references to the White League highly offensive, however, not only because of the group's pro-Confederate leanings but also because the White League had been responsible for other acts of terrorism, such as the post-war Colfax riot, in which inno-

cent blacks who had gone to vote for the first time were surrounded and shotgunned to death.

The stone obelisk erected at the site of the riverside battle
was dedicated to the honor of men who died there in defense
of liberty—a reference not to the militiamen and Metropolitan
Police (whose ranks included African-Americans) but to the
white-supremacist White League. In case there was any doubt,
this sentiment was clarified by an 1874 pedestal addition that
praised white supremacy.

The monument became a rallying point for the Ku Klux
Klan in the 1970s and 1980s. Later it was removed from its site
to facilitate highway repair, but the city had agreed to return it.
There was considerable foot-dragging, however, until an uptown pharmacist whose family had fought on the side of the
White Leaguers sued to have it returned. The pharmacist had
been a major contributor to the failed presidential and guber-
natorial campaigns of former Ku Klux Klan Grand Dragon
David Duke, who himself took an active role in the fight to
have the statue restored.

Reluctant city officials had no choice after the court order
was issued, and in 1992 the obelisk—with a new plaque that
sought to water down the offensiveness of the old plaque—
was returned to a new site at the foot of Iberville Street.

A rally at which Duke was a featured speaker was held at
the obelisk that summer. Black demonstrators converged on
the area as well, and the badly undermanned police contingent, fearing violence, called for reinforcements.

Among the demonstrators was eighty-two-year-old Avery
Alexander, the dean of Louisiana's modern civil rights movement. Alexander had been dragged up a city hall staircase
twenty-five years before by the New Orleans police when he
attempted to desegregate the lunch counter at City Hall, and
was the first black man elected to the state legislature.

The black demonstrators grumbled about what they saw

as preferential treatment for the whites during the event. That the police officer reservists were all white didn't help matters any. Minor scuffling broke out. One of the reservists, armed with a nightstick, placed Avery Alexander in what appeared to be a chokehold. A close-up color photo of the incident ran on the front page of the *New Orleans Times-Picayune* the next day, and an investigation was ordered by the city council. The action of the officer reservist, though not illegal, was ill-advised at best, considering the circumstances. The specter of an elderly black man being dragged off from a peaceful demonstration in Louisiana by uniformed officers made for a chilling *déjà vu*.

The response of the city council was swift and very public. The news media reported extensively on the situation, and in the wake of the incident the council declared the obelisk to be a public nuisance. The black community seemed confident that the council had done what was necessary to address the offensive situation. Some observers suggested that protests over the Rodney King verdict that occurred in the New Orleans area never had the chance to escalate into violence, as they did in other cities, because the new city council seemed to demand accountability from the police.

———

What is most remarkable about the New Orleans Police Department is the job it does controlling crowds—especially during the annual Mardi Gras bacchanalia. Their tacticians are consulted by governments all over the world.

Problems involving intoxicated persons are not unique to New Orleans, but are shared by other jurisdictions where the inebriati are present but more thinly concentrated. The public record consistently demonstrates that the least perilous situations often result in the greatest risk to people who are beaten (not shot) by the police. Very often these people are intoxicated, otherwise unruly, and have made the grave mistake of challenging an officer's authority by words or actions, which is perceived immediately as a threat.

Findings of the 1987 New York State Commission on Criminal Justice and the Use of Force included this statement, which could certainly apply in New Orleans as well as other cities:

> The vast majority of incidents requiring the use of physical force by police officers do not, in the first instance, involve the commission of violent felonies or indeed, felonious conduct of any kind. Most such incidents escalate from minor order-maintenance confrontations or other enforcement efforts where the offender challenges or otherwise resists the officer's authority, and the officer responds with such force as may be necessary to handle the situation. It is not irrelevant that in the majority of these cases, the citizen-offender is under the influence of alcohol . . . One court described the typical situation as one in which "words led to more words and then to action by the police in effecting the arrest" or "the oft-encountered situation of an officer attempting to vindicate a perceived affront to his dignity."

One problem in New York state has been confusion over the right of a citizen to attempt to negate an illegal arrest or other police action. This could be done up until 1968, when the legislature changed the rules of the game.

Section 35.627 of the penal law in New York now states that "[a] person may not use physical force to resist an arrest, whether authorized or unauthorized, which is being affected or attempted by a police officer or peace officer when it would reasonably appear that the latter is a police officer . . . "

The law also states, however, that a civilian who uses physical force to resist an officer's use of excessive force to effect a legal arrest cannot be prosecuted for assault, but still may be prosecuted for resisting arrest.

A study cited in the New York commission's report was based on 3,200 hours of patrol-work observation in New York. The study made the following findings, which concur with those of researchers in several other jurisdictions: "The type of force most commonly used was physical restraint, that is, pushing, grappling or wrestling with an unruly citizen, as opposed to beating with fists or striking with nightsticks or batons. In the majority of incidents neither the citizen nor the police were injured; where injuries did occur most were superficial."

It's necessary to remember, too, that police officers are not machines; they are living, breathing human beings with emotions and feelings and pride. Most consider themselves to be authorities as to what they do, and most object strongly to criticism. This was evinced in 1987 when Andrew Karmen, a professor at John Jay College of Criminal Justice, observed transit police officers effecting an arrest at the Columbus Circle subway station. John Jay College is attended by many law enforcement officers, and the fact that some of these officers were his students might have influenced Karmen to act in a less than diplomatic manner when he admonished the officers for what appeared to be the use of excessive and arbitrary force. Karmen was arrested after making his comments on charges of disorderly conduct, resisting arrest, and obstruction of governmental administration, all of which are typical charges police officers will use to justify holding a "troublemaker."

What is important to recognize is that an arrest in and of itself, if not grounded in a true violation of law and public order, can constitute an act of excessive force—even if hand or glove is never laid on the defendant. Such abuses of the legal process—so-called "asshole collars"—are rarely met with resistance by prosecutors. The defendants in such cases usually plead guilty to a violation and do not demand a trial. The plea may be to disorderly conduct, but the underlying offense was usually "contempt of cop."

Police work that emphasizes restraint, particularly in crowd control situations, rarely makes headlines unless something goes horribly wrong. Yet public recognition of police work that results in minimizing violence on all fronts rather than inciting it is necessary to encourage its practice.

Some officers visibly bristle in sensitive situations where they are unusually well supervised, because their unique weapon—the power to take someone's liberty away on their allegation alone—must be holstered on such occasions. The police in New York were sharply criticized for their failure to stop rioting in the Crown Heights section of Brooklyn in 1991 after a black youth was struck and killed by a car whose driver was a Hasidic Jew. But observations of police in testy encounters with groups of civilians suggest that there can be a benefit when police—sometimes reluctantly—are ordered to hold the line and refrain from making unnecessary arrests.

On a summer night in 1993, a celebration of Colombia's clinching of a World Cup qualification by defeating Argentina spilled out of bars and onto the streets of the New York City community of Jackson Heights, in the borough of Queens. The entrenched Colombian population of the area—sometimes referred to as "little Bogota"—doesn't always have a lot to cheer about. Most of the Colombians are honest, hard-working people and avid churchgoers, but Jackson Heights has long been a northeastern hub for American cocaine distribution, and thus the adopted home of American factions of the Colombian drug cartels. Public perception of Colombians is not always positive and often mired in stereotypes, so the opportunity to express national pride was a welcome release, especially for the exuberant young.

Similar celebrations in the past had gotten out of hand, but this time around community leaders had planned ahead, determined that this would not happen.

"We met with the police and worked everything out," said city councilman John Sabini. A plan had been devised for the celebration to be directed toward the nearby community of Woodside, in order to help thin out congestion. But somehow the crowd, with a mind of its own, remained in Jackson Heights. Thousands of the cheering, flour-throwing throng remained, many growing increasingly intoxicated as the night wore on. Close to midnight all but the most stalwart celebrators had left the streets, but there were enough of those remaining to make police officials nervous.

Something almost happened at 37th Avenue and 84th Street, a shopping area where most of the stores are closed at night. Luigi's restaurant, however, remained open on the normally quiet block. At midnight only a handful of diners were left inside when some of the soccer celebrants appeared, indicating they wished to use the bathroom. A waitress said that one of the men attempted to urinate in the dining room. There were angry words exchanged and the police were called.

During the course of the evening hundreds of task force police officers wearing riot helmets had stood by, awaiting any possible orders to disperse the crowds. Such tactics might have served to create acts of destruction against lives and property rather than prevent them, but cool heads at the command level had prevailed.

A single police car from the 115th precinct went to the restaurant in response to the owner's call. Most of the interlopers had already left by that time, and the officers attempted to soothe the visibly upset and shaken hostess. A crowd had gathered outside the restaurant; some of its members might well have been those who locked horns with the restaurant staff earlier, although this was not entirely clear. A shouting match between a handful of the Spanish-speaking crowd and the restaurant manager ensued, with the police acting quickly to defuse the situation by talking the manager back inside. But there was still the crowd to contend with.

An officer stood in front of the restaurant door, and there was the unmistakable sound of a breaking bottle somewhere nearby. A moment later an empty beercan sailed through the air and landed at the officer's foot. Anger flashed in the officer's blue eyes.

"You want a story?" he asked an observing reporter. "Put this in your story. We can't make a fucking move. We can't do anything about this. Nothing. They want us to stand here and take it."

The crowd grew to over a hundred people, most speaking Spanish, as helmeted reinforcements arrived, backed up by officers on horseback. They could easily have waded into the growing crowd, swinging nightsticks, but instead separated the most unruly and loudest (who were also the most intoxicated) of the group in a nearly surgical procedure. Within minutes the crowd dissipated. The angry officer who had first responded to the restaurant call simmered down.

"I know they want to celebrate," he said. "But people live here. They see all this and they're afraid. They don't know what's going on. They should have let us get them off the streets as soon as it started getting late and we would have avoided all of this."

The officer and his partner got into their car and left. What they may not have realized was that their fortitude in the face of considerable unpleasantness—a situation that could have easily escalated into violence—was what prevented a tragedy from occurring.

Police administrators have won praise for their use of hostage-negotiating teams, which have proved successful. Yet it is the beat officer or radio car operator who first requests such tactical assistance, rather than acting recklessly, who is the true hero. The New York City Police Department had come a long way from the night in 1988 when all hell broke loose on Manhattan's Lower East Side. By all accounts the rioters that night were not the sometimes obnoxious denizens of the area, but the police themselves.

SIX

FORCE EN MASSE:
THE TOMPKINS SQUARE LEGACY

MANHATTAN'S LOWER EAST Side was once dominated by inexpensive tenement apartments that, in the mid-1980s, began yielding to the wrecker's ball, or else echoing the blows of renovators' hammers. Once-squalid heaps were transformed into condominium and co-op housing accessible only to New York's monied classes.

For the well-heeled newcomers, the neighborhood's "renaissance" meant lower prices for Manhattan living space, especially in comparison to the more affluent communities uptown, or nearby Greenwich Village. The crunch of rents and apartment prices in other areas of the borough was not as keenly felt on the Lower East Side, although living costs were still pricey by most other cities' standards.

Some positive aspects of this demographic change had come about when young people were able to buy co-ops at relatively cheap prices, or for sweat equity invested in abandoned buildings on blocks considered highly undesirable. For this reason, some of the professionals living in the area felt they had every right to reap the fruits of their investments, especially in terms of the rise in property values.

But for the artists, writers, musicians, and poor families evicted as a result of this rehabbing, the transformation was catastrophic. In the late 1980s, while homelessness was emerging as a major urban policy issue, developers driven by profit were constructively creating a new underclass of people without roofs over their heads. Such "gentrification" was only one aspect of the homelessness problem, of course, substance abuse and poverty in general being important factors as well. But that was small consolation for those most directly affected by the Lower East Side's transformation. Many camped out in Tompkins Square Park, an urban oasis of trees and playgrounds that had itself become symbolic of tensions between the older, less-monied residents and the more affluent newcomers.

Of course, by this time the urban crack cocaine invasion was in full swing, and the Lower East Side, already drug-prone, was not spared. Open-air drug dealing occurred in Tompkins Square Park with rampant frequency, to the dismay of the area's new residents, who thought that the influx of co-ops and the raising of rents would have had some greater positive effect on their surrounding community. Repeated complaints to city officials of Tompkins Square Park's reputation as a mecca for low-level dealers, and as an open-air toilet and sleeping quarters for the impoverished, eventually found the ear of then-Mayor Ed Koch. As July of 1988 sweltered its way into August, the powers that be decided that something had to be done.

August 6, 1988 was selected as the day that a 1:00 A.M. curfew on occupancy of city parks would be enforced—albeit selectively—at Tompkins Square. Because the park's occupants were by then so entrenched, any police action geared toward expediting their departure would be regarded not as a mere sweepstroke of the municipal broom, but as an outright eviction. Tensions between the park denizens and the police had been building up for days, even, according to some accounts, weeks. A bizarre alliance of punk rockers, homeless men and women, neighborhood eccentrics, poets, and musicians—

many fitting more than one of those categories—had been oc-
cupying the park, harassing area residents, and occasionally
trading insults with police officers. Unlike more celebrated
standoffs between the police and the public that would take
place in later years, the tension between the park demonstrators and the police had little to do with race and everything to
do with class. In the eyes of the parkies, the cops represented
everything they were against, including the so-called "yuppie
scum" who had been gentrifying the neighborhood. (The
phrase "Die Yuppie Scum" was chanted rhythmically and incessantly to the accompaniment of bongos and whistles
through a good part of the evening.) As the zero hour—one o'-
clock—approached, the demonstrators grew more vociferous
as an increased police presence was noticed near the park's
gateway at Avenue A and East 7th Street.

The Lower East Side's reputation as a high-crime area has
been well deserved, although that part of Avenue A was too
busy to add much to the statistics. Teenagers from Long Island
and New Jersey, dressed in punk drag made more outlandish
by the surreal glow of sodium vapor street lamps, scouted out
alternative music nightspots armed with fake proofs of age.
The line outside the Pyramid Club resembled nothing less
than an open casting call for the *Rocky Horror Picture Show*.
Many of the street oddities, sensing the approach of an
"event" at the park, hung around the perimeter, some joining
in the mounting hand-clapping and whistle-blowing to chants
of "It's our fucking park."

Sweeping the park was not going to be an easy task for the
assembled police officers, who included a full column of
mounted troopers, their horses nervously pawing the sidewalk. Deputy Chief Thomas Darcy, a thirty-one-year NYPD
veteran, was in charge of the operation, and would ultimately
be held responsible for its success—or failure.

At around 1:00 A.M. some demonstrators were told to

leave by helmeted police officers. While some of the crowd in the park complied, others remained—attempting, it would appear, to force the hands of the enforcers. If the police weren't sure what action was to be taken next, they were helped along in the decision-making process when at least one firecracker was thrown at the mounted column, ostensibly in an attempt to frighten the horses. It was the only excuse the officers on foot needed. Already fed up to the breaking point with the slurs and catcalls thrown at them for hours by the street denizens, and supported by supervisors who knew that their emotional state was heightened, they began clearing the park and the street in front of it.

It began slowly at first. Working west (away) from the park, officers urged bystanders to move along, in sometimes harsh language. A young man with spiked blonde hair, obviously drunk, his white shirt open in front, berated one of the officers, who finally struck at the man in the knees and legs with his baton. The young man, although obnoxious in behavior, had at no time struck at the officer. Soon after the young man retreated to some corner there were more incidents of baton use, and the crashing of glass breaking on the pavement. Officers began pursuing bystanders and demonstrators alike, herding them west toward First Avenue. At the corner of First Avenue and Seventh Street the cops continued striking out, as the wails and whoops and flashing lights of police vehicles bearing reinforcements came closer. A police helicopter, charged with looking for people who might be seeking to throw rocks or other objects, hovered ominously just above the rooftops, and its whirling blades drowned out the screams of protest from frightened men and women, some of whom had simply been walking home when they were confronted by the baton-wielding police.

Breaking glass was heard on many surrounding blocks, although most of the shattered bottles that glistened on the pavement were the result of police efforts to prevent bottles from being used as weapons. The police broke them themselves with their batons as a pre-emptive measure. It was one of the few well-advised tactics that law enforcement would employ this night, but it also served to panic other officers who didn't know the smashing and crashing was only the sound of friendly fire.

The vicinity of the park swiftly resembled a war zone, and pedestrians crossing First Avenue lowered their heads in the summer heat as if in a blizzard to shield their eyes and noses from the debris stirred up by the chopper blades. There were numerous calls to 911 reporting police officers beating people on the street. The violence only escalated the anger of some protesters, who set fires on Avenue A—mostly in trash cans, or else to their dumped contents. Responding to a supervisor's command to restore order in the area, the mounted troops galloped full speed down East Seventh Street, the horses nearest the curb sharply cutting the corner. James O'Connor, a freelance video photographer for a local news service, was shocked when he looked away from his viewfinder and saw how close the horsemen had come to him as they rounded the turn.

There were only a few reporters out on the street; the local media had in large part been taken by surprise. What they saw was mass confusion, disorder, and physical confrontations, some resulting in acts of brutality in the immediate park area (from the park to First Avenue). But the real show was going on a block or two east. Perhaps because of the countercultural bent of many of the brutality victims, the senseless acts committed by some officers, or a combination of these factors, the confrontation evoked strong reminders of Chicago's Grant Park during the 1968 Democratic convention.

Blocks away from the scene of the first conflict, an amateur video photographer had been rolling tape on police officers, many with their badges and nametags covered to obscure their identities, swinging wildly at pedestrians with their nightsticks.

Upon noticing the video photographer's activity, a contingent of officers chased him to a fire escape, where they attempted to arrest him and seize his camera, grabbing at his legs and striking at him with clubs. It was only after this videotape was aired on local television stations, three days later, that the full impact of the police riot was realized.

By 5:00 A.M. the situation was tense but had quieted down considerably. Platoons of officers nervously awaited orders. The police had unquestionably encountered resistance from the park demonstrators and bystanders; they had been taunted verbally, and some had even been assaulted. But like a child's game of telephone, the officer-to-officer accounts of these assaults escalated far past the real degree of violence. What many of the officers closest to the park had not realized was that most of the violent street confrontations that night were initiated by the police themselves. The tense atmosphere made for rumors among the ranks, and some officers appeared under the impression that they had been assigned to suppress a full-scale civil disorder fomented by unruly and perhaps dangerous civilians.

One officer, surprisingly young for his assignment to highway patrol (as indicated by his unit collar bars and high black boots) was convinced that he was in the midst of an urban Armageddon.

"I don't know why they have us just standing here," he said, fidgeting, the leather on his new uniform unscuffed and shiny. "They ought to let us in there and kick some ass."

He had absolutely no idea where "in there" was—and even less of who had actually been doing the ass-kicking.

Sociologists, psychologists, and anthropologists have long recognized the phenomena that occur when individual consciousness is replaced by groupthink, particularly in volatile situations such as civil disorders. The mere *idea* that one's group is in danger can set in motion a series of events that can lead to death, sometimes on a huge scale. Police officers are not immune to mob-related hysteria. Knowing that they were in a volatile predicament at Tompkins Square Park, some officers who might not have dreamed of perpetrating violence on innocent civilians may well have found themselves attacking Lower East Side residents without a second thought, convinced it was what they were supposed to be doing. Such behavior by individuals charged with enforcing the law can only occur when officers are undisciplined and poorly supervised. The facts would later reveal a massive void in the upper chain of command.

The siege of Tompkins Square Park lasted into Sunday, August 7, with occupation of the park's grassy turf by police officers. But repercussions rapidly echoed through the halls of One Police Plaza, the waffle-iron-shaped building across from City Hall that is the police department's multi-story command center.

In all, 121 civilian complaints of brutality were processed. A total of fifty-three people had been injured. The Manhattan district attorney's office began an investigation into what happened, as did then-Police Commissioner Benjamin Ward. The injuries and arrests were spread across all ethnic and economic lines, reflecting the multifaceted neighborhood's demographics.

The official police department report was released in late August. In a *New York Newsday* article by Richard Esposito, the report was described as "firmly placing the blame on the three commanding officers at the scene and prompting the retirement of the deputy chief who was supposed to be in charge at the . . . park."

The "appalling behavior" of some officers, the report

stated, "caused a significant portion of our citizens to lose faith in our ability to respond in a controlled, disciplined fashion."

Deputy Chief Darcy was absent for several hours during the battle of Tompkins Square; other commanders were unsure of their role or unwilling to communicate effective orders of any nature to their troops, even if it was just that they should "hold the line" and not pursue the park people or bystanders—many of whom were already heading in the direction the police wanted them to go. It was Darcy who was the target of some of the strongest criticism. He agreed to resign, rather than face what would eventually become, Esposito reported, the certain disintegration of his career.

"It is reasonable to expect that once a deputy chief of police is on the scene of such a disorder he would in fairly rapid order consolidate his forces, identify his personnel, and assume control," the report stated.

Newsday quoted Commissioner Ward as saying that he had been asleep through the melee, and that he had not been notified of its occurrence.

Of the 121 complaints received by the Civilian Complaint Review Board in the wake of the Tompkins Square Park incident, seventeen were substantiated and referred to police officials for action; twenty-nine additional complaints were substantiated but the officers complained of were not identified; and only six indictments were brought in United States District Court for the Southern District of New York by the office of Rudolph Giuliani, who became New York City's mayor five years later. Prosecution never went forward.

The police department realized, upon reviewing what had happened, that it had been many years since city cops had been forced into a physical confrontation with members of the public. As is often the case, those who bore the brunt of the cop-rioters' wrath were persons from outgroups. Only this time, instead of being blacks or other ethnic minorities, the victims (initially, at least) were people with shaved heads, green and purple hair, and biker outfits. Racial tensions in the city were already quietly simmering in August of 1988, although incidents that occurred that year—including the deaths of emotionally disturbed persons in custody, among other allegations—did not provoke sufficient ire to bring things to a flash point. Police administrators realized, however, that some action had to be taken to prevent future problems. A new training program focusing on civil disorder was put into effect; new directives on command procedures at civil disorders were formulated. It appeared, as the scepter of city government changed from the hands of Edward I. Koch to David N. Dinkins in 1989, that there might be little fear of any other Tompkins Square-style fiascos in the future. But that would change in 1991—in photo-negative image.

It happened in the Crown Heights section of Brooklyn, which was called Crow Hill back in the early nineteenth century when the area was settled by free black farmers and craftsmen. Crow Hill did not retain its rural character for long, however, as it became a desirable place for newly arrived immigrants from northern and western Europe to settle. Scatterings of comfortable row-houses sprang up throughout that century, but the building industry really boomed in the next, with the establishment of a subway line in 1920, and the coming of the Jews, Italians, and Irish.

After World War II, Crown Heights—or more accurately, its white population—went the way of the rest of Brooklyn, which was out. Coming in were northward-migrating African-Americans, as well as English-speaking blacks from some Caribbean nations. Most of the whites who remained were members of the Lubavitcher Hasidim, a sect of strictly orthodox Jews, many of whom maintain that the spiritual leader of their community, their Grand Rebbe Menachem Schneerson, is the promised Messiah of the Jewish people, with a faith so strong it outlived his June 1994 death. The Lubavitch had built a world headquarters on Eastern Parkway, a broad boulevard that stretches through the width of central Brooklyn. With their long black coats, beards, and broad hats, the sight of Hasidic men flocking to prayers each morning calls to mind eastern Europe in another century rather than Brooklyn in this one. The Hasidic way of life is fiercely protected by its adherents, who have traditionally bought up available property adjoining their immediate neighborhoods as insurance against intrusion.

Long-standing disputes, and equal doses from each side of anti-Jewish prejudice, anti-black prejudice, and overall mutual mistrust have clouded the relationship between the blacks and the Jews in Crown Heights—people who have more in common when it comes to social problems than either cares to admit. These tensions exploded on August 19, 1991.

Until he suffered a stroke in 1992, Grand Rebbe Schneerson made regular visits to the graves of his wife and father-in-law, and would travel to the cemetery and back again with a New York Police Department escort. The police escort, and other concessions to the Hasidic community, such as the closing of the streets on Sabbath days, were a source of resentment to the blacks in Crown Heights, who saw them as evidence of preferential treatment.

The three-car Schneerson motorcade, which included a radio car from the 71st precinct that covers Crown Heights, was returning from the cemetery on August 19 at an average rate of speed. The last car was a Mercury station wagon driven by a man named Yosef Lifsch, and occupied by three other members of the entourage.

At 8:20 P.M. the lead patrol car and Schneerson's auto were on President Street crossing Utica Avenue, a two-way commercial thoroughfare. Lifsch's station wagon, however, was struck by a Chevrolet traveling on Utica, and it careened onto a sidewalk, where two seven-year-old black children, Gavin Cato and his cousin Angela, had been playing. Horrified witnesses ran to the corner, where both children were pinned beneath the Mercury. Members of the predominantly black crowd tried to extricate the children; some attacked Lifsch when he exited the auto to help.

At 8:32 P.M. Gavin Cato was rushed by ambulance to Kings County Hospital, where he was pronounced dead. Little Angela was extricated and placed in another ambulance several minutes later, and survived the ordeal.

As police investigated the accident scene huge crowds of blacks and Hasidim gathered, hurling epithets at each other. A rumor that a Jewish volunteer ambulance squad had ignored the children and instead tended to the relatively unscathed Hasidim from Lifsch's station wagon, allowing Gavin Cato to die, circulated throughout the neighborhood. By 9:10 P.M. the first phone calls were received by 911 reporting rioting. Rocks and bottles were being thrown. Police officers on the scene radioed for help. At one nearby location shots were fired; at another, a police officer was beaten by an angry crowd.

At 10:30 P.M. the throwing of debris continued at President and Utica. The police on the scene made no move to stop the violence, if indeed they were in any position at that time to do so at all. Robert Brennan of Mayor David Dinkins's community assistance unit arrived on the scene and reported back to the City Hall police desk that the "shit is hitting the fan."

While pandemonium was breaking loose virtually unchecked at President and Utica, there were nearly 100 available police officers nearby, assigned to a B.B. King concert at a local park called Wingate Field. Three sergeants and thirty officers were ordered from the park to the scene of the disturbance by the 71st precinct's newly installed commanding officer (it was his first day serving in that capacity), Captain William Kennedy.

Captain Gerald McNamara was on assignment as the Brooklyn duty captain that night. A duty captain's job is to respond to unusual situations and provide supervision from the borough level. McNamara, well connected politically within the department, was no stranger to civil disturbances. Three years and ten days before, he had been the commanding officer of the 9th precinct on Manhattan's Lower East Side, and had been censured for failing to assume a leadership role during the Tompkins Square Park riot.

McNamara responded to President and Utica and upon exiting his car was struck by a hurled bottle and cut on the bridge of his nose. He went from there to the stationhouse, where he notified higher-ups of the situation.

Ironically, recent retirements and other shuffling of the command structure at the highest levels in Brooklyn had left the borough with a slate of top police supervisors who were relatively inexperienced with the immediate area of the disturbance. This was later to be cited as a problem in achieving the needed mobilizations of police forces in response to the rioting.

While the top cops huddled, mayhem was breaking loose on the streets of Crown Heights. One of Captain Kennedy's major concerns, considering the anti-Jewish sentiment of the most vehement black protesters, was the Lubavitch world headquarters on Eastern Parkway. As additional patrol officers responded to the area around midnight, Kennedy thought it wisest to post them in a perimeter surrounding the affected area as well as at the site of the headquarters. As the cultural and spiritual center of the Hasidic community, it could be reasoned that the headquarters might be a likely target for attack. The Lubavitch also had a well-deserved reputation for defending their community against crimes of violence. An attack on the headquarters, then, could have doubly disastrous consequences.

By the time at least one car had been burned by a roving mob; store windows on President Street were being shattered. On one street corner a Jewish man was surrounded by a crowd of fifteen blacks who kicked him, stoned him, and struck him with bottles. Other such beatings of Jews occurred, with the assailants making remarks like, "Jews get out of here" and "Death to the Jews."

At 11:20 P.M. at the corner of President Street and Brooklyn Avenue, a twenty-nine-year-old visiting Australian rabbinical student named Yankel Rosenbaum was assaulted and stabbed four times. Police apprehended sixteen-year-old Lemrick Nelson and brought him to the scene. After identifying his alleged assailant, Rosenbaum was taken to Kings County Hospital, where he later died of his wounds.

Mayor Dinkins and other officials personally responded to the precinct station house at around 1:00 A.M. Community workers were ordered to circulate throughout the neighborhood to try to restore calm. Police Commissioner Lee Brown maintained to the press that a "strong police presence" was being kept in the area.

Because of the nature of the disturbance, normal dispatching procedures were severely hampered. The volume of 911 calls, coupled with the deployment of personnel for crowd control (there were large groups of Hasidim being kept behind barricades at some locations), served to deplete police resources. Police also attempted to break up brawling between blacks and Jews. Adequate police response to heart-rending pleas of assistance from the Jewish community was next to impossible.

Behind the closed doors of their apartments and private homes, frightened Hasidim, terrified by what was going on in the streets, vainly phoned 911 for help.

One caller described the rioting to a 911 operator and told her, "It's a pogrom! Do you know what that is? It's something very bad . . . "

Things had gotten considerably worse by Tuesday night, August 20. Uniformed officers were pelted with rocks and bottles, including some at sites where they separated Hasidim and blacks from each other. One television reporter praised the restraint that cops employed during one such confrontation.

Police officers without helmets or riot shields, overwhelmed by hurled debris, retreated—actually ran—back to the 71st precinct. The effect of the rioting on the Jewish population was overwhelming, and the unquestionable wickedness of the attacks was not lost on non-Jews, who were terrified—and angered—as well. Here is one example:

911 Operator: Police 884. What is your emergency?
Caller: Yeah, um, there are some guys . . . stoning
               Jews on the corner of Lexington? Stoning
               the Jews!
911 Operator: What are they doing? They're stoning the
               Jews?
Caller: Yes! They're throwing a lot of stones at the-
               Jews.

At 8:52 P.M. the following call was received from a woman:

911 Operator: . . . need assistance?
Caller: You need to send some police back around
               Union and Utica, 'cause these people are
               going crazy out there!
911 Operator: A unit for Union and Utica Avenue?
Caller: Yes. Every car that comes down the block—
               they bombing 'em—they, they've got this
               one man down—they're pulling him out of
               his car!

911 Operator: Union and Utica? And what are they doing
                with the car?
Caller: They're pulling the people out of the cars.
                All the Jews that come down the block, they
                take them out the car and beating 'em up.
911 Operator: Is there anyone injured?
Caller: I don't know. I just ran in my house and I
                said it don't make no damn sense. All these
                people they don't even know what the fuck
                they out there for.
911 Operator: How many people are out there now?
Caller: I don't know, Miss, it's a whole crowd of
                people out there! It's a army of people! You
                need to send somebody back around.
911 Operator: Listen Ma'am, we have police out there,
                okay?
Caller: Okay.
911 Operator: It's a lot of police out there. Why don't you
                go and speak to one of the police? It's police
                out there, Ma'am.
Caller: I just came from outside!
911 Operator: Ma'am, as you say, it's a lot of crowd out
                there at the location. Anyone out there got
                got injured?
Caller: I don't know.

Earlier, at 8:26 P.M., another woman had called.

Caller: They're tearing up the stores and there's fire
                in the street . . . they starting fires in the
                street!
911 Operator: How many people?
Caller: Maybe a thousand.
911 Operator: One thousand, right?
Caller: Probably a thousand people out here. A
                thousand. They tearing up . . . starting a fire.
911 Operator: Your last name, Miss?

Caller: Huh?
911 Operator: Your last name, Miss?
Caller: [NAME]
911 Operator: . . . what is your phone number, please?
Caller: Huh? I don't want to give up my phone
                 number 'cause I don't want to get involved.
911 Operator: I see. Oh, let me give you the fire depart-
                 ment. Hold on . . .

What happened during this same caller's conversation
with the fire department operator has thoroughly frightening
implications.

FD: Hello, fire department.
Caller: They're starting a fire over here on Utica Avenue,
          behind the riots.
FD: Yeah, well . . . we're unable to come there.
Caller: You're unable to come?
FD: That's right. That's on President and Utica, right?
Caller: Yeah.
FD: Unable to respond right now, but we will get there
          as soon as we can.
Caller: Okay, thank you.
FD: You're welcome.

Mayor David Dinkins's highest-ranking deputies were on
hand in Crown Heights, but if the later testimony of the mayor
is to be believed, they never fully appraised him of the serious-
ness of the events. The police remained badly outnumbered.
Dinkins claimed he was advised through police commissioner
Lee Brown, and Brown was advised through the chain of command from borough supervisors that the situation was "under
control."

One of Brown's chief concerns was a demonstration led by
black leaders on Tuesday afternoon, August 20, which could
conceivably have resulted in even greater protection prob-

lems. Indeed, the marchers were pelted with rocks and bottles thrown by Hasidim, as well as by some members of the black community who yelled that they wanted, "No more talk, just action." However, both the marchers and the more violence-prone residents were angered by the same thing—which was that Yosef Lifsch, the driver of the station wagon that struck and killed Gavin Cato, had not been the subject of criminal charges.

From the beginning of the Crown Heights troubles on August 19, City Hall focused chiefly on community outreach to both Hasidim and African-Americans, while Lee Brown relied on reports from the command. Brown maintained that if the Brooklyn supervisors needed more resources he would have complied, but they did not ask for any.

On Wednesday, August 21, Mayor Dinkins returned to Crown Heights, only to be attacked with bottles. Only then, perhaps, did Dinkins realize the scope of the problem. First Deputy Commissioner Raymond Kelly (who later replaced Brown as commissioner) had been on the sidelines Monday and Tuesday, but he took on an active role in directing operations on Wednesday, which included a crackdown on the roving bands of black youths besieging the neighborhood. Reinforcements were called in, and by Thursday morning, August 22, order had been essentially restored.

It is difficult, however, to assess whether things calmed down in Crown Heights because of the efforts of the police, or because the violence was about to fizzle out anyway. Within this context a serious question looms, which is whether a more aggressive use of force might have resulted in more injury, more property damage, and perhaps even in deaths—apart from the murder of Yankel Rosenbaum, which occurred early in the conflagration and thus may not have been preventable no matter how much force police had shown.

The most effective way of determining the impact of the

Crown Heights riot is not by examining the number of 911 calls made. In many cases numerous calls may have been received regarding the same incident, and a certain number of 911 calls on any given day or night in New York, in any neighborhood, are unfounded. Likewise, the mere number of police complaints filed during the period of the disturbance cannot be the most accurate indicator, since various crimes occur on any given day or night in the affected areas as in the rest of the city. One reasonable way to determine the effect is to examine the increase of criminal complaints for the four-day period of the disturbance as opposed to the same four weekdays the prior week. Overall complaints of crimes during four days in the prior week within the effective area totalled 148. The total jumped to 411 during the four days of the disturbance.

In the week prior there were no assaults on police officers reported, but during the course of the riot 141 such complaints were filed. Other assaults rose from nine to twenty-six (the murder of Yankel Rosenbaum originally was classified an assault, not a homicide, and so is included here as an initial assault complaint); there were seven complaints of arson, up seven from the previous period. Criminal mischief rose from twenty to ninety, and robberies from fifteen to twenty-eight. As with any crime figures, allowances must be made for the "dark figure" of crimes that were committed but not reported to authorities. The disturbance, it should be noted, was concentrated within a mile-square area.

In August 1993 Richard Girgenti, New York State's Director of Criminal Justice, released a report on the riots that was commissioned by Governor Mario Cuomo. Although critical of the mayor and top police brass, the report found unsubstantiated the charges that Dinkins or other officials had "handcuffed the police" by ordering them not to make arrests. Rather, the commanders at the scene, realizing that the numbers of available officers were not sufficient to stop the disturbance itself (this was the result of their own lack of understanding about what was occurring on the streets, communications glitches, and other difficulties), had ordered their officers to remain at fixed posts and not to take individual actions.

The Girgenti report characterized the reported increase in criminal activity during the disturbance as "substantial." The police were neither properly nor sufficiently mobilized to contain this activity.

> The officers in Crown Heights lacked a clear understanding of their mission. While the Field Commander initially ordered officers to exercise restraint, he was unprepared to alter their tactics when that approach failed . . . The police were unable to maintain control of the marches and demonstrations which frequently resulted in group conflicts and criminal activity . . . On Tuesday and Wednesday the police permitted large unruly crowds to form at President Street and Utica Avenue. When violence erupted, they were unable to control it. Attempts late on Wednesday to disperse mobs on Utica Avenue merely drove these groups into nearby areas.

The more successful control tactics were also cited by Girgenti:

> On Wednesday, violence erupted at President and Utica and on nearby streets at about 5:30 P.M. Although the police attempted to clear the area, they merely pushed the unruly demonstrators onto adjacent streets. At approximately 10:00 P.M., a 100-officer detail cleared Utica Avenue of demonstrators. When they met resistance at Montgomery Street, officers in patrol wagons penetrated the crowd, trapping rock and bottle throwers from behind. This response to lawlessness demonstrated that aggressive tactics could be effective, that they would not lead to further violence, and that a specific tactical plan stressing dispersal could work

... On Thursday, the Department increased the size of its
force and adopted aggressive tactics from the start. Supervisors were told explicitly to "take back the streets" and to arrest anyone violating the law. Crowds were dispersed at the
first signs of trouble and mass arrests were made for unlawful assembly. As a result, order was restored.

What the comparison of Crown Heights and Tompkins
Square indicate is that the key to proper police action is re-
sults-oriented leadership on the part of superiors. But this necessary comparison should not stop there.

While clashes at Tompkins Square were between *police* and
the public, the violence in Crown Heights was directed against
one group of civilians (for the most part, Hasidic Jews) by another group of civilians (blacks, for the most part—more
specifically, Caribbeans rather than African-Americans).

There was minimal public furor over the excesses of
Tompkins Square when such reaction is compared with that
attending the Crown Heights incident—with the bulk of criticism regarding Crown Heights surfacing not immediately, *but
two years afterward.* The Girgenti Report was not released until
1993, just in time for the mayoral election, and very conceivably helped put Republican challenger Rudolph Giuliani over
the top, costing David Dinkins reelection to the mayoralty.

What is most important in considering Crown Heights,
however, is the fact that order was eventually restored
through a use of police force that was not considered excessive. The public perception, gleaned from radio talk shows,
letters to the editor, and other media, was that police should
have immediately used maximum force to contain the incidents of violence. In fact, a *minimal* use of force, when finally
utilized, did the job just as well.

Proper training of police officers, and, even more important, better preparation of superiors for effectively dealing

with such a disturbance, would have minimized problems in both situations. However, the NYPD under Raymond Kelly seems to be coming around, eschewing either extreme in terms of force and landing squarely—and properly—in the middle on crowd-control efforts.

At a November 1993 demonstration, thousands of Haitians took to the streets of midtown Manhattan while exiled Haitian president Jean-Bertrand Aristide addressed the United Nations. Late that afternoon approximately 200 Haitian supporters of Aristide, many of whom loudly blame the U.S. for the turmoil in that nation, broke off from the main group and occupied Third Avenue—a heavily traveled thoroughfare lined with luxury high-rise buildings.

Under the command of Assistant Chief Charles Reuther, phalanxes of helmeted police officers appeared with a column of mounted troopers. The demonstrators were hemmed in on all sides, effectively placed under temporary containment. Leaders of the group ignored police pleas for dispersal, and the uniformed forces began preparing for mass arrests. Contingents of helmeted back-ups awaited orders, hidden four blocks away. A most unlikely peacemaker emerged, however, to prevent what might have turned into a disaster. Sergeant Arthur Smarsch of the community relations unit prevailed on supervisors to permit him leeway to negotiate with the demonstrators until they finally agreed to disperse voluntarily. What made Smarsch an unlikely hero was the fact that while one might assume such an able tactician to have a wall full of degrees, he was at the time only pursuing undergraduate work at a night school. His background as a cop included assignments to high-crime areas in high-risk capacities. His example is one of many displayed by police professionals every day across the country, who know that the most successful police riot operation has more to do with the one that's been prevented rather than the one that's already begun.

The entire world was watching the U.N. appearance of Aristide. If operations on Third Avenue had degenerated into violence, pitting police against people who had already fled a totalitarian government, the videotape could have seriously affected U.S. credibility in the world community.

The only difficulties arose after the demonstrators were dispersed, and then only when one errant young man had refused to follow the orders of a Metro North Railroad police officer in front of Grand Central Station. The Metro North officers were not involved with the demonstration control efforts, and had no way of knowing the delicate series of dialogues that had taken place. Five of them pounced on the miscreant youth, which panicked other Haitians in the area. Some arrests were made. Sergeant Smarsch, Assistant Chief Reuther, and other police leaders responded quickly to defuse what could have become yet another disaster. The incident at Grand Central, which involved unnecessary but not excessive force, resulted in minimal overall problems.

Crowd situations are inherently difficult for police supervisors to address, because they are often complicated by underlying first amendment issues of freedom of assembly. Many such events have been historically associated with left-wing causes, and the use of excessive force, when it occurs, is sometimes seen as the expression of police indifference to minorities (as embodied by particular demonstrators) or specific political causes.

However, evidence emerged at congressional hearings held in the wake of the Rodney King incident that shed new light on accusations against officers of excessive force. These accusations were the product of a thoroughly different kind of demonstration, pitting police against people who may well have shared some of their own personal ideologies.

SEVEN

OPERATION RESCUE AND LESS-THAN-LETHAL FORCE

THE FIRST AMENDMENT TO the United States Constitution states that Congress shall make no law abridging freedom of speech or freedom of the press, or of the people to assemble peaceably in order to redress grievances. But Congress, has, in fact, made such laws, after weighing freedom of expression issues against considerations of public interest. The case law that has developed over the years in regard to freedom of expression issues provides an interesting picture of how Americans have sought to deal with the conflicts that arise over this problem.

There may well lurk within the hearts of people who would otherwise regard themselves as "good Americans" a desire to see free expression minimized in some way, especially when the individual doing the expressing is in disagreement with their particular views. Others balk when the target of protest is the very government that permits such dissent to begin with.

This was the case in 1977, when a group of self-avowed Nazis sought to hold a rally in a Chicago suburb called Skokie. Many of Skokie's citizens were not only Jews but also Holocaust survivors, and the municipality refused to grant a permit to the Nazis. Skokie's refusal, however, was struck down by a federal appeals court. The American Civil Liberties Union had brought the suit against Skokie, drawing considerable criticism. The principles upon which the ACLU case was based had sound foundations in American constitutional law, however, and our courts have traditionally been loathe to permit anything less than absolutely necessary government trampling upon the rights of those seeking to be heard—no matter how unpopular their views.

In the 1950s and 1960s nonviolent protest was one of the most effective weapons employed by the civil rights movement. Marches by opponents of racial segregation gained national headlines. The ensuing beating of demonstrators by police, brought into American living rooms through the magic of television, made for a dramatic display. Because they were intentionally breaking the law, the people who staged lunch counter sit-ins went beyond freedom of expression. And their strategy worked.

The use of nonviolent protest—and using the system against itself by forcing government's hand—has extended to other arenas of challenge. Most recently, civil disobedience tactics have been used extensively by Operation Rescue, a national organization whose members are opposed to legal abortion.

The abortion issue is an emotional one. Proponents of a woman's right to choose whether a pregnancy should be terminated see that decision as purely personal, between that woman and her doctor. For the most part, ever since the Supreme Court's decision in the case *Roe v. Wade*, the law in recent years has upheld a woman's right to choose to have an abortion. Congress has passed laws limiting access to abortion in some cases, but the Supreme Court has stood firm in stating that the procedure itself is legal and constitutional; thus, the individual states have had to legislate within that context.

Operation Rescue activists see the abortion procedure as nothing less than the murder of a human being, and gather at places where abortions are performed to give public expression to their feelings. These "rescues," as partisans call them, involve much more than the carrying of signs or chanting of slogans. Anti-abortion adherents maintain that laying motionless on the ground, nonresistant, yielding—like dead weight, as it were—is in itself a form of metaphorical speech, symbolizing the helplessness of the womb-bound fetus during an abortion procedure. The demonstrators attempt—aggressively and en masse—to interest women seeking abortions in alternatives, and activists have often disrupted clinic operations.

No matter how questionable their tactics may be, and no matter how legal the actual procedure of abortion may be, and no matter that some people associated with the anti-abortion movement have even taken the life of a doctor whose practice included abortion procedures, a gathering of Operation Rescue activists cannot, in and of itself, be criminalized. The group's members have every right to express their views—up to the point where they are not unreasonably interfering with the liberty and freedom of others. This fact, coupled with the sheer number of activists who show up for the rescues, has resulted in major problems for law enforcement agencies.

Charges of impropriety by police agencies have been made by Operation Rescue activists in many jurisdictions. At the Westchester County Jail in New York state, activists calling themselves "Baby Jane Doe" or "Baby John Doe" were allegedly held for weeks without being processed. These claims don't necessarily represent an abuse. After all, proper identification is required for processing arrestees. Persons engaging in civil disobedience, precipitating their arrests as well as processing delays by their own actions, are not looked upon kindly by either the courts or their jailers.

The rights afforded inmates of jails or prisons have been the focus of considerable attention by the courts, although allegations of beatings and other forms of mistreatment do still occur from time to time. There is an entire body of correction law that addresses the conduct of jailers, and while there can be little doubt that abuses do occur, the mechanism is in place for adequate investigation. The Rodney King case, however, raised concerns among some federal lawmakers that little was known about how detainees are treated *before* they ever enter prison walls.

Congressional authority to investigate the question of police brutality, which is clearly provided for the United States Code, was utilized in March 1991 when hearings on the police brutality question began before the subcommittee on civil and constitutional rights of the committee on the judiciary of the House of Representatives. Rep. Don Edwards, the subcommittee chair, presided over a fact-finding endeavor that was clearly inspired, as stated in the record, by the Rodney King incident.

"Police work is dangerous, difficult, and often unappreciated," Edwards said in his opening statement on March 20. "But there is no excuse for the type of behavior recorded on videotape in Los Angeles. Seeing that man being beaten was offensive to all Americans, particularly to the tens of thousands of dedicated law enforcement officers who would not engage in such conduct."

The subcommittee's mission, Edwards said, was not to focus on the King incident in isolation, but to examine the issue more broadly: "We want to know how effective the federal government's response has been. We want to look at the question of training and the question of internal discipline. We want to look at the federal laws and whether they need to be strengthened."

John R. Dunne, assistant attorney general of the U.S. Justice Department's civil rights division, then began his testimony with an opening statement in which he stressed the importance of civil rights prosecutions, which the department is authorized to pursue under the United States Code, and noted that the federal government's role in such cases is to serve as a "backstop" for situations where local law enforcement agency resources have been demonstrated as inadequate.

At the conclusion of Dunne's testimony, Rep. Henry J. Hyde asked about the alleged use of nunchukas—a martial arts weapon consisting of two rods attached with a brief chain—against anti-abortion demonstrators.

Dunne replied that his office had investigated the claims: "The basic determination in our conclusion that there was no basis for a federal criminal civil rights violation is that the use of chukka sticks, or nunchukas, or Orcutt control devices, as they might be called on the West Coast, is a technique which is authorized and recommended under certain FBI training programs. So, that being the case, you could not prove a willful intent to do injury to a victim."

"I'm told there was a fractured arm using one of those?" Hyde asked.

"Indeed there was," Dunne replied.

"You don't deem that excessive use of force?" said Hyde.

"Not in our judgment," Dunne responded. "It was not in the context and the use of the device and the events leading up to it, which I viewed twice very closely on the video. That was our conclusion, Mr. Hyde."

A little more than a month later, Don Edwards sent a letter to William R. Sessions, then director of the FBI, citing Dunne's testimony that FBI training programs endorsed use of nunchukas.

"Is this statement correct?" Edwards wrote. "Has the FBI recommended the use of nun-chukkas (nun-chuks) [sic] or the use of pain-compliance techniques with demonstrators in any of its training programs?"

The April 24 missive was replied to one month later.

"The FBI does not authorize or recommend the use of

nunchukas by Special Agents in . . . basic New Agent Tactics training and (SWAT) training," Sessions personally wrote. Sessions went on:

> New agents are briefly shown the device, along with numerous other weapons and pain-compliance devices, during defensive tactics training at the FBI academy. The purpose is strictly to familiarize agents with these weapons and other items they may encounter and have to defend against in the field. Special agents are not trained to use nunchukkas. Further, no recommendations are being considered to incorporate training on the use of this technique into any of our training including our training programs that focus on state and local law enforcement programs.

Dunne admitted his error in a June letter to Edwards, in which he stated that Justice Department lawyers had witnessed a demonstration of pain-compliance techniques at the FBI training academy in Quantico, Virginia, and that they were told there that the devices could be used to keep greater distance between an arrestee and an officer, or to help an officer expend less energy in effecting an arrest.

That may have been the goal when the devices were used on Operation Rescue demonstrators, who are notorious for becoming dead weight (a time-honored civil disobedience technique) when the time comes for cops to haul them off to the paddy wagons.

A number of police departments do indeed make use of the devices. The homemade variety were popular with some gangs, and these were improved upon to where they are now described in *Deadly Force: What We Know*, a reference book published by the Police Executive Research Forum, as:

> Two cylindrical polycarbonate cylinders joined by a four-inch nylon rope . . . primarily utilized as a pain-compliance

tool and not as a striking weapon . . . placed on the wrist, arm or ankle. When brought together the sticks exert pressure and cause intense pain which leads to compliance.

The Police Executive Research Forum also makes a reference to Kevin Orcutt, a Colorado police officer and martial arts expert, who was consulted by some police departments on the device's uses, and who first began marketing a police version of something that originally was used to cut down rice stalks—hence the earlier reference to the "Orcutt control device." The San Diego Police Department, for one, has made extensive use of the tool, resulting in a number of subsequent brutality complaints. Some of the reported damage to complainants included everything from wrist sprains to nerve damage.

During the course of litigation arising from the use of nunchukas and pain-compliance techniques on Operation Rescue activists, Los Angeles Police Chief Darryl Gates had been shown a videotape recording of eighteen such applications of the nunchukas. The video clearly showed people writhing in agony, and one man's arm breaking with an audible snap. Gates's response, taken in deposition, was that he saw no violation of LAPD policy on the tape. Other LAPD supervisors gave similar responses under oath.

David L. Llewellyn, president of the Sacramento-based Western Center for Law and Religious Freedom, shed further light on the use of pain compliance against Operation Rescue when he gave testimony before the House subcommittee on April 17, 1991. The Western Center has defended hundreds of anti-abortion protesters in legal actions arising from Operation Rescue demonstrations, including 500 such cases brought in California. (These were prosecutions of demonstrators for the violations of law for which they were arrested.)

Llewellyn testified that it was the official policy and practice of the LAPD to inflict excruciating pain upon anti-abortion

demonstrators, and permitting the use of nunchukas—possession of which by a private citizen in Los Angeles is considered
a felony. "In Los Angeles," Llewellyn said, "hundreds of passive and nonthreatening demonstrators blocking the entrance
to abortion clinics have been arrested by the use of brutal pain-
compliance techniques." Referring to the videotape shown to
Gates and other officials, Llewellyn testified that the tape,
though furnished as evidence by Operation Rescue, was actually made by the LAPD, and demonstrated officers using the
nunchukas in a "tourniquet torquing manner."

In this case, the trial court declared pain compliance to be
"whatever force is necessary to overcome resistance"—a definition that Llewellyn suggested might have been employed by
medieval inquisitors, tagging it "an authorization for torture."

"The Los Angeles Police Department policy cannot tell officers how much pain and force will be necessary to obtain
compliance," Llewellyn testified before Congress. He continued:

> Their policy of ever-increasing pain until compliance is
> achieved with no upward limits virtually mandates the re-
> sultant injuries. The pain produced by nunchucks is so in-
> tense as to be counterproductive. Many demonstrators have
> reported that the pain was so severe they lost the ability ei-
> ther to comply or to communicate their desire to comply.
> The force and pain effectively disabled the demonstrators
> due to reduced blood circulation, nerve interference, nau-
> sea, muscle failure, loss of feeling, focusing of the mind and
> body in the areas of this excruciating pain, shock, fear of
> further injury, surges in blood flow and nerve activity due
> to pressure and release, and even loss of consciousness.

The logical leap of faith made upon witnessing such pain-
inducing techniques can only be that the officers are not
merely making arrests, but actually dealing out punishment,

which is a role (as previously discussed within these pages) clearly beyond the purview of the law enforcement agency involved. Indeed, Llewellyn cited the claim by an LAPD police captain in one of the litigated cases that "some demonstrators appear as a young child, welcoming punishment for past transgressions."

Llewellyn suggested that the level of force used in the Operation Rescue protests was determined by a desire that these *specific* demonstrators—anti-abortion activists—be singled out for this "punishment" by police officers. Llewellyn argued that less force was historically employed during, for example, antiwar sit-ins.

"If a department of animal control used pain-inducing techniques on dogs or coyotes like those used by the Los Angeles Police Department when other means were available, they would be universally excoriated as inhumane," Llewellyn said during completion of his congressional testimony. "The Los Angeles Police Department authorizes inhumane treatment of human beings because of their belief and demonstration against abortion and belief in the sanctity of life."

Llewellyn pleaded with the members of the committee, "Let [the demonstrators] be arrested. Let them be carted off to jail. But do not permit them to be put in the hands of police officers who have been taught that it is acceptable to break their bodies in order to break their wills."

The Western Center submitted to the congressional subcommittee a statement of appropriateness of legislative action against brutal pain-compliance techniques. Such techniques, the Center suggested, provide police with unregulated discretion to hurt or injure people and are thus an invitation to use excessive force.

Standing case law cites four factors meriting use of force in effecting arrests of suspects: the severity of the crime committed, the threat posed to officers or others, the attempt to evade arrest by flight, and the active resisting of arrest. Opponents of pain compliance as used against peaceful demonstrators argue that such force is unwarranted in terms of all four criteria. Non-violent demonstrators, by definition, intentionally avoid any action that would fulfill any of these different police concerns.

An inference might be drawn that all police officers who use weapons such as the nunchukas against nonviolent dem-onstrators must be sadists. Yet even opponents of the use of pain compliance state that this is not necessarily so. Even those police officers who do not intend to cause undue pain might end up doing so because they have no way of knowing exactly what effect the devices might have on the individuals they are engaging. A legislative support synopsis from the Western Center lawyers stated:

> People's ability to endure physical force and tolerate pain varies widely. The use of nunchucks and other pain-compli-ance techniques causes some people to comply but many people to break. The police do not know how much pain it will take to break the will of a passive demonstrator. The police do not know whether any amount of pain will be suf-ficient. Even a conscientious police officer cannot know in advance who will comply before breaking. Even a conscien-tious police officer cannot know how much pain is being in-flicted. Even a conscientious police officer cannot know when such pain-compliance techniques will produce tem-porary or permanent injury. But an unscrupulous police of-ficer can induce pain to teach people a lesson, pain to intim-idate and silence civil rights protests, pain to vent passion or prejudice, pain to punish. An unscrupulous police officer could even induce pain for the sake of pain.

The authorization of *any* devices that specifically inflict pain, then, is what makes that last scenario possible. Most other devices used by the police are, of course, designed to force compliance—the discomfort of tear gas and the net shot from a special gun, and even the use of the baton, certainly fall within this category. But the pain or restriction these tools of law enforcement generate serve an understandable goal in aiding officers in the detention of violent offenders. Obviously, the nonviolent Operation Rescue demonstrators are not tear-gassed, or tasered, or clubbed with batons, for all of the reasons already cited. Their demonstrations are usually nonthreatening by nature. The use of any instrument specifically designed to cause pain, then, in a situation such as a nonviolent demonstration, plays right into the hands of the abusive officer.

Under questioning from Rep. Hyde, Llewellyn was asked whether he had sought assistance from the Justice Department on behalf of Operation Rescue. Llewellyn replied that he and other public-service lawyers handling the Operation Rescue cases had first hoped they could deal with the issue effectively through litigation at the local level. They were not successful, however.

Llewellyn noted that the problems involving use of force against Operation Rescue and other anti-abortion groups was not limited to nunchukas.

"In addition to that," Llewellyn told Hyde, "people face down on the ground, handcuffed, officer's knee in the back holding them down while another officer is trying to lift them up from the nose, for example, a technique which the Los Angeles Police Department says is only to distract people's attention toward their nose and face in order to get their hands free. These are people totally subdued and on the ground."

"Now wait a minute," Hyde interrupted. "Someone is on the ground with their hands handcuffed behind them?"

"Yes," Llewellyn replied. "And officers around. And the

person is making no apparent effort to move except to respond to try and get away from the pressure."

"And the officer has a knee in the back," Hyde asked incredulously.

"That is correct," Llewellyn replied.

"And another officer is trying to pick the person up by his nose?" Hyde asked.

"Well, yes." Llewellyn said. "He is pulling the head back by the nose, and there is no evident reason for this. And there are similar kinds of things."

"You can hardly get up if someone has a knee in your back," Hyde suggested.

"It is obviously impossible for the person to rise," Llewellyn agreed. "The chief difficulty is that the Los Angeles Police Department has justified it, saying, 'well, if we use pain compliance we use fewer officers. We don't have to carry [the demonstrators], and that sort of thing.' But, if you look at the video tapes, what actually happens is that these nunchucks are placed on people's arms and they are lifted by the nunchucks, so that the weight of the person is added to the torquing effect of the officer's grasp and it causes, you know, people—you can see, they can hardly react if they wanted to. They appear to be limp, and they are limp. Some of them are limp not because they don't want to walk but because they cannot walk."

"Now," Hyde asked sarcastically, "what are these arch-criminals doing that requires this torture? What laws are they violating?"

"Well, they are trespassers," Llewellyn conceded. "They are intentionally, as many other people in many areas, anti-nuclear, animal rights protesters, they are sit-in demonstrators. The only thing that is distinctive about them is that they are entirely passive."

Llewellyn noted that low-level pain compliance, such as wrist and thumblocks, have been used on some of the other groups he mentioned, but that nunchukas and other high-level pain compliance efforts, to his knowledge, had been reserved in recent years solely for use against the anti-abortion activists.

The line of questioning Hyde employed with Llewellyn was not to be confused with objective fact-finding—as a legislator whose record has been decidedly anti-abortion, it is understandable that he would want to eke out every last horrific episode or anecdote Llewellyn could muster. Yet the unexpected bipartisan tone that the hearings took on demonstrated that no matter what side of the political fence someone might be on, if excessive force is tolerated in one set of circumstances, then its use can also be justified on other occasions.

Rep. Craig Washington brought that point home when he addressed Llewellyn: "There is one clear message; and that is, [if the] police use excessive force against one group and other groups stand idly by and let it happen, then the next time it will be another group and then another group and then another group."

This was an obvious slap at some of the more conservative members of Congress, including Hyde. He, among others, had speechified extensively at the outset of the hearing on how, despite the Rodney King debacle, he did not expect to discover widespread abusive tactics practiced by police officers. These conservatives claimed, too, that Congress should give its unflagging support to law enforcement officers.

"I apologize for myself," Washington went on to say, "that I wasn't more aware of what was happening in Los Angeles, but I abhor [it] as much as I do any other form of police misconduct. And whatever remedy we attempt to fashion, I assure you . . . will include protection for people without regard to what cause they espouse and what their political persuasion or nonpolitical persuasion may be."

Were it not for the baton blows that struck Rodney King,

the allegations of abuse against anti-abortion activists might never have made it to the halls of Congress, and by Rep. Washington's own admission, certainly not to his ears. What this demonstrates is that police procedures that are inherently wrong, no matter how little publicity they may generate, must be addressed in a proper and public fashion. The use of ostensibly nonlethal force for compliance purposes must be scrutinized; the ill will that the misapplication of that force is capable of creating can be devastating for a community.

———

Kingston, New York is a normally peaceful city of 50,000 on the banks of Rondout Creek, near the Hudson River, about ninety miles north of New York City. Its police chief, James Riggins, is a capable administrator whose job has been made more difficult in recent years by the rapid proliferation of drugs and weapons, which make their way to Kingston by way of I-95, the interstate highway connecting Kingston a two-hour drive from the Big Apple.

During the summer of 1991, Riggins and his officers had to contend with drive-by shootings and other violent incidents. There were pleas from churchmen in the city's black community for police intervention, and the Kingston P.D., which had in the past paid no more than ordinary attention to the central Broadway area, where problems were rife, had to devise a counter-attack against the drug trade. The plan they conceived involved the placement of undercover officers acquired through a "swap-a-cop" program with adjoining jurisdictions, in order to prevent their identification. This tactic has proved useful to many small police agencies.

The new interdiction effort had rocky beginnings. Tension grew between the police and the neighborhood residents because many of the residents, with no way of knowing of the undercover effort taking place on their very blocks, saw police cars driving past drug dealers who were brazenly operating on the dimly lit streets. The message seemed to be that the police did not care about what was happening, but were only too willing to harass "decent folks" who were minding their own business. The presence of the uniformed officers, in large part ordered to protect the undercovers operating in the area, resulted in increased police-citizen contact that wasn't always pleasant. One such incident involved the pursuit and apprehension of a young man (believed to have affiliations with Los Angeles gangs) who was in possession of a pistol. A crowd gathered after the arrest (mostly angry relatives of the young man) and in the brief melee that ensued a fourteen-year-old was bitten by a police dog.

This incident substantially increased community tensions, which were only resolved after the undercover operation was made public and the police embarked on a community outreach program developed by Chief Riggins and local clergymen, which had positive results.

The dog bite incident could have escalated into something far more serious, however, and in some less-balanced communities could have conceivably led to the type of negative rumors—and overall ill will—that cripples good police work. It was one of the few such incidents recorded in Kingston; other jurisdictions have seen more. Indeed, police dogs can and have killed people.

This was not the case with the first dogs pressed into local police service, in New York City in 1907. They were imported from Belgium, and were trained to wrap their legs around those of a suspect until reached by an officer. The dog's bark was incorporated into training as a device for alerting the officer that an apprehension had been made and intimidating the suspect into compliance. What is generally regarded as proper use of a police dog (when dealing with the civilian population) is a procedure called "find and bark." "Find and hold" training, however—meaning, essentially, "find and bite"—is not uncommon. "Find and hold" has traditionally been reserved for military use, and no one has ever suggested that the primary use of a police dog is to inflict purposeful injury on the suspect.

The use of a dog is not regarded as a deadly use of force. Doubtless, animal rights activists might well object to the use of a dog for the purposeful infliction of pain or injury (which jeopardizes the dog), and no one is suggesting here that police dogs should not be trained to respond to specific commands or situations with the required force when life is threatened. There are police officers who owe their lives to dogs who have apprehended suspects—including situations where injury or death has resulted directly from the dog's actions. There are also police dogs who have actually laid down their lives to protect those of their human partners.

But, conscious of the intimidating effect a dog can have on a suspect, some officers have been documented making less than desirable use of man's best friend. Between 1989 and 1991, over 900 bites were inflicted by police dogs in Los Angeles. This record is far from typical. Philadelphia, which has twice as many dogs, reported only twenty bites during the same period.

In San Diego, Philadelphia, Indianapolis, and other cities that routinely use canine patrols, officers also issue a verbal warning before releasing a patrol dog—a practice that Los Angeles has been urged to adopt.

Progressive law enforcement chiefs tend to regard dogs as tools rather than weapons, and dogs can indeed be used—even in the most crowded situations—effectively and safely, as evinced by their deployment in the tunnels under the streets of New York by the transit police. The canine patrols' task, however, should be to *reduce* violence and attendant injury to officers and suspects, rather than create additional problems. This is the reason why less than lethal tools and weapons are used in the first place.

Nets designed to be thrown over a flailing or resisting suspect or emotionally disturbed person, minimizing risk to all parties, have made some headway in recent years. A form of net was field-tested by the Los Angeles Sheriff's Department (a separate agency from the LAPD) but was not put into wide service there because of budget restrictions—an ironic twist when one considers the money that has been paid out in lawsuits for use of excessive force.

A body blanket that works like an old-fashioned straightjacket has also met with some approval by police departments. Further study or development of the blankets may be warranted, though. Although the blankets are effective in their intended use, there is the possibility they may cause overheating, which in some cases can be fatal.

Although recently cited as the cause of a fatality in Westchester County, New York, a new chemical tool, oleoresin capsicum (OC), or "pepper gas," seems to be gaining favor as an alternative to more lethal weaponry. The gas, which comes in a small, personal-sized sprayer, is usually isopropyl alcohol-propelled and is considered superior to chemical mace. Mace is intended to irritate mucous membranes and other sensitive areas, including skin, but that effect is sometimes lost on suspects who have ingested large amounts of alcohol or drugs because their nerve receptors are blocked. Use of OC, on the other hand, induces *swelling* of the skin and other tissues (which is especially effective on the respiratory system and the eyes). In one police department, officer training with OC is routinely videotaped, with officers actually being sprayed themselves (in a short burst) so that they can experience the effects of the gas.

There have been some problems associated with the substance, however. In New York City, emergency service officers shot one suspect with OC but, being in a highly agitated state and severely influenced by drugs, he did not respond quickly enough. They then fired a taser dart, and the electric charge ignited the OC's alcohol propellent, engulfing the suspect in flames.

All in all, however, some of the most progressive police organizations support the phasing in of OC. The NYPD is doing just that. The possible hazards posed by environmental variables (as with other forms of lethal and nonlethal force) are being approached and dealt with in training.

Taser guns also have a continued future in policing, although they are not always up to snuff. Rodney King, for instance, was tasered with little beneficial effect. Although Los Angeles police officers attempted to cite the ineffectiveness of the taser on Rodney King as evidence of their need to use continued force (later ruled excessive), the fact is that police professionals in the field report a 50 percent effectiveness rate for the device.

The taser (acronym for Thomas A. Swift Electronic Rifle) is a hand-held device that shoots a pair of darts for a distance of anywhere from eight to fifteen feet. The darts are propelled by a smokeless gunpowder charge. When the darts make contact they conduct an electrical charge to the body that should result in the temporary immobilization of the suspect. Both darts must attach to the suspect or the person's clothing, or no electrical arc is created.

Tasers and electric stun guns can be extremely hazardous if used near water. But tasers are employed with success by many law enforcement agencies and there is no reason why, especially as the technology advances, their use should not increase as well. This will undoubtedly take time, as the general public has an aversion to weapons that use electricity. It is interesting to note that while the taser (under optimum conditions) is far less capable or likely to cause serious injury or death than the primitive nunchuka, the mass tasering of Operation Rescue demonstrators would no doubt cause serious public alarm and controversy.

—————

The development of nonlethal technology could well usher in a new era of law enforcement practices, increasing safety for officers and their civilian subjects alike. The general rule seems to be that the more an object is looked upon as a *tool* rather than a weapon, the much less the chances are it will be used improperly, or with deadly results. Of course, this is not always the case—and many simple tools have the capacity to be used as instruments of harm. Flashlights, for example.

The portable light is an important policing tool. Officers often respond to dangerous situations with a minimum of available light, and even on day shifts a flashlight is standard equipment on most officers' belts. In recent years heavy, multicelled flashlights have been employed by some departments, and their potential for use as a weapon has not gone unnoticed by some officers.

There are some considerations concerning the use of flashlights that transcend mere issues of improper force and brutality. Research indicates a right-handed officer will almost invariably reach for the flashlight before a threat—perhaps to be illuminated by the flashlight—becomes obvious. But the flashlight cannot just be dropped to the ground if the officer needs to unholster the gun, as it could then be a potential weapon for the perpetrator, and reholstering the light might cost precious seconds off the draw of the gun or the nightstick in an emergency. Some law enforcement agencies have actively sought out a flashlight that could also be used as a baton. To date, no such product is known to be on the market.

Nonetheless, flashlights have been used as weapons, causing injury to suspects in 96 percent of cases in which officers chose to use them as such. In one recent case the result was fatal. So egregious were the circumstances surrounding the death of Malice Green in Detroit that even a prosecutor and chief medical examiner sympathetic to the police position could not prevent criminal convictions of the officers responsible.

EIGHT
THE MALICE GREEN CASE

The Negro is in the hands of the enemy when he is in the hands of the police.

—Clarence Darrow, during the Detroit murder trial of Dr. Ossian Sweet in 1926.

THE CITY OF DETROIT RE-sides upon the banks of a river bearing the same name, which means "of the strait" in French. Its strategic location in the industrialized Great Lakes region made it a blue-collar mecca for migrating southern blacks, along with poor whites from the Appalachian and Ozark regions, ever since the advent of the automobile.

Detroit has a reputation for being a tough town; its "Motor City" nickname has been revised to "Murder City" by many. According to some community leaders, however, the city has gotten a bad rap. "Devil's Night," which involves young people setting fires on Halloween Eve, has been widely exaggerated in the national media, according to many life-long Detroit residents.

The Rev. Clayton Smith, pastor of Detroit's Central Baptist Church, is one of those who thinks the city has been unfairly singled out as an exemplar of urban violence.

"I walk out my door and I don't see it, and I'm right here,"

Smith said. "Unless you associate with those types of people you're not going to be a victim of many of these crimes. The everyday citizen trying to make it doesn't have that much to fear . . . nobody is going to shoot you in the back of the head."

One of the more curious aspects of police-community relations in Detroit has been the fact that in some historic cases, both past and present, justice has actually prevailed in the courtrooms when blacks came up against the establishment. That is not to say that there haven't always been problems. Detroit *is* a tough town, and its police department has earned a reputation over the years for being equally tough. But the two cases presented in this chapter certainly indicate that "happy" endings are sometimes possible.

In the very early days after the turn of the century, relations between the races in Detroit were not good. They were exacerbated by the first great wave of black migration that began around 1910, when approximately 6,000 blacks called the city home. The black population crested at over ten times that number after World War I. Throughout the northeastern United States there was sporadic rioting; in some cases the violence was sparked by particular incidents, but more often than not it simply welled out of discontent over lack of decent housing and jobs. Detroit was no exception. The city's tensions were escalated by the preexisting enmity between blacks and formerly southern whites, as well as attendant labor difficulties stemming from the segregated nature of the trade unions.

The housing shortage that occurred in the years after World War I unbalanced the de facto racial segregation that existed in many neighborhoods. The black ghettos could not support any additional homes or people, and so their borders began expanding into marginal neighborhoods occupied by poor whites, who organized "neighborhood improvement associations" and "clubs." Some of these were little more than fronts for the Ku Klux Klan. Some officers of the Detroit police department, if not actually members of these groups, were at the very least sympathetic to their goals.

Dr. Ossian Sweet, however, was not one of the blacks competing against whites for auto industry jobs when he and his family relocated to Detroit in 1924. At the age of thirty, Sweet had just completed a lengthy European stay that had included studies under Madame Curie. His medical practice soon began to thrive, and he decided to purchase a two-story house at 2905 Garland Avenue, in an all-white neighborhood. Word spread that a black man had bought the house, and the local residents were not happy.

On September 8, 1925, Sweet moved into the house with the help of his brother Otis, who was a dentist, and another brother, Henry, a law student. Fearful of the possible reactions of his new neighbors, and well aware of the racial tensions in Detroit, Sweet moved a supply of guns and ammunition into his home.

Sweet, his brothers, and seven friends were in the house when a mob began to collect on the first night; no trouble erupted, however. On the second night, the size and attitude of the mob had grown. Perhaps out of concern for Sweet's safety, the moving party had continued staying with him. Some of the mob yelled angry racial epithets as others threw rocks and stones at the house, shattering windows. The police, who were present, took no action against the crowd, whose members were trespassing on Sweet's property. Reacting to the situation, some of the moving party fired shots from Sweet's upper windows, taking the life of one white man, Leon Beiner, and wounding another. As a result, all of the men in the house were arrested and charged with conspiracy to commit murder and other crimes.

The case of the *People of the State of Michigan v. Ossian Sweet et. al.* began in 1926. The prosecution believed it could win the case handily on its apparent merits, charging that the defen-

dants "premeditatedly and with malice aforethought con-
spired that one or more of them would kill if there was threatened or actual trespass."

The Sweet case was handled through several trials, all of
which kept the city on edge. Dr. Sweet himself testified to the
history of American race riots—particularly those that occurred within the century—and the defense tried to make the
case that Sweet and the others in the house were victims of
grave psychological fear.

The prosecution claimed that the police had come to Garland Avenue to protect Sweet and his home; that contention
was rejected out of hand by the defense team, which included
the great Clarence Darrow. In order to represent Sweet, the old
lion had denied himself sabbatical from high-profile cases that
he had promised himself after his participation at the Scopes
"monkey trial" in Tennessee.

"The officers of the law were in sympathy with the
crowd," Darrow announced during his trademark seven-hour
summation for Sweet's defense.

> If the police had done their duty and dispersed the mob
> Beiner would not be dead today . . . No matter what the
> laws we pass, no matter what precautions we take, unless
> the people we meet are kindly and decent and human and
> liberty loving then there is no liberty. Freedom comes from
> human beings rather than from laws and institutions . . . I
> am the last one to come here to stir up race hatred or any
> other hatred. I do not believe in the law of hate. I believe in
> the law of love and I believe you can do nothing with ha-
> tred. I would like to see a time when man loves his fellow
> man and forgets his color or his creed. We will never be civi-
> lized until that time comes.

The all-white jury deliberated for three and one-half
hours, and returned a verdict of not guilty.

———

The Sweet case is recounted here for two reasons. For one thing, it echoed what would later become long-standing allegations of collaboration between white police officers—many of them migrated southerners—and white supremacy or hate groups in Detroit. These allegations created a mistrust among the public for the police that has continued into the present. It is also mentioned because, as will soon enough become apparent, Darrow's message of love and caring was in more recent times strongly exemplified by the father of a man who became the city's most prominent victim of police brutality.

Some of the worst racial violence to hit Detroit after the Sweet years occurred during World War II, at the Belle Isle recreational area in the Detroit River. Rioting between groups of young blacks and whites there resulted in thirty-four deaths. Twenty-five blacks were killed, nearly three-quarters of the total fatalities, and seventeen of those were killed by the police. In the post-war, post-riot years, distinctions between the city's white and black communities remained clear, although the black ghettos grew and expanded during the 1960s.

It was not until 1967 that serious mass violence returned to the streets of Detroit, when rioting broke out in its ghettos as it did in other American cities. Block after block of Detroit was reduced to rubble; some areas looked like ghost towns. Like other rioting during that period, the 1967 Detroit riots were precipitated by police action, in this case the closing of an after-hours club.

In spite of Detroit's many problems, however, people still came there in search of work. One of these, in 1968, was Jesse Green, Jr. He had raised his young family in Arkansas, where—although some work was available for a man willing to do it—the pay scale was extremely low. Like the immigrants of old he left his family behind while he sought shelter and the means to pay for it. He landed a job at the brake drum manufacturing plant of a firm called Kelsey Hayes.

"I came here and within the week I was working," Jesse Green said. "The wages was good here."

He remained alone from October through June of the following year, when he sent for his wife Patricia and their children. Life was good for the Green family, despite the threat of occasional layoffs. One of the couple's six children, Malice, had grown up adopting his father's quiet ways, and understood that in order to succeed in this world you must find worthwhile employment. But as Malice Green grew to manhood, he realized that the mammoth auto industry held little promise for him.

"He was brown-skinned with long, shoulder-length hair, nice shoulder-length hair," Jesse Green said when asked to recall his son, who stood 5'7" tall. "Quite a women's man—everybody who saw him fell in love with him right away. He was in Illinois since he graduated from high school."

It was after moving to Illinois that young Malice became a steelworker. Before long he married, then divorced, then married again. Along the way he fathered two children.

In 1974 Detroit elected a black mayor, Coleman Young. Young pledged to make the police department more sensitive to the needs of the community, and to eradicate police brutality. Detroit still had a reputation for being a violent town, and such violence was not unknown to the Green family. In 1982, while Malice Green was working in Illinois, his younger sister Brenetta, with whom Jesse Green said he was "very close," was tragically killed. Brenetta Green was shot to death by a boyfriend, who then turned the gun on himself, while she was still a college student. Malice returned to Detroit for the funeral at a cemetery on Woodward, near Fourteen Mile Road. Changes had been at work in the city during the time Jesse

Green and his family had first moved there, including an ambitious urban renewal program.

Malice Green lived the simple life of a midwestern working man, and enjoyed fishing on the Great Lakes. And he liked listening to the blues. "My kids never cared for none of that rap stuff," Jesse Green recalled. "All my kids and grandkids like the blues." But Malice also indulged in a few less than healthy pursuits, however, including occasional use of cocaine and alcohol. Malice Green also had some confrontations with police, according to published reports, although none were described as serious.

He stayed with his mother during his Detroit visits, which became more frequent after he was laid off from the steel mill in 1990. Patricia Green had separated from Jesse Green years before and lived in a small apartment. There were no ill feelings between father and son; Malice saw Jesse at least three times during his last stay in Motor City during the fall of 1992.

Patricia had kept an old car around for some time, a red 1980 Mercury, and she gave it to Malice. Although it was old, it was still reliable. Malice left his mother's home on the night of November 5, and was driving down a street called Warren when he spotted a friend, Ralph Fletcher, a former Chrysler worker who was returning from a trip to the store. Green drove Fletcher two blocks to his residence at 23rd and Warren. Fletcher's neighborhood was a model of urban decay, prone to heavy drug traffic and other criminal activity. As Fletcher got out of the Mercury another vehicle glided to a stop behind it.

Two veteran Detroit police officers, Larry Nevers and Walter Budzyn, had been patrolling in an unmarked car and suspected that the driver of the red Mercury might have been involved in a drug transaction. It was also possible that the two officers had received a report of a "missing" auto similar in appearance to the Mercury, although the stated reason for the initial confrontation between Malice Green and the two officers was, ostensibly, the possibility of a drug scenario.

According to court testimony and early media reports of the case, the officers, dressed in civilian clothes, came around to the side of the car and ordered Green to produce his license and automobile registration. Green reached for the Mercury's glove box, with his fist clenched, and the officers, after receiving no response to their shouted demands that Green open his hand, began beating at his hand with a two-pound flashlight. A struggle ensued, according to witnesses, with the officers beating Green in the head and other parts of the body with both the flashlight and their fists until all of them ended up on the sidewalk in front of the former Beauty Salon storefront that Fletcher called home. As back-up units arrived the beating of Malice Green continued, even after he was handcuffed.

The unconscious steelworker was rushed by ambulance to Detroit Receiving Hospital, where he died in the emergency room. The sidewalk near Ralph Fletcher's house was stained with Green's blood, and the stains remained for many days after the incident. The site became a shrine of sorts for angry protesters who had learned the specifics of the case.

The telephone rang at Jesse Green's West Graham Boulevard home at around 2:00 A.M. It was Patricia, who had been notified by Ralph Fletcher. She had just finished the gruesome task of identifying her son's battered corpse at the hospital. "She called me and said the police had beat his brains out," Jesse Green said. "I was shocked. Everybody knew he was a good guy—he didn't bother nobody, never get in no trouble or nothing like that."

An autopsy was initially performed by Dr. Kalil Jiraki, who found the cause of death to be head trauma inflicted by the flashlight; Green had suffered fourteen blows to the head and a torn scalp. In the wake of the beating of Rodney King in

California, the beating death of Malice Green touched deep emotional chords across the nation.

Green's funeral was held at a small Baptist church, a service simple in its poignancy despite the fact that it had reached event status.

"There was music and they sang a couple of songs; the preacher preached," Jesse Green remembered. "Thousands of people white and black, they came." Malice Green was laid to rest at the Fourteen Mile cemetery next to his beloved sister, as the furor over his death continued.

That Detroit knew well the lessons taught by the Rodney King case was fully documented in local and national media. Comparisons between the two cases were inevitable.

"I think the Rodney King situation did impact this particular case," Central Baptist's Rev. Smith said. "I think it helped play a part because there was pressure."

For whatever reasons—and one might hope that a sincere desire to see justice done was one of them—officials acted swiftly in announcing an investigation into the incident, which Police Chief Stanley Knox was quick to condemn. He called it a disgrace and an embarrassment to the good police officers of Detroit, and said that such behavior would not be tolerated. The swift police and prosecutorial response to the Green incident was considered surprising in criminal justice circles. Certainly, police departments and prosecutors have never been anxious to bring down one—or more—of their own.

The Detroit policemen's union was critical of public statements made by the chief, who suspended Nevers and Budzyn without pay within days of the incident.

"I must've done something wrong; a guy died," Nevers himself was quoted as saying in the *Detroit Free Press*. "If I can ever sleep again I'm going to wake up and say this was a dream, that it didn't happen, it didn't happen."

Both Nevers and Budzyn are white; another four white of-

ficers and a black sergeant who all watched the incident but
did nothing to stop it were suspended as well. And then came
the news that four of the seven suspended officers would be
criminally charged. Incredulous criminologists interviewed on
television news programs and quoted or alluded to as sources
in newspapers spoke of the relative rarity of such legal actions.

On November 16, 1992, suspended Detroit police officers
Nevers, Budzyn, Freddie Douglas, and Robert Lessnau were
arraigned on criminal charges. Four of the "new untouchables"—big city cops who for the most part are never brought
to task for taking the lives of people they are sworn to protect—had become eminently touchable, at least in Detroit.
Prosecutors felt they had a strong case. More than one Detroit
civic leader said that the quick moves by city officials kept further tragedy from occurring, a la Los Angeles.

Nevers and Budzyn faced life in prison if convicted on the
second-degree murder charges brought against them. They
were bonded at $100,000 each. Sergeant Freddie Douglas, the
black officer, was charged with involuntary manslaughter and
neglect of duty, and faced a maximum of sixteen years and
posted $25,000 bond; Robert Lessnau faced ten years in jail if
convicted of his charge, aggravated assault, which drew a
bond of $100,000.

The officers' attorneys, as well as the police officers' union,
said that the trial should be moved out of Detroit because a
fair hearing could not be given due to the case's publicity.
John D. O'Hair, the Wayne County prosecutor who had
brought the charges, said he would vigorously fight any such
action. He knew full well that the tragedy of Los Angeles was
due in great part to the successful motion by defense attorneys
to move the trial of the officers who beat Rodney King.

O'Hair was successful in his fight to keep the trials in
Detroit. Also, Freddie Douglas prevailed in his quest to have
the most serious charge against him dismissed. He faced only

the misdemeanor charge of neglect of duty, which would be decided at a later time.

Nevers and Budzyn had requested separate juries and the motion was granted. Lessnau was to be tried by the court, meaning he had requested the trial judge to decide on his guilt or innocence rather than place his fate in the hands of a jury.

Judge George W. Crocket III presided over the case. The son of a prominent civil rights lawyer, Crocket had a reputation for integrity—and for wielding a fair but iron-clad hand in his court room. The *New York Times* reported that he had been hospitalized in 1977 for acute manic paranoia; by all accounts Crocket was a success story of a man who overcame mental illness, among other adversities, maintaining at all times the respect of his peers and of the lawyers who practice before him.

For the *Times* article, Crocket consented to be interviewed while the trial was going on—a request not many judges will grant while in the midst of a high-profile case. He was asked to describe his judicial philosophy. "I try to treat people as I would like to be treated or as I like someone I care about to be treated," Crocket said.

Malice Green might well have taken part in a drug transaction, or might even have been in possession of crack cocaine at the time he was arrested. Green's resistance to questioning— his refusal to open up his hand—was certainly suspicious. Several small vials were recovered at the scene, although there was nothing to link them to Green directly. There was never any conclusive evidence presented to indicate what it was Green was holding in his hand that cost him his life. The circumstances of the incident certainly lend credence to such a contention. The boarded-up storefront where Fletcher lived was not your typical Detroit residence, but it was often used by homeless people as a place of shelter.

But there was no evidence presented to indicate that the lives of the officers were in jeopardy. Emergency medical technicians who arrived at the scene testified that Green was punched and kicked as he was removed from the automobile. There was testimony that he was also beaten after he was handcuffed. Sergeant Kenneth Day, a Detroit P.D. veteran, testified that he had become angered with Douglas at the crime scene when he learned that Green's car was moved by officers, and that blood had been wiped from more than one officer's flashlight.

If those actions were intended as part of a cover-up, information would surface later—after the trial—indicating that despite the apparent eagerness of county and city officials to bring the prosecution, there might have been other cover-up attempts in an area that was crucial to the case. Forensic evidence constituted the single most important weapon at the disposal of the prosecution team. The defense lawyers would attempt to prove that drugs—not the flashlight blows—had been the key factor in causing Malice Green's death. The idea of drugs being responsible for a suspect's death was not new, and not always difficult to maintain with credibility. It would be a battle of medical credentials over what specifically caused Green to die, and the defense pulled out all the stops in its attempts to prove that contention.

———

Dr. Kalil Jiraki, thirty-nine, the assistant medical examiner, testified for the prosecution. He is a native of Lebanon who studied at the American University in his home country before emigrating to the United States, where he maintained a general practice before going to work at the office of the medical examiner in Cleveland. He has claimed since the trial that he has long been disheartened by his knowledge of the adjustment of autopsy records to take the heat off of police officers in beating cases. He began his testimony in the Green case by presenting his credentials and explaining the autopsy procedure.

An autopsy is the systematic examination of the body of a deceased person by a qualified pathologist. In Wayne County, as in many other jurisdictions, autopsies are performed by pathologists authorized by the chief medical examiner, who is an appointed county official. The body of the deceased is routinely checked for disease or injury; specimens of the vital organs and body fluids are taken for microscopic and chemical tests, which are usually performed *after* the body has been prepared for release. Written records are made of all procedures and their results, and the oral report of the pathologist during the procedure is often tape-recorded for transcription and record-keeping purposes. Jiraki stated unequivocally that the flashlight blows—blunt trauma to the head, according to the testimony—had caused Green's death. What Jiraki had to say months after the trial was more fascinating, however, than anything he presented on the witness stand—and more frightening as well.

According to Jiraki, the prosecution of the four officers was a public show done not for the sake of justice but for appeasement; once the case was in court it could be lost on the forensics, and the public would have the impression that the best possible efforts had been made to bring the defendants to justice. This is a serious charge made even weightier by the fact that Jiraki stood to lose much by not complying with pressure he claimed came directly from the top echelons of Wayne County government, including his boss, Chief Medical Examiner Bader Cassin.

In November 1993, Jiraki said that the day after he performed the Green autopsy his boss reviewed his work. "I have not seen the injuries you have seen," Jiraki said he was told by his boss, in an attempt to discourage Jiraki from testifying. Jiraki, however, had photographed the injuries himself. The only way for his findings to be changed—short of an assault by experts on the witness stand sufficient enough to affect the credibility of Jiraki's findings in the mind of the jury—would be for Jiraki himself to change them.

"There was lots of pressure on me to change it," Jiraki said of his findings and the testimony he gave in support of them. He was later instructed, he said, to ignore the head injuries, which left the presence of cocaine in the deceased's system to account for the death. "Ignore the injuries and you are left with natural death," Jiraki said. But he could not ignore the injuries. The cocaine, he said, would have been entirely incidental.

Jiraki said that the Green case—and subsequent cases in other jurisdictions he has since heard about from colleagues—has soured him on the role of pathologists in medical examiner offices. "We protect the system," he said. "Doctors, hospitals, everything works together to keep the status quo. But if it is my case—and this was my case—I do not change my opinion."

The defense was unable to shake Jiraki on cross examination, and rolled out some big forensic guns when the time came to present its side of the story. The chief medical examiner for nearby Oakland County was called to testify. Dr. Ljubisa Dragovic said he had reviewed the materials prepared by Jiraki, and said that since there appeared to be no evidence of swelling to the brain, it was not likely that Green died of the wounds caused by the flashlight. Green's death, according to Dragovic, would have been attributable to cocaine and alcohol in combination, in addition to "bruising" of the brain. All of these in combination would have caused a fatal seizure, Dragovic testified.

By all accounts, Dragovic's testimony conflicted with Jiraki's chiefly in terms of the role any cocaine in Green's system might have played in his death. In other words, according to Dragovic, if Green had not ingested cocaine and alcohol, the brain swelling would not have resulted in death. Conversely, according to Jiraki, if Green had not received the blows, any effects of the cocaine and alcohol in his system would not have been fatal. Jiraki later said that even with Dragovic's testimony taken at full face value, one would have to conclude that were it not for the intervention of the police, Green would not have died.

The Green trial continued to generate public attention throughout its duration. To the surprise of many courthouse veterans, Judge Crocket had permitted cameras in the courtroom. This gesture should not have been taken as a blanket assessment of relations between the judge and the press, however. Crocket ordered a twenty-three-year-old *Detroit News* intern jailed for five days for calling up a juror at home. A *Free Press* photographer, Richard Lee, was threatened with contempt charges for photographing a witness outside the courthouse—on a public street.

As the case drew to a close, Detroit palpably held its breath. Despite the attacks on the forensic evidence offered by the prosecution, their case was a strong one.

One aspect of the case that did not become much of a factor during the trial was race. Perhaps because of the alleged complicity of Douglas in Green's beating. But it might be more logical to conclude that even if race had played a role in any of the actions committed by the defendants, such claims would not have furthered the legal arguments for conviction and may even have harmed them.

Judge Crocket had reached his own verdict on Lessnau, but had sealed it pending the juries' findings on the other two defendants. In Budzyn's case, the jury reached a verdict on the afternoon of August 20. Deliberations continued among the jurors weighing the evidence against Nevers.

On August 23, 1993, the verdicts were announced. Lessnau was acquitted of assault charges by Judge Crocket. Nevers and Budzyn were not as lucky. The juries announced murder convictions against both officers, and word spread quickly. Horns honked in some neighborhoods. There was a celebration on the block where Green had been killed, where his face had been painted on a cinderblock wall. There were more honking horns and the boom of rap music. Sherry and Monica Green, Malice's sisters, prayed at the site with at least fifty other people while patrol cars cruised close by and a police helicopter circled overhead.

Not everyone was happy, however, particularly when Judge Crocket allowed the convicted officers to remain free until their sentencing. The president of the police union, Tom Schneider, said that the verdicts did not bode well for Detroit, and that they would affect the work performance of officers on the street.

Nearly two months later, on October 12, 1993, Judge Crocket told the convicted officers that he did not believe they had intended to kill Malice Green. Nonetheless, he told them, "You did use excessive force in the extreme." He then announced his sentences. Nevers was given twelve to twenty-five years. Budzyn received eight to eighteen.

Jesse Green reflected on his feelings about the case and the juries' decisions shortly after the anniversary of his son's death. Patricia, he said, did not care to talk. "This was especially hard for her," he explained. "After all, he was her first son."

As for himself, Jesse said he had been angry in the beginning, when he first learned that Malice Green had been killed. "At first I was angry," he said. "But by then me being angry wasn't going to help anything. I didn't want anything to happen to the city. I think the verdict was pretty well justifiable. They're going to be old people when they get out anyway. I wouldn't have felt right if there was no justice done at all, but I couldn't afford to take the law into my own hands. All in all I think they did a pretty good job."

NINE
THE CRACK PANIC ATTACK

FORT TOTTEN IS AN ACTIVE
military base in eastern Queens, New York on the southern
shore of Long Island Sound at Little Bay. Gently rolling hills
and tree-lined pathways lend it the appearance of a college
campus, and there is an inviting green expanse of athletic
field. People spending time on the base might be able to forget
that they were in New York City at all, if not for the distant
spires of the city skyline. This is just fine with the many young
men and women who make the trip from area high schools for
dialogue sessions with officers of the NYPD Community Relations Unit's Youth Services Division.

Officer Eddie Rivera, dressed in sneakers, jeans, and a ca-
sual shirt, looked just like the people the small group of students from Bushwick High School were used to seeing on a
day-to-day basis in their Brooklyn neighborhood. The young
people had been promised an afternoon of air hockey, basket-
ball, and touch football in exchange for listening to Eddie
Rivera's rap during the morning hours.

Rivera's street-level patter endeared him to even the
toughest students; their laughter at his jokes gave strong indications that he was "reaching" them—that the barrier between
cops and teenagers that runs so high in the inner city had been
eroded ever so slightly.

"Okay," Rivera, animated, kinetic, and smiling, said with a clap of his hands. "So what do you think of the police?"

There were twitters of nervous laughter in the room. One boy whispered something to another.

"Come on man, share it with all of us," Rivera said. But the young man grew silent and sullen.

A Latino girl, perhaps about fourteen, raised her hand timidly.

"Yeah, go ahead, Sonia," Rivera said, gesturing toward her. Each time he addressed one of the students by first name during the morning session there were stifled gasps of surprise. "So tell me what you think."

"They're okay, most of them," the girl began slowly. "Most of them. But some aren't no good. They boss you around. They think because you're young and black or Spanish you sell drugs even if you don't."

Rivera felt that Sonia had more to say, and he worked to draw it out of her. If she opened up then others would, too.

"Tell me more," he said, arms folded across his chest, looking like a protective big brother. "Go ahead. It's okay."

The other students began prodding her, and finally she related her story.

"Well, on my block these two black guys, they were young, in a white Lexus, and two white cops pull them over," Sonia began, her voice and confidence level rising as she continued. "So they pull them over and tell these guys get out of the car, and they get out, and one of the cops, he says, 'how'd you guys get this nice car, you selling drugs?' So they said 'no, we ain't sellin' no drugs.' An' then the one cop says 'yeah, right.' So the other cop he takes his stick and he hits the lights in the back and breaks one of them, and then he hits the door of the car, and the two guys they're just lookin', and then a black cop pulled up behind them and says, 'what's going on.'"

Eddie Rivera was taking it all in and looked extremely concerned. The room had grown silent.

"That's bad," he said. "Did you tell anybody?"

"No," Sonia replied. "I didn't tell nobody."

"Well, cops like that aren't my friends," Rivera said. "Guys like that make it hard for me to do my job. They don't do any good for anybody. And somebody needs to know when something like that happens."

When something like that happens (and it happens more than people who live outside neighborhoods like Bushwick might realize), it is a result, in large part, of the crack epidemic. The introduction of crack—a cheap, smokable form of cocaine that some experts believe to be a direct attempt to meet market demands by Colombian druglords—has had a measurable effect on the quality of life in America's cities. Crack and the culture it has spawned has also severely affected relations between police officers and the communities they serve.

The perception by some police officers is often that everybody in a given neighborhood is either dealing drugs or knows someone who is. Cops who don't live in the cities they patrol are especially vulnerable to this. Manners of dress, speech, and other behaviors prevalent among particular members of a community are lumped together by the officer as the signs of the enemy. In much the same way, people in that community tend to view men and women in uniform as a hostile threat, even after they themselves have asked for more "blue" on the street.

The crack revolution's effect on neighborhoods has been a subject of study for Terry Williams, an author and sociologist who teaches at the New School for Social Research in New York. His book, *Crackhouse*, gives an excellent picture of the effects of cocaine on neighborhoods. Williams is well aware of how community frustrations with the problem of drugs and related criminal activity can be a harbinger of inappropriate actions by police against the community itself.

"When people say bring the police in, they don't realize that this is a cause of their victimization," Williams explained. "The police don't make a distinction between the BMW-driving middle-class working person and the BMW-driving dealer. There is a certain kind of victimization that occurs because you initiated it."

The war on drugs has in some cases become a war on drug-prone communities themselves. In some cases residents tolerate, and even tacitly encourage police violence and impropriety. Community residents made fearful by the wanton violence perpetrated by street thugs, and painfully aware of the shattering effect drug use has had on families, have publicly expressed willingness to allow police to "take back the streets" by any means necessary.

In Kingston, New York the friction between police and community that existed during the summer of 1991 left many church leaders puzzled. Drug trafficking was left seemingly unchecked while police prepared to carry out a major sweep of arrests; unknown to the public, many of the drug buyers in the small city's central Broadway area were police officers themselves on undercover assignment.

There were allegations that these Kingston cops had used excessive force on some young people. However, when these were presented to local leaders, some said quite frankly that they didn't wish to hear about any of it. These were the same individuals who ordinarily might have questioned such police actions, but they did not do so there because they were willing to "pay any price" to get the drugs off the streets. The Rev. James Childs, a respected Kingston clergyman, said that so long as the police were stemming the flow of drugs he wasn't concerned about what methods they used. His voice was only one of several raised in similar words by local churchmen.

The serious nature of the crack epidemic cannot and should not be minimized or sugar-coated. But the latter part of this century is not the first time in our nation's history that drugs have been a major social concern. The use of morphine as a cure-all by army doctors during the Civil War was so rampant that addiction among returning soldiers was referred to commonly as "army disease." The prevalence of opium dens in California prompted San Francisco to prohibit use of the drug at the turn of the century. The substances of choice nationwide, morphine and cocaine (originally sold as a wine product), led to such widespread addiction that after the turn of the century, an estimated 250,000 Americans were addicted, and the government sought new ways to control their use. Much of the federal legislative response focused on the importation and distribution of opium, such as the Opium Exclusion Act of 1909 and the Harrison Narcotics Act of 1914, which taxed and regulated the distribution and sale of narcotics. The Harrison Act was challenged, but upheld by the U.S. Supreme Court in 1919.

Most interdiction efforts, then, were concentrated at the federal level, with the exception of any dealings with drug addicts themselves, who were classified as criminals and dealt with accordingly. Most of the nation's concerns by 1920 were focused on alcohol, however, with the passage of the Volstead Act and the advent of Prohibition. Alcohol and drugs were regarded as substances that undermined national security. Federal bureaus were developed to deal specifically with narcotics use and traffic, but the bulk of narcotics enforcement had shifted to the states by the end of the next decade. Of course, by this time the unstable condition in Europe was commanding much of the federal government's attention.

World War II effectively halted the international drug

trade. In the post-war years little attention was paid to an ever-so-slow escalation of the domestic drug business, although there were still some legislative landmarks that included harsher penalties for drug dealing. In 1956 the Narcotics Control Act further increased those penalties and established once again the federal government's role in targeting drug traffic.

It was only at the dawn of the Kennedy years that drug use again made major inroads into the national consciousness, with treatment centers being established for the first time since the turn of the century. Street trade in amphetamines and barbiturates began to grow, as did use of LSD and marijuana. An upsurge in heroin addiction resulted in the establishment of pilot methadone maintenance programs.

Through the next two decades the use of drugs—especially marijuana, cocaine, and heroin—made a major impact on society, and public consciousness of drugs was raised to the highest level ever with the assistance of mass media. But it was not until the mid-1980s that the use of smokable cocaine changed both the perceptions and the reality of how drug use was affecting our urban centers.

The "free-base" smoking of cocaine was in vogue before the so-called advent of crack (which itself is essentially pre-packaged free-base) in 1984, at least two years before the mainstream media first "discovered" its proliferation in the inner city, and later began to understand that it was not restricted to those environs. Concurrently, AIDS was first being described in medical literature, with its path of transmission via shared needles soon to create a stir; a series of high-profile cocaine-related deaths, including those of athletes Len Bias and Don Rogers, further focused public attention on the problem.

Peak drug use was reached not in the mid-1980s but much earlier, according to some accounts. The federal National Household Survey on Drug Abuse reported a crest that began in 1979; by 1988, the use of most drugs had declined or remained stable, a decline that has continued to the present. One of the most dramatic drops in drug use occurred among military personnel, from 28 percent in 1980 to 5 percent in 1988. Jail inmates, however, were reported to have had significant increases in usage from 1983 through 1989, up from 12 percent to 24 percent. Declines in drug-related medical emergencies reinforced the findings of such surveys, rising dramatically from 1986 through 1988 but falling from 1989 through 1990.

The tracking of drug use was an invention of the 1980s, and so comparisons with earlier decades are difficult to compile. Empirical evidence conflicts with the cited survey findings, however, indicating that drug use *increased* during the 1980s, with the popularity of crack. This was most clearly evinced by the erosion of the quality of life in many big-city neighborhoods. Most police departments in major cities—and by extension their personnel—adopted a siege mentality regarding the drug trade. Officers felt more vulnerable and more at risk. Residents of some neighborhoods gave up hope, and those neighborhoods deteriorated visibly.

The proliferation of children in foster care born of drug-addicted mothers and fathers was certainly a measurable indication of how drug use had increased. Yet the presence and availability of drugs, while serious problems, were really only the tip of the iceberg. The mere use of drugs was not the only factor affecting this neighborhood decay. Rather, drug use and abuse constituted proof of underlying social problems, particularly unemployment, which continued to go unaddressed throughout the decade. But the most *visible* indicators that something was wrong were the legions of young men gathered on street corners, ostensibly to peddle product. Often their customers were outsiders (many white and middle-class) who "took a walk on the wild side" to feed their developing habits.

Despite the wild media attention paid to the riches made

by street-level dealers, the facts do not support the contention that the way out of the ghetto for most young men was street sales of drugs. Most of those who sold drugs openly did so as a creative way of feeding their own habits. Any cash earned went directly up their noses, into their arms, or down their lungs.

The mere presence of drugs on the street, then, was not the problem posing the greatest danger to police officers, no matter what the perceptions might have been. The drug trade was merely the smoke of a long-smoldering fire rather than the other way around. Tensions caused by the underlying problems of the inner cities continued to fester, all but forgotten by the soldiers of the war on drugs and their commanders.

The developing "gangster" or "outlaw" culture of the street, polarizing the police and the neighborhood, took its deadliest form in the amount of guns that began making their appearance. And while millions were spent on studies of drug traffic and use, scant attention was paid to the weapons of death. These were used mostly against other drug dealers or street people, and often to solve disputes—sometimes disputes *not* specifically related to drugs. The introduction of high-powered weaponry like assault rifles and semi-automatic handguns, wielded by inaccurate and inexperienced marksmen, made matters far worse.

The statistics tend to show that police officer deaths and injuries due to gunshot wounds did not increase substantially during the "crack epidemic"—at least not during the time the public perceived the crack menace as being at its worst. Enforcement efforts at the street level, however, did place officers at severe risk, especially those working in undercover operations. The emphasis on street-level enforcement also made for more incarcerations than ever before, packing jails to their limits. Stiff drug laws mandating maximum penalties were followed grudgingly by federal judges, who realized that someone threatening the life of the president could get out of a federal lock-up quicker than someone charged with possession with intent to sell of a laughably small quantity of cocaine.

Our greatest fear concerning drug use, quite understandably, has had to do with its prevalence among the young. Trends vary from city to city, and the only firm indicators are tests done of persons taken into police custody. Yet federal data on drug use indicates that the young have consistently shown less of a propensity for drug use than do people in their thirties, who may have switched to cocaine use from heroin, marijuana, and alcohol.

For example, in 1991 in Atlanta, 23 percent of fifteen to twenty year old males arrested for any offense tested positive for cocaine use, compared with 74 percent of those men arrested who were between thirty-one and thirty-five years of age. New York City's borough of Manhattan had a higher positive test rate among arrested males in the fifteen to twenty range (63 percent) than anywhere else in the country, yet that was still lower than the 78 percent of arrested men testing positive who were between the ages of thirty-one and thirty-five. The Atlanta figures were far more representative of the national norm, however.

The purpose of this thumbnail history of drug abuse facts and perceptions—or misperceptions, as the case may be—is not to downplay the role drugs have played in the deterioration of many neighborhoods, nor to minimize the quality of life issues which have weighed so heavily on inner-city neighborhoods. Rather, its purpose is to look at the "drug epidemic" in proper context, because hysteria over the situation has, perhaps more than any other factor, led to severely fractured relationships between community residents and police over the past two decades. If the federal figures on drug use and abuse

are to be believed, conditions in many of America's neighborhoods had never been so bad. And yet the truth of the state of
the cities could more accurately be pictured as an ongoing
blight stretching at least from the post-World War II years
through to the present, with the biggest change being the
greater attention paid to inner-city neighborhoods by the
media and the police after crack became king. Instead of benign tolerance of illegal activity in neighborhoods nobody
cared about, police departments and federal agencies waded
in waist deep, paying unprecedented attention to areas previously neglected. The number of people arrested—and jailed—
for offenses like loitering for the purpose of soliciting drugs increased dramatically.

The deployment of the Tactical Narcotics Team (TNT) in
the late 1980s in New York City resulted in the closing off of
entire blocks while wholesale arrests were made, with the emphasis on quantity rather than quality. This caused serious
problems for residents of some neighborhoods, who may not
have been involved in any illegal activity but were swept in
right along with offenders. One Brooklyn legal aid attorney related the story of a man who was an apartment building
porter who spoke little English. He was charged with loitering
for the purpose of narcotics trafficking because he and some
other men were sitting on a stoop drinking beer—a common
activity among many people in the low-income neighborhood.

The man argued with his court-appointed attorney at arraignment, who had advised him to plead guilty to disorderly
conduct, a violation. But the man was adamant in his insis-
tence that he had committed no crime, and therefore should
not say that he had. After taking his not guilty plea, the judge
released the man on his own recognizance, and he returned to
the block where the raid had taken place, determined to gather
witnesses for his trial. There was another raid, however, and
the hapless porter got caught up in a sweep once again. Upon

appearing before the same judge at arraignment, he was jailed in lieu of $500 bail. Not a lot of money, but an unreachable figure for the porter, who remained in jail, lost his job, and now had two "drug-related" arrests against his name.

During the 1960s, when widespread rioting broke out across the United States, conditions in the inner city were as bad if not worse than they are in the 1990s. But with the invasion of the television cameras into these neighborhoods, Americans saw first-hand the result of problems that have existed all along. The "drug epidemic" created easy villains—young men emblematic of blight—and so the war on drugs became a war on the community, with the consent of the community leaders.

There is no clear evidence of any conspiracy here, as some have claimed, but certainly the results of a greater focus on neighborhood drug trade, rather than on such root causes of poverty as lack of education, have let administrations local and national off the hook. This concentration on attacking the symptoms rather than the real problems was a hallmark of both the Reagan and Bush presidencies.

For the officers on the street, violations of the most basic civil liberties were in most cases committed with the very best of intentions. Young people, especially those fitting the "profile" of alleged drug dealers, are often stopped and searched without probable cause in some neighborhoods. The goal of "cleaning up the streets" in this fashion is enthusiastically supported by beleaguered residents. This tacit support leads to a feeling that improper conduct, including violence, can be tolerated if it is committed in the name of the war on drugs.

There was a flip side to all of this, however, that became painfully obvious in 1993 during the hearings conducted by the Mollen Commission in New York City. Acting under the guise of "restoring law and order" to crime-plagued neighborhoods, small pockets of NYPD officers engaged in systematic robberies of drug dealers' product and cash, in order to deal the drugs themselves in suburban areas.

Claims that police officers were using violence and intimidation (and their badges) as part of their involvement in illicit drug trade had been circulating through inner-city neighborhoods for years, but went largely unreported and uninvestigated. Certainly reports of police officers taking graft from drug dealers were nothing new. In the 1970s the NYPD was rocked by the allegations of Frank Serpico, a cop who turned his back on the force and testified before a commission on police corruption headed by attorney Whitman Knapp; his life story, *Serpico* by Peter Maas, became a best-seller, and a movie starring Al Pacino as Serpico became a box-office classic. Later, the film *Prince of the City*, starring Treat Williams, explored another true story of police corruption. But in 1993, when then-mayor David Dinkins appointed a blue ribbon panel to investigate present-day corruption, the findings were astounding. The Mollen Commission—named for its chairman, appeals court judge and deputy mayor Milton Mollen—took testimony from corrupt cops who admitted to both stealing *and* dealing drugs. The decision by Dinkins to convene the commission was fueled by the 1992 indictment of six police officers accused of trafficking in narcotics in suburban Suffolk County on Long Island.

On September 29, 1993, the commission heard from an admitted rogue cop, Bernard Cawley, who testified that brutality against civilians was encouraged in order to get out the street message that the police were "in charge," and that such behavior was not only condoned by superiors but encouraged.

Cawley said the supervising sergeant nicknamed him "the mechanic" because, in Cawley's own words, "I used to tune people up." The tune-ups, Cawley testified, were beatings. When asked by the commission's associate counsel, David A. Burns, whether he was concerned about being arrested or dismissed from the force because of his activities, Cawley replied, "Who's going to catch us? We're the police. We're in charge."

Cawley testified how he and thirteen other officers—some wearing sapgloves (leather gloves with lead in the knuckles)—swept into one Bronx building and began beating people wholesale. There were hundreds of other raids of homes and apartments, he said, conducted by officers looking for money, or drugs and guns that could later be sold. The sapgloves, a violation of department policy, were worn openly by some officers on their equipment belts, with the knowledge of their supervisors.

The star witness who appeared before the commission was Michael Dowd, a veteran cop who had lost his badge in disgrace. Dowd told lurid tales of widespread police brutality in Brooklyn and other boroughs. One common medicine dispensed to civilians who disrespected officers or failed to abide by their wishes was a beating referred to as an "attitude adjustment." Dowd testified that rookie cops are taught from the get-go that such beatings are necessary in order for the community to respect officers working in the area. Community leaders in East New York, the crime-plagued Brooklyn neighborhood where Dowd was once assigned, said they were not surprised by his testimony, and that none of what he said was new to them.

The common thread running between the Mullen hearings and past corruption probes was the certainty that officers who engaged in such vicious conduct could not have done so without a "nod" from higher-ups, who were themselves so steeped in police culture that they were inured to tolerance of misdeeds.

In its controversial report, issued the day Rudolph Giuliani was sworn in as the new mayor of New York, the commission concluded that a permanent, independent monitoring agency was the solution to the NYPD's problems.

"Twenty years ago police officers took bribes to accommodate criminals, primarily bookmakers," the report said. "Today's corrupt cop is often the criminal." The entire department was described as separated into three groups: "A few determined offenders, a few determined incorruptables and a large group in the middle who could be tilted either way and who are, at the moment, tilted toward corruption tolerance."

Although Chairman Mollen himself said the majority of police officers are honest, he also said that corrupt officers flourish in part because of the "shocking incompetence and inadequacy of the police department to police itself." Such conclusions did not draw much public acclaim in an atmosphere that saw the election of a "tough on crime" mayor who hinted at wanting to reinstate TNT-style sweeps at the street level.

"I don't care what they do," one elderly woman in East New York said when asked about police misconduct. "Long as they get the drugs off the streets. These kids make our lives hell out here."

While one might expect minority residents of inner-city neighborhoods to frown upon excessive use of force against minorities, that is not always the case. The old concept of a cop on the beat administering "street justice" is a longed-for panacea by some residents, whose own experiences have turned them against their neighbors.

That young men congregate on street corners in bad neighborhoods is nothing new. But their immediate identification as possible participants in the drug trade, which made them easy targets for constitutional violations by overzealous or just plain brutal officers, went largely unaddressed by the police and the community.

The perceived violence that endangers the city streets is misunderstood by many in leadership positions as a rebellion against authority, some experts suggest; the reality may be that the violence is part of a suicidal bent that is consuming whole communities. The New School's Professor Williams defined the subculture of violence that goes hand in hand with the drug epidemic as a "lack of a culture of civility within a larger culture of refusal.

"By that I mean young people who grew up with certain values need to have something that's scarce—respect, power, money. These scarce values create a great deal of competition," Williams said. "If you put it inside of a culture of refusal, what you have is people who are struggling to get those scarce values. If a person doesn't have money, power, or prestige they want something very basic, which is respect. If they cannot get that, then that's what they fight for."

The employment situation affects the situation in this way, according to Williams: "You go for that which you can get. You want a job. A job gives you the scarce values that you want— money, a sense of respect, or prestige. The basis is economic, and when the economic side falls more violence occurs."

The violence Williams described is the interpersonal violence now so common in our cities, anger-rooted violence that is evinced at the smallest levels. Gunfire might erupt from someone stepping on someone's foot or giving the wrong sort of glance. "This is because people have so little to hold on to," Williams explained.

When Colin Ferguson opened fire on a Long Island Railroad train in December 1993, killing six and wounding fifteen, he was exhibiting the same type of rage, according to Williams. "Ordinarily," he explained, "you have the Ferguson factor inverted. You take the anger and resentment and you internalize it because what you do is harm somebody else who looks like you. So you're really doing it to you. The black kid who kills a black kid is killing himself."

The menace of cocaine, coupled with the public perception that things are even worse than they are, has created a fertile ground for tolerance of police abuses of power. If the residents of a community do not demand accountability from police supervisors, then they can hardly expect governmental authori-

ties to demand it for them. This climate of tolerance is complicated by the fact that many deaths of persons in police custody
that are attributed to drug use, but could just as easily be
chalked up to improper handling of particular situations by
police, do not ordinarily draw great protest from established
community leaders. The victims in these cases are considered
to blame for the violence; if they had not been doing drugs, the
reasoning goes, then they wouldn't be dead. This reasoning
has allowed for widespread abuses, and encouraged police
authorities (as in the case of Kevin Thorpe) to use drugs as a
catch-all excuse for inadequate standards of care.

Lack of understanding about the physiological influence of
drugs on individuals who come into negative contact with the
police has led to unnecessary deaths. In situations where these
deaths could have been prevented, there has been little public
clamor for changes. The lack of accountability in such cases,
such as might be enforced by the courts, has led to a continuing
pattern. It is therefore difficult to discern accurately whether a
given death is due to actual police abuse, or else the product of
conditions that are relatively new to our cities, such as acute cocaine intoxication or so-called "sudden death syndrome."

Misunderstanding and plain ignorance of these factors
may well have resulted in police officers who were criminally
negligent in their duties to go unpunished. At the same time,
other officers who have been conscientious in their treatment
of prisoners have been wrongfully accused of crimes, or at the
very least been frightened to the point where they might have
wondered whether they could effectively discharge their
duties.

The specter raised by the Mollen Commission of a police
department unable to police itself was one further blow to official credibility. To the dead and maimed and their grieving relatives, the commission hearings fueled the belief that police
officers' shields were merely licenses to kill with impunity.

TEN

SUDDEN DEATH SYNDROME AND THE LONG ARM OF THE LAW

DR. E. BERNARD JORDAN, pastor of a prophetic congregation known as the Zoe Ministries in New York City, is a far cry from the rabble-rousing, media-savvy preachers that people have come to associate with public anti-police pronouncements. Soft-spoken and always impeccably dressed, Jordan, thirty-four, looks like a man ten years his junior. His prophetic ministry draws a multiracial, multi-ethnic congregation, and the services, held at 103rd Street and Riverside Drive in Manhattan, are always well attended. His sermons, portions of which are televised by local broadcast and cable stations with an estimated combined audience of 32 million, carry a positive, uplifting message that encourages personal success. Jordan has preached in the United States, Europe, the Caribbean, and South Africa. He has spoken before the Royal Family of Swaziland and addressed a special session of the United Nations.

Generous donations from churchgoers permitted the expansion of the church facilities on Manhattan's Riverside Drive to the first and second floor of a luxury apartment building. Those without money to give, or who had already donated and wished to give something more of themselves, did much of the physical work alongside paid staff members. In the summer of 1993, one of the most dedicated workers was the pastor's younger brother, John Gregory Jordan. He used his abilities, talents, and strong back to paint walls and doors, tape plasterboard, and perform other necessary duties.

"He was always smiling, always happy, and he never had a bad thing to say," recalled Sandy Hill, a congregation member and aide to the pastor. "I was always happy to see him."

No one could have been happier to see the good work John was doing than Bernard, his pastor brother. Both men had been raised in the same household, but while Bernard Jordan had little difficulty adopting the attitudes and values of their hard-working carpenter father, things had gone differently for John. He had taken up with a few bad companions, and experienced some bad breaks that sapped both his physical and his spiritual strength. His wife Jacqueline, who directed the church's youth group, became pregnant with their first child in 1989, but suffered a miscarriage. The death of Walter Jordan, the family patriarch, during that same year, was another blow that John took quite hard.

Finally, later that year, John was riding in a car with some friends in Brooklyn when the vehicle was pulled over by police, who discovered it was stolen. John Jordan and his companions were arrested, and the minister's brother was sentenced to a prison term. His wife remained loyal to him and eagerly awaited his release from prison. They were reunited in 1993, and with the financial and emotional support provided by his family, his job, and his church, John Jordan attempted to put his life back together.

On August 27 of that year, Dr. Jordan was in St. Thomas, preparing to deliver a sermon on the coming Sunday. In the Bedford-Stuyvesant section of Brooklyn, John's wife Jacqueline was expecting their second child and had gone for a sonogram during the afternoon. After returning home that evening she was cooking dinner, waiting for John to come home. The two had lunched together before her doctor's appointment, and he had said he'd be home early. He had been painting the foyer doors of the church for most of the afternoon. One woman who was active in church affairs remembered speaking to him. "You watch your pretty dress by the wet paint, [he] told me, not to back up into the paint because it would be hard to back out," the woman said.

At 8:00 John was still not home, and Jacqueline began to worry. He wasn't usually late. Shortly before 9:30 the telephone rang. The man on the other end of the line was someone from a hospital who said there was bad news. Jacqueline felt a sickening feeling in the pit of her stomach as she waited for the taxi that would bring her to Brooklyn's St. John's Hospital.

"He was on a stretcher laying on his stomach with the back of his head bashed and with handcuffs on," Jacqueline recalled of the form she encountered in the emergency room. "First I saw that his fingers were purple from the handcuffs and I checked him for a pulse but there wasn't one and he wasn't breathing. He wasn't especially warm, but he wasn't cold either and it was like he was already dead so I started shouting and screaming 'bring him back, bring him back, bring him back.' He had blood on his face . . . "

The doctors told her they had injected him with drugs to calm him down, but nobody could tell her from what. The police officers who stood over the lifeless form offered no explanations.

Dr. Bernard Jordan was advised of the situation when he landed in St. Thomas that night, changed his plans immediately, and caught the next plane back to New York.

"I didn't know what to think," he later said. "I've always trusted the police, trusted the system. And maybe if things hadn't been handled the way they were I wouldn't have been so suspicious. But the last people who saw him alive were the police. They were, altogether, very curt, very unhelpful, and anything but comforting."

———

The initial police radio call was for a robbery in progress on a bus, at Malcolm X Boulevard and Fulton Street. Two officers on patrol in the 81st precinct, one of Brooklyn's toughest, responded to the radio call; there they ascertained that what they had on their hands was an "EDP"—emotionally disturbed person—who was leaning against the wheel well of the bus, which was stopped at the curb. The man, it turned out, who was behaving erratically, was John Jordan. The bus driver told the officers that the man had chased the bus, and that when he got on he began harassing the driver and the passengers, ripping up transfer tickets and acting in an incoherent manner. The officers handcuffed Jordan and placed him in restraints—not without difficulty, according to the most generous accounts of witnesses—then radioed for an ambulance. According to the police officers' official report, Jordan still managed to injure himself despite being restrained. The officers stated that Jordan's injuries were the result of his banging his head against the bus wheel.

Upon hearing what scant details of the situation were made available, Dr. Jordan said he was shocked into near disbelief. He contacted Dr. Arthur Davidson, a private Brooklyn physician recommended by someone in the congregation, to be present at the autopsy, which was performed on Sunday, August 29.

"It was shocking," Davidson said of the injuries he observed on John Jordan's body. "He had bruises on his lungs, which would be consistent with being kicked. Injuries to the head and the back could only have been from severe direct force." Davidson also noted a cut on the skull and a bruise under the brain. Scrapes on the wrist would have been consistent with struggling against handcuffs. But more troubling to

Davidson were injuries to the larynx, which to him suggested choking.

"It was utterly ridiculous," Dr. Jordan said. "If they restrained him then he shouldn't have hit the wheel of the bus. And none of that explains any of those other injuries. And they said it might be weeks before we know the exact cause of death that the medical examiner had found."

The New York City medical examiner's office needed to perform chemical tests on tissues from Jordan's body. One important test, which takes at least a week, involves freezing a segment of brain tissue and then running a chemical analysis on it. For most cases such exhaustive testing is not required, but when an allegation has been made that police use of force might have been involved in a death, every precaution is taken. Also adding to the delay was the fact that many of the chemical tests are done by other laboratories outside of the medical examiner's offices.

During the Mollen Commission hearings in New York there were repeated claims as to how corrupt or brutal police officers stick together, at all costs foreswearing any information leaks to unfriendly superiors. When a municipality is subject to potential lawsuits, the circling of wagons heavy with their bureaucratic burdens can be a mind-boggling event. It is not that an individual police supervisor, assistant medical examiner, municipal hospital nurse or doctor, or any other city employee has a specific personal stake in whether the city gets sued successfully. The problem has to do with the "CYA"—literally, "cover your ass"—nature of civil service, which forces employees to tolerate wrongs that may have been committed, because if anything is said, one's job could be in jeopardy. None of this was acceptable to Bernard Jordan.

"I believe the police beat my brother," he stated emphatically before officiating over a church service. "There is no other explanation that I can see for it, and if there is then they haven't told me."

When a death in police custody occurs, there is no one available to guide grieving family members through the maze of bureaucratic red tape. The situation is uncomfortable for all concerned, certainly, and the relationship between survivors and officials is almost chemically mutated into one of an adversary nature. Mistrust is bred on both "sides," and communication becomes difficult if not impossible.

This is one of the reasons why often controversial "community leaders," such as New York's Rev. Herbert Daughtry and Rev. Al Sharpton, have gained notoriety in some cities. They are familiar with the system, able to communicate with officials, and able to draw media attention. Sometimes an appeal to the media is a family's only hope when the family members feel they have been wronged and that officials have no desire to respond to their pleas for assistance. One method of calling attention to such cases is through "creative confrontation," marches or other demonstrations specifically designed to generate maximum media attention.

"There won't be any marching in the streets," Dr. Jordan said a week after his brother's death. "We'll take to the streets but it won't be to march, it will be to knock on doors. We expect to find answers, but we shall obtain our answers with dignity."

The sermon Jordan delivered that Sunday survived the philosophy behind that statement. Information, he said, is the ultimate weapon, and the ultimate key to power. The man or woman with the greatest amount of information is the man or woman with the greatest amount of strength. Information, first hand, from witnesses, was what would be sought at Fulton and Malcolm X by church volunteers.

If information was power, then Dr. Jordan was relatively powerless in the quest to find out what had happened to his brother. With no liaison available to him from the police department or any other city agency, he had no way of knowing whether delays in autopsy protocols were strictly routine, or evinced a conspiracy. He spoke to a *New York Post* reporter about the situation, and claimed that he believed a cover-up was indeed afoot.

The police department began investigating John Jordan's death as soon as it occurred, but with the delayed medical examiner records essential to any real fact-finding, they were limited to interviews. Dr. Jordan claimed that no attempt was made to contact his family or interview them. Church volunteers worked tirelessly—and unsuccessfully—to ascertain where John Jordan might have gone after he left work at the church on the night of his death.

Under Commissioner Raymond Kelly, responsibility for investigation of all deaths in police custody fell to the Field Internal Affairs Unit (FIAU). Later events would indicate that, perhaps this policy, while well intentioned, also raised the risk of tunnel vision on the part of the investigators. Whatever the case, the distinction between regular precinct detectives and internal affairs investigators was lost on Dr. Jordan.

"How can they possibly be objective?" he asked, becoming rapidly convinced of his conspiracy theory's validity. "They're using the same people who killed my brother to investigate themselves."

Morton Portnoy, a Manhattan lawyer retained by the family, was uncharacteristically low-profile for someone taking on such a sensitive case. But that was the way of Dr. Jordan, and so it would be the way of those who worked on the case for him.

"Dr. Jordan is a dignified man," Portnoy explained. He does not wish to make a circus out of this. He only wants to know the truth."

What is interesting about Dr. Jordan's demurring posture

on public spectacle or controversy was that he became living proof of why the very people whose behavior he eschewed— the marchers and the protesters—were so successful at keeping individual cases in the limelight. Dr. Jordan wanted media attention, which he believed would help bring the facts of his brother's death to light. But there was little motivation for the media to involve itself in the Jordan case past a few cursory stories. When Rev. Al Sharpton led marches in the Howard Beach and Bensonhurst neighborhoods and television camera crews flocked to the streets like sharks to blood, the news was not that people incensed at what they considered to be injustice were exercising their first amendment rights. Rather, it was the air of confrontation that drew interest. The violence that threatened to explode, given the volatile circumstances, was the real drawing card. Without the specter of such societal peril, widespread coverage of the Sharpton-led marches would have been nearly nonexistent.

Dr. Jordan's sense of propriety dictated to him that playing by the rules was imperative, and in interviews he communicated an implied belief that if indeed he did play by the rules, if he tried to work within the system, if he tried to accomplish his goals through lawful and proper means, he would be rewarded with the truth he sought so diligently. But Dr. Jordan was to learn that the system was geared for him to receive anything but the truth; the more questions he raised, the fewer answers he received.

"We went to city hall," Jordan said. "We had a few contacts there. And I explained to them that I wanted the answers, I wanted the truth. They said they would look into it."

There were personal assurances made by Mayor David Dinkins that the case would be looked into. The Jordan family and the congregation considered these hollow at best, and the assurances were never fulfilled. Dinkins would soon lose his election battle against Rudolph Giuliani, and would not serve a second term as mayor. The family never heard back from Dinkins, nor from anyone else in city government.

If Dr. Jordan's brother had been the victim of a street criminal, then public interest might well have been higher. That he suspected the *police* of committing the crime stripped the story of sympathetic luster. He already knew that authorities were focusing on the issue of what drugs John Jordan might have taken prior to his arriving at the hospital, and this was a bitter pill for the minister to swallow.

"Even if he did," Dr. Jordan said, "that wasn't the issue. Drugs didn't give him internal injuries and bruises. Dr. Davidson said that those could only have come from being beaten—not from being restrained, even if he was acting inappropriately."

On September 4, 1993, Jordan and about twelve members of the church gathered at the corner of Malcolm X and Fulton Street with their questionnaires and photocopied requests for assistance from the public. A few television camera crews showed up, as did a *New York Post* reporter who had been covering the story. The street corner is a busy one. At least four bus lines cross it, and there is a well-traveled subway station underground. Near a small pedestrian plaza, where the beating incident occurred, people drawn to the excitement—in particular the cameras—came forward and spoke with the volunteers. Some said they didn't recall seeing anything. Others said they saw a police officer striking a man in handcuffs on the back of the head with a portable radio. Two or three people provided new information that church members continued to investigate.

The autopsy studies on John Jordan were completed on September 14, 1993, under the supervision of Dr. Charles Hirsch. "Mr. Jordan had a two-inch tear of his scalp at the left rear part of his head," a statement from Hirsch's office stated. "His skull was not fractured and his brain was uninjured. Mr.

Jordan also had bruises of his left upper back, and he had small scrapes of his wrists, left elbow, and right knee. There were no fractures, the vital structures of his neck were not injured, and there was no injury of his chest or abdominal organs. Mr. Jordan's physical injuries neither caused nor contributed to his death. Toxicological testing disclosed that Mr. Jordan was under the influence of cocaine. Mr. John Jordan died as the result of cocaine intoxication with agitated, violent behavior."

The results of the autopsy as stated by the medical examiner were unsatisfactory. Dr. Davidson's notations regarding, for example, bruises to the lungs, were entirely discounted by the medial examiner's statement. If indeed the behavior of John Jordan was "agitated and violent," then how much of that behavior was due to the ingestion of a drug? How much was due to his treatment at the hands of police officers—or, for that matter, with anyone else who might have come in contact with him prior to their arrival?

————

There is no doubt that cocaine has affected public perception—and the perceptions of public officials—when a person's death in police custody is presumed to be in any way drug-related. Any individual who is a cocaine user and who comes in contact with the police is presumed to be a "bad guy," unworthy of concern from either the public or public officials. The presence of cocaine in such an individual's body at the time of death would seem to exonerate police officers automatically from any culpability in terms of negligent or improper use of force. But overall, the presumptions inherent in such cases merit far closer scrutiny.

It is a generally accepted legal principle that when a crime of violence is committed, the perpetrator takes his victim as he finds him, and thus can be considered criminally culpable for a death that occurs even if his actions, under normal circumstances, would not have caused a fatality had the victim been in perfect health. For example: Jones accosts Smith on a dark street, pulls a gun on him, and demands his money. The two men do not know each other and so Jones, the robber, certainly has no way of knowing that Smith has a serious heart condition. At the sight of the gun, fearful for his life and thoroughly excited, Smith has a sudden heart attack as he reaches for his money and collapses to the ground. Jones grabs the money from the stricken man's hand and flees, unaware that his victim is actually dying as he lies on the street.

If he is apprehended, Jones will almost certainly be charged with the murder of Smith, and there would be little argument of the propriety of such an assessment. If it were not for the unlawful action of Jones—which under normal circumstances would not result in a death unless he pulled the trigger of his gun—then Smith would probably have continued to live a normal life, and his heart condition might not have been triggered.

The actions of a police officer who employs force, *unlike* the actions of Jones, are and must be considered lawful in most situations. The officer, after all, has the legal authority to use such force. He is thus shielded from any presumption of wrongdoing, at least initially.

The circumstances surrounding the death of John Jordan must be reassessed, then, with these considerations in mind. If John Jordan was brought to the hospital by John Doe, an acquaintance, who said that the two had struggled prior to his having been brought there, and an autopsy revealed bruises to Jordan's lungs indicative of a beating, then the mere fact that Jordan died with cocaine in his body does not let John Doe off the criminal hook. In fact, John Doe might well find himself up on criminal charges, and it would be up to prosecutors to prove their contention of criminal indifference on Doe's part to

Jordan's safety and well-being. The Jordan case, as the facts indicate, does not immediately necessitate a criminal action against police officers—indeed, the facts may eventually indicate that the actions of a third party might well have been responsible for Jordan's death—but should, one could argue, result in a suspension of those involved from active duty on the streets until the facts can be ascertained.

Among the facts *not* ascertained through the police investigation of the Jordan incident were those suggested by witness accounts stating that *prior* to the arrival of police, Jordan had already met with foul play. These witnesses, independent of each other, told church investigators that the driver of the bus had ejected John Jordan from the vehicle for behaving in an irrational and potentially violent manner. The bus driver, who according to the witness was a hulking man who outweighed Jordan considerably, struck and repeatedly stomped Jordan on the sidewalk prior to the arrival of police. Yet no mention of any of this was made in the initial police report. As of this writing, the only action taken by New York City Transit Authority officials, according to sources who have asked not to be identified, was the placing of the driver on desk duty. No criminal charges have been filed against the driver. When the driver was questioned by police it was as a witness, and not as an assault suspect. A death that might have been caused—at least in part—by the possible criminal action of a municipal employee *not* licensed to use force, represents the extension of privileges and protections granted to police officers to someone who is licensed merely to drive a heavy vehicle. On its face, the paranoia of government officials fearing civil litigation would seem to be the motivating factor for protecting the driver from criminal investigation.

It is difficult to determine how many people die each year while in police custody for reasons other than gunshot wounds, according to officials in most municipalities. "When

you have someone who dies in custody it could be from anything," one explained. "You have someone that will have a
heart attack, or something else wrong with them, which has
nothing to do with how they were handled while they were in
custody. It just happens, and it's unfortunate, but some of
those same people might have died if they were just walking
down the street."

When it comes to the criminal and civil culpability of public officials accused (or, in too many situations, *not* accused) of
wrongdoing in custody death cases, there are many unfortunate pitfalls contrary to the interests of justice. If, for example,
a chokehold is misapplied to an individual who has drugs in
his system, and he dies as a result, the cause of death could
well be attributed to cocaine intoxication rather than the
chokehold. This may never become an issue in the investigation except in those municipalities where chokeholds have
been banned.

A 1993 ban on chokeholds by the New York Police Department, on orders of then-commissioner Raymond Kelly, not
only eliminated the use of specific techniques such as the
carotid and bar-arm holds, but also banned other practices,
such as standing on suspects' chests, overlaying, and the
transportation of prisoners face-down in the back of radio
cars. What is particularly interesting about this positive move
by the nation's largest police department (which was met less
than enthusiastically by the uniformed rank and file) is that it
represents an acknowledgment that such practices were at
least tacitly *sanctioned* by top police officials.

Confusion over the cause of death in cocaine-related cases
is reminiscent of the chokehold issue for obvious reasons.
Ominously, the two are often intertwined.

The Police Executive Research Forum (PERF) cites a statement by St. Louis forensics expert Dr. James Cooper:

> Most of those whose deaths have been attributed to choke-
> holds by coroners have actually succumbed to what doctors
> call "sudden death syndrome," in which death occurs unex-
> pectedly in a person who seemed previously healthy. The
> extent of our present knowledge is that discharge of the
> adrenal glands excites them so much that they develop car-
> diac arrhythmia and die from that and the heart appears
> normal.

PERF also cites a study by the International Association of Chiefs of Police which claims that many deaths attributed to chokeholds are in fact instances of "sudden death," thus claiming that the chokehold is not to blame.

But Dr. Michael Baden, special forensic investigator for the New York State Police and former New York City medical examiner, takes an entirely different view. Baden has been called to testify in wrongful death cases all over the world, and has done more than his share of investigation into police custody deaths. It was Baden's testimony, shoring up the testimony of Dr. Kalil Jiraki, the assistant Wayne County medical examiner, that contributed to the conviction of the officers involved in the Malice Green case. Baden scoffs at the "sudden death" theory.

"Sudden death syndrome is usually applied to babies," Baden said in an interview. "There is a question of whether the same thing exists above one year of age. It is simplistic to say of the chokehold death that it is a physiological reaction of chemicals. Usually the basis is injury to the neck, the muscles, and the windpipe, fractures and hemorrhage in muscles. It is misleading to say that people who die during police takedowns die of an 'adrenal surge' or something when this doesn't happen in other adrenalin-producing situations."

Baden applauds the elimination of the chokehold by New York and other municipalities, explaining, "It is the use of potential deadly force, and police are misled to think it is a physiological reaction. Using a chokehold is just like drawing a weapon. It is a potential use of deadly force; it has to be monitored because it is so potentially lethal."

A landmark chokehold case involved the death of Federico Perriera in Forest Hills, New York, a suspect stopped in a stolen car who may have had drugs in his system, and who died during a routine arrest of what was called "traumatic asphyxia." Five police officers were criminally charged in connection with that incident, but the Queens County district attorney's office dropped charges against four of them, ostensibly because of credibility problems with witnesses. The remaining officer was acquitted of criminal charges. Yet if it had not revolved around a police chokehold, attorneys involved in the case agreed in private conversations, the other officers, who permitted the action to take place, would undoubtedly have been tried as well.

A drug overdose is a toxic reaction to a substance that has been introduced into the body. Many heroin-related deaths have had much to do with the unstable quantities of the pure drug when mixed with other "stretching" substances such as lactose, when they are "stepped on" by dealers as the drug moves down the distribution chain. This particular problem was rampant with the intravenous use of heroin in the 1960s and 1970s, and has been less of a problem with cocaine ingested by snorting or smoking.

Cocaine increases heart rate and blood pressure, and induces chemical and electric changes in the central nervous system. Cardiovascular and respiratory failure can occur in reaction to the drug, as well as convulsions. Aortal rupture and central nervous system complications can occur in reaction to the drug, even from a single dosage. Paranoid psychosis can also result.

A total of 5,830 deaths were reported by medical examiners as a result of *all* illicitly and/or illegally obtained drugs nationwide in 1990, 76 percent of which were classified as the result of multiple drug-use episodes. The most frequently reported deaths involved heroin and morphine. During that same year 22 percent of drug-involved emergency room episodes in twenty-one major cities involved cocaine abuse. The figures presented by the Drug Abuse Warning Network, to which emergency rooms and coroners supply data, involved few deaths specifically related to cocaine in 1990. The data have not changed considerably in subsequent years. Actual death due to cocaine intoxication when no other drug is present—despite highly publicized cases involving athletes and other celebrities—are rare. These numbers seem to increase only when a police confrontation has somehow been involved in a particular case as well.

No definitive or conclusive studies on the relationship between police action and the sudden deaths of persons in custody are available. Understandably, there is little motivation for government agencies to dig into the problem. Examination of the figures available would indicate, however, that the number of times cocaine or other drugs were cited as causative factors in deaths of persons brought to emergency rooms after confrontations with police are statistically unbalanced. The initial public statements made by police after the death of Kevin Thorpe (caused it would seem, by the very sort of behavior now *banned* by the same police department) were only too quick to cite drugs as a factor, even though Thorpe had no such drugs in his system.

"We used to see this with drinkers in the old days," Baden said. "They would become obstreperous and would have to be subdued. Later on it was heroin addicts, now it's cocaine users. Of course if there was an attempt to cut off breathing ability with an arm around the neck or standing on his chest and something went wrong the police didn't intentionally kill them that way. The window of time is a very small, safe time to control somebody."

Baden explained similarities between this sort of situation and the "thrill-sex" technique popular for a while with some teens—cutting off the air supply at the point of orgasm—that claimed a number of young people in the 1980s. The practice was part of the defense offered by "preppy killer" Robert Chambers, now doing time for the murder of Jennifer Levin in 1986. Chambers's defense attorney, Jack Litman, maintained that Chambers cut off Levin's air supply during "rough sex" in New York's Central Park.

When asked about cocaine intoxication and its relation to custody deaths, Dr. Baden recalled his testimony in the Malice Green case. "He [Green] died while being pounded in the head and had eleven separate tears to the scalp, and still three medical examiners came in and said he died *while* he was being beaten on the head; three medical examiners came in and said he died of cocaine taken an hour or two hours earlier, even though he didn't have any symptoms of agitation," Baden said. "The problem with the cocaine syndrome is that while people can die from cocaine, it doesn't happen suddenly."

Baden said that in true cocaine intoxication cases, the body temperature rises and there are major metabolic changes. "Then a person can die," Baden said. "And that is rare as hell."

"I think it is unfortunate," he continued, "that a lot of people who come in contact with the police, especially minority people . . . often it is in those cases that when police are called [and] there are drugs on board, that the death would be attrib-

uted to drugs. The danger of neck compression . . . isn't addressed."

"Many of the cases where I have had to testify have involved situations where death occurs during the take-down,
or while a suspect is being controlled," Baden continued.
"Maybe the person has been acting bizarre in some way—
[maybe] because of the drugs themselves—but statistically the
likelihood of their dying if there was no attempt to subdue
them is very remote. Often times what is needed is someone to
talk the person down, rather than strap them down." Even if
Baden's claims were to be discounted, despite his recognized
expertise in the field: and even if it was a given that sudden
death syndrome, a biological reaction caused by extreme excitement, could occur as a result of the use of illicit drugs,
heightening a victim's risk factor: still, the failure of police
agencies, and the municipalities they serve, to take these risks
into account evinces a serious question of liability.

In the case of John Jordan, no explanation was offered for
the marks around his throat. If a chokehold had been used on
Jordan by police officers, or even some other form of restraint
(not even taking into consideration the alleged striking on the
head with the radio), and if such treatment contributed to
physiological changes in Jordan's body, and these changes
were perhaps even accelerated by the use of the drug, then
what would be the *moral* (if not legal) responsibility on the
part of law enforcement for Jordan's death? Certainly, the results of the medical examiner's report would not take such
factors into account. The medical examiner's job is to report
the condition of the body and to refrain from passing judg-
ments. Yet it is exactly these moral and ethical issues that are at
the root of the chokehold problem.

The salient question arising out of the Jordan case, as with
many other custody deaths, is: What is a municipality expected to provide for a victim's survivors in the way of conso-

lation and explanation? At the same time, a thorough, objective finding of the truth is often at odds with the problems medical examiners face, considering how closely they must work with police officers.

"Medical examiners spend an awful lot of time working on cases with police agencies," Dr. Baden noted. "We tend to rely on the police in death investigations and it gets tough when you've got to investigate yourself from within. The officer who tells you freely about the details involving a little old lady you're examining who's been killed by a stranger has less incentive to give his perceptions on a case involving one of his own. It is too hard for local people to investigate themselves. If there was a police officer and we had been involved with some interesting homicide investigations and he was involved in a possible neck compression death, I might be subtly biased. I might be more inclined to see the cocaine as the culprit and not his actions. After all, I know that he didn't intend to do this when it happened. It is a case of a police officer maybe reacting or overreacting but it isn't cold-blooded murder. It is an inadvertent death, because ordinary people—and the police—don't realize how sensitive the brain is to lack of oxygen. If the officer uses a sleeper hold and it cuts off air for twenty seconds, the person may be permanently brain damaged or dead."

Baden knows this conflict problem only too well. After the inmate uprising at the Attica Correctional Facility in 1971 resulted in heavy loss of life and serious questions about who was to blame, Governor Nelson Rockefeller impaneled a commission to investigate the deaths of all persons in correctional custody in New York State. The program, in which Baden played an integral role, was highly successful. The number of detainee deaths declined, and the number of questionable cases for which no cause of death could be found were effectively eliminated.

This situation changed in 1985, when the case of Michael Stewart, the graffiti artist killed in custody by transit police, went to trial. Robert Morgenthau, the New York County district attorney, refused to be bound by the Rockefeller ruling in the Stewart case, and he was eventually able to cause a change in the standing law. Michael Stewart had lingered in a coma after he was beaten, at Bellevue Hospital. He was not placed in the hospital's prison ward, but rather kept in a nonsecure ward while being guarded by police officers. The state attorney general, Robert Abrams, eventually agreed that Stewart was not in custody per se (since he was under charge of the police and not the corrections department), and that the New York State Commission on Corrections thus had no authority to conduct its own inquest.

From that time on, the Manhattan district attorney's office has considered itself immune to the interference of the State Commission on Corrections in all but the most clear-cut custody status cases. The commission does not investigate much in the way of New York City death-in-custody cases anymore, although it has looked into as many as 2,000 in the past decade. There are procedures by which a bereaved family seeking answers can request the intervention of the commission, but there was nobody in the Brooklyn precinct interested in informing John Jordan's family that they could request such assistance—although since then the family has begun investigating the possibility of getting such intervention.

When an individual is in the custody of police, especially when that person is in distress and needs assistance, then officers have assumed a duty to safeguard that individual and see that he or she receives proper care. In the Jordan case, this was not done. Worse yet, the police department's failure to provide answers to vital questions has led to suspicion in the minds of the survivors. These sorts of suspicions can severely hamper the perception of what kind of job the police are doing and create hostility in the community.

Baden says it is unquestionable that a municipality has a vested interest in the outcome of a custody death inquiry. "The family might sue the municipality, it might make the local police look bad, it might anger one group or another group," he said. "The police have a hard job to do. But occasionally people die when they are being subdued who shouldn't die. And it causes friction in the community."

———

In John Jordan's case, Dr. Bernard Jordan has not suggested, openly at least, that race played a part in his brother's death. Indeed the bus driver who may have contributed to John Jordan's injuries was himself African-American. But while there are no hard figures on custody death cases, anecdotal evidence definitely supports the idea that these deaths have occurred with greater frequency in minority neighborhoods. As in the Kevin Thorpe case, the overriding issue becomes the standard of care used in the treatment and transport of individuals in need of assistance. Whether detained individuals are perceived as "good guys" or "bad guys" by the police makes all the difference in the world in terms of how they are treated. In the grip of the fear of substance abuse so prevalent across the nation, the drug user who crosses the line and acts in a manner that invites police intervention is a "bad guy," and treated as such.

The possibility that the bus driver may have used force against John Jordan—complicating the issue of who may have caused Jordan's death—would have gone unnoticed had the volunteers from the church not sought information from witnesses. Every aspect of the handling of the police investigation, family members charge, has worked against the finding of the truth. Investigators satisfied with the "cocaine death" verdict of the medical examiner wished to look no further, fearful, the family claims, of finding police culpability.

If John Jordan died of "sudden death syndrome" (not something one would diagnose on an autopsy report or summation), then how much did drugs contribute to this syndrome? How much did the treatment John Jordan received at the hands of the bus operator and, subsequently, the police play into this syndrome? The police self-investigation system is designed to minimize potential pecuniary impact on municipalities through lawsuit claims, which means that the truth of a case like Jordan's must be concealed whenever possible.

"Dr. Jordan has taught us constantly that patience reveals deception," said Sandy Hill of the Zoe Ministry congregation. "He has been very patient in this case, and he believes that eventually the truth will be known. He has provided us a strong understanding of this through his example."

And so Dr. E. Bernard Jordan, haunted by the memory of a brother who was starting to take his life back again only to mysteriously lose it, continues to seek answers, ever so patiently, and says he will not stop until he has found them. As of this printing, his attorney was completing the legal briefs necessary for a lawsuit to be filed in connection with John Jordan's death.

"The ordinary citizen cannot find the truth without a lawsuit to find out what transpired and what reports were made and what has been conducted," attorney Morton Portnoy said while preparing the Jordan case, to be filed in state supreme court. "I got stonewalled from the police department to the transit authority to the medical examiner. We will get subpoenas in the proper course and obtain that information. We only hope that it is not altered."

ELEVEN

MIAMI VISE

Over the past few decades, Miami—and its surrounding environs of Dade County Florida—has become emblematic of the late twentieth-century version of the American melting pot. A recent history of problems between the Miami police department and the city's citizens are exemplary of the difficulties inherent in coping with America's combustible new racial make-up.

Many African-Americans have argued that when immigrant Europeans came to this country, they ended up with a far larger slice of the pie than native-born blacks. While Italians, Irish, Germans, and Poles (to name just a few) were climbing up the economic and social ladder in the early part of the twentieth century, such opportunity remained elusive for the people whose ancestors helped build this nation while bound in chains. This legacy continues to wreak havoc on black families, and by extension, our great cities. Miami is certainly no exception, particularly when one considers the fact that Florida is, after all, a southern state, with a history of racial oppression no less real than that of its proximate Confederate cousins. The difference in Miami, however, is that when other cities were beginning to open doors to blacks as a result of the civil rights movement, a wild card was thrown into Miami's racial deck that complicates race relations in that city to this day.

Refugees from post-revolutionary Cuba flooded Florida in the late 1950s and early 1960s, the first major immigrant wave into the U.S. after World War II. Many of these people held positions of distinction on their native island, and in no time, through hard work and perseverance, they had created the vibrant Miami community now known as "Little Havana."

South Florida's tropical climate suited the Cubans well, and anti-Castro sentiment in the United States tipped public and political sentiment heavily in the refugees' favor. Meanwhile, many of Miami's impoverished black citizens stood by, while blacks in other cities made greater strides in terms of social and economic advancement. To some of Miami's African-Americans it seemed as if their long-deferred American dream had been purloined by the Spanish-speaking newcomers, and there was fear among those who had waited for so long that for them, that dream might never materialize.

As the decades passed, new immigrants from Puerto Rico, Columbia, Haiti, and, later, Nicaragua would also carve off their slices of the American pie, Miami-style. Following the blueprint laid out by European immigrants generations before, such as the Irish and Italians of New York, Chicago, and Philadelphia, the sons and daughters of Cuban exiles and the other new Hispanic immigrants established a strong presence in the municipal services fields. This included, of course, the one public employer whose workers interact most with other citizens at the community level—the police department.

We have already explored the racially based tensions that exist around the nation between the policed and the policers. In Miami, the tensions between African-Americans and Spanish-speaking police officers have laid a new stress on these existing difficulties. Hispanics, themselves oppressed and the objects of scorn in many other parts of the country, have found something of a haven in south Florida; some have difficulty understanding why blacks, who could have reaped the benefits of being American citizens for so much longer, could continue to wallow in poverty and squalor. This attitude would evince itself in a variety of ways, to the consternation of blacks. Many blacks saw the Latinos as responsible for the drug epidemic, yet saw themselves as bearing the brunt of the enforcement effort, often times at the hands of the people they considered to be the real perpetrators.

The 1979 Mariel boatlift, which flooded Miami with thousands of new Cuban refugees, aggravated the existing tensions. These newcomers were despised by many blacks who already thought they were getting the short end of the stick, and who saw the new immigrants being received favorably by the powerful and established Cuban community. The perceived attitudes of white and Hispanic police officers came into play as well; the situation worsened in 1980, when three white officers and one Latino officer were acquitted in federal court of charges that they beat a black businessman to death with their flashlights and then covered up the murder. The businessman, Arthur McDuffie, had committed a traffic violation, but then made the fatal mistake of committing one much more serious crime—"contempt of cop"—by not pulling over his motorcycle when asked. Critics charged that once the police discovered that McDuffie had died, the officers went a step further to make it appear that McDuffie's injuries were the result of a traffic accident, by driving over him with a car.

The reaction of the largely black Liberty City and Overton communities to the McDuffie verdict was a harbinger of things to come, both in Miami and elsewhere. Rioting tore up the neighborhoods. As with the riots that swept the nation in the 1960s, black-owned businesses bore the brunt of the damage. The Police Executive Research Forum cited the Miami incident as a "frightful forewarning of the sequence of events that would occur more than a decade later in Los Angeles." As is customary after such disorder and disturbance, there were frantic efforts by civic leaders to determine why the destruction had occurred, and promises of attempts to increase community relations efforts. But the tensions didn't go away; neither did the perception among blacks that Miami's police would often shoot first and ask questions later.

As history throughout the country has indicated, the lodging of criminal charges against a police officer for a death occurring during official police action is the exception rather than the rule. However, this has not held true in the Miami area. The Dade County prosecutor's office demonstrated that questionable police shooting cases could well be brought to trial in that jurisdiction. But the outcome of those trials was another matter. Acquittals were more frequent than convictions, the exception being when an inexperienced officer was convicted and sentenced to jail time in 1984 for the shooting of a black man. Three other officers charged with manslaughter in the same incident were found not guilty, and rioting once again ripped through the city. The acquittal of one officer (a Latino) was deemed particularly suspect, since he had been scrutinized in the past for committing another controversial shooting.

One allegation that gained currency through the 1980s— the "Miami Vice" years—was that officers would sometimes intentionally place themselves in front of moving vehicles, in order to justify the firing of shots to stop a vehicle; ostensibly, the driver was trying to run down the police officer. That was the exact scenario that occurred in 1989 on a day that began in celebration but ended in death.

———

That death came to two black men on the streets of Miami as the result of a police officer's actions on, of all days, the

birthday of Dr. Martin Luther King, Jr. This was a bitter pill for
the city's black community to swallow, literally the insult on
top of the injury. These deaths occurred on January 16, 1989, as
the Miami sun was setting somewhere in the direction of the
Gulf of Mexico. The police officer involved was William
Lozano, a Colombian immigrant. Like the McDuffie case, this
incident also involved a motorcyclist, one who police had attempted to pull over for a violation. The officers' warnings
were not heeded, and the bike's operator, twenty-three-year-
old alleged drug dealer Clement Lloyd, ignored stop signs and
continued on, traveling at a high rate of speed. Also on the motorcycle was Alan Blanchard, twenty-four. With the other officers in pursuit, the two men were speeding in the direction of
Lozano's patrol car.

Lozano was in uniform, standing near his patrol car at the
time. He later said that as the bike veered toward him, he fired
the single shot that killed Lloyd. In the ensuing accident, Blanchard was also killed. Both men were unarmed, and as word
of the incident spread through Miami's black neighborhoods,
violence erupted for the fourth time within seven years.

Miami's police chief, Perry Anderson, gave his troops high
marks for containing the violence, crediting them with active
intervention. Looting, arson, and other crimes were stemmed
as rapidly as possible. However, the rioting was still bad
enough to tear the Overton area apart, and it portended havoc
for the economy in Miami, where tourism reigns supreme as
the city's premier industry. Matters were complicated by the
fact that the Super Bowl was scheduled to be played in the city
later that month. Sportswriters found themselves doing double duty, covering the riots as well as the football players. The
riots—predictably, perhaps—had no discernible effect on the
swarms of tourists in town for the Super Bowl. But the city's
reputation for trouble, according to some accounts, began to

generate fears that Miami could be out of the running as a site for subsequent Super Bowl games.

By the second day of the riots, 230 people were reported arrested. One person was killed by gunfire and another eight were wounded. An independent commission was established to study the violence, and the Dade County district attorney's office made plans to prosecute Lozano.

The question of how much danger Lozano was in as the motorcycle veered toward him was not something that could be resolved easily. A grand jury decided that sufficient grounds existed for an indictment, and an announcement was made that Lozano would be brought to trial.

Like the lawyers for the officers in the Rodney King case, attorneys for Lozano sought a change of venue. The possibility of violence in the face of an acquittal, the lawyers felt, could result in less than fair proceedings. But Lozano's lawyers were rebuffed, and the trial remained in Miami. (The lawyers representing the officers in the McDuffie case, however, had been more successful, as they had won a move to Tampa.) The entire city was captivated by the Lozano trial, which was televised live. Some Latinos believed the entire proceeding was a farce engineered to placate blacks. According to supporters of Lozano, and his defense attorneys, the driver of the cycle, Lloyd, was merely a drug dealer evading arrest; he would have wasted no opportunity to escape—even if it meant running down a police officer.

The jury patiently viewed the evidence and listened to testimony. On December 7, 1990, the jurors issued their verdict: guilty of manslaughter. Lozano was sentenced to seven years in prison, but was allowed to remain free pending appeal.

Police officers in Miami and elsewhere were flabbergasted. They saw the verdict as a clear indication that before deciding whether use of force was necessary to protect their lives or those of others, they would have to think twice before deciding to pull the trigger. The possibility of criminal sanctions for causing a wrongful death while executing their professional responsibilities was, they argued, too much of a burden to be expected of them. The bitterness between Miami's black community and the city's police remained.

The Miami case unfolded under the shadow of potential civil disturbance, and Lozano's attorneys wasted no time preparing their appeal, which noted the possibility that a fair trial may not have been possible before a racially mixed jury in a town so weary of wholesale violent unrest. It was even more difficult to try Lozano's case fairly in a city whose very economic existence depended on good public relations with the rest of the nation. This time Lozano was successful. The conviction was reversed on appeal and a retrial ordered.

Given its history of unrest between blacks and Latinos, Miami was caught in a vise grip of tension and anger by the Lozano case. Indeed, rioting blacks were far from the only concern of city officials, who had feared problems in the city's Latino communities if a conviction was brought. But such violence never materialized, or at least, not as a result of the Lozano case.

Meanwhile, the proceedings in the Lozano case began taking a toll on the defendant himself, who attempted suicide while the appellate papers were pending. He survived, but the greater question facing civic leaders in the Miami area was whether the city itself would survive the case's next legal hurdle.

Like the McDuffie case, the second Lozano case would be tried in a different city, this time in Orlando. Jury selection for Lozano II began on May 17, 1993. When the trial began, prosecutors once again portrayed the defendant as a trigger-happy cop gone wild, a man who irresponsibly and unlawfully used his authority to take lives. The defense predictably painted him through testimony elicited from several witnesses, including his mother, as a solid citizen who was being persecuted only to appease lawless elements and loud-mouthed activists.

There were still fears in Miami that an acquittal of Lozano the second time around would spark more violence. But that was not to be the case. Overton and Liberty City, along with the rest of Miami, remained calm after an acquittal was announced on May 28, 1993. More than a thousand police officers had been placed on stand-by for possible riot duty, yet no riots materialized—much to the relief of agents, publishers, authors, and other participants at the annual American Booksellers Association conference, which was being held in the city at the same time.

The fears of violence, and the violence itself (the mob violence, that is, as opposed to the initial violence that made legal proceedings necessary) in Miami give rise to several important questions concerning our attitudes about police violence. Mob violence—or the threat of such—in response to legal actions is nothing new in this country, and is certainly not limited to cases involving police officers. In 1928 Clarence Darrow argued for the lives of two young men who were accused of a heinous murder. His three-day plea for Nathan Leopold and Richard Loeb was widely criticized, and protesters appeared regularly outside the courthouse urging that the two defendants be hung. Darrow prevailed, and the threatened violence, though certainly feared, never materialized. Over a decade earlier, a man named Leo Frank was tried in Georgia for the alleged kidnapping and murder of a young woman. Protesters surrounded the courthouse bearing signs threatening the judge hearing the case, which bore messages such as, "Hang The Jew Or We'll Hang You."

More recently, during the first trial of defendants in the racially charged Bensonhurst case in New York City in 1990, Rev. Al Sharpton was quoted by the *New York Post* as saying that people would take to the streets if gunman Joseph Fama and provocateur Keith Mondello were not convicted. There was some intermittent violence when Mondello was cleared of murder, but nothing serious.

Using the potential for violence to influence whether prosecutions against law enforcement officers should be brought is a ludicrous undertaking that undermines the very core of our concept of justice. Violence that occurs when a verdict viewed unacceptable by the mob—repugnant as it may be and always has been—is caused by factors that run far deeper than a decision by a jury. Even the murderous act of an errant police officer is not in itself enough to inflame a neighborhood. There must be underlying, preexisting tensions to which the addition of the death is "the last straw."

In Miami, a history of violent, unauthorized, and unwarranted police actions had more to do with the violent public response to the Lozano case than just the isolated incident. A number of recent magazine and newspaper articles indicate that aggressive outreach programs aimed at disaffected communities in Miami are helping to quell public unrest. Doubtless such efforts will make the difference the next time a questionable action is taken by a Miami police officer.

TWELVE

LOCAL MOTION

NEW YORK CITY'S 34TH precinct is located in the Washington Heights section of Manhattan at the island's northern tip, where the majority of the population hails from the Dominican Republic and speaks Spanish. Geographically, the area bears a great resemblance to the Bronx, with its palisades and hills. The apartment buildings are newer and airier than the tenement houses found further to the south on the Upper East Side or midtown, perfect for the large families who once occupied them in what was seen as an oasis from the crowding and squalor downtown. The apartments are just as ideal for the large families who occupy them now. As the eastern terminus of the George Washington Bridge, the suspension span that links New York with New Jersey, Washington Heights is also the perfect place for out-of-state suburbanites to come for illicit drugs. On a Friday night many cars cruise the streets, already crowded with double-parked vehicles. Many of these cars have Jersey plates.

The three-four, as cops call the place where they work, is housed in a modern brick building on Broadway, surrounded by apartment buildings and bodegas that blare salsa music day and night. Livery cabs, unmarked as taxis except for their special license plates beginning with a "T" and bright yellow, dash-mounted "car service" signs, parade incessantly in front of the station house as they pass north and south looking for fares.

There are so many guns in Washington Heights that it was chosen as the first community in which to hold a corporate-sponsored "toys for guns" program. It's a likely spot, since within the 34th precinct confines 171 murders had been committed during 1991. As part of the program, residents could turn in a weapon—any weapon—during the holiday season of 1993 and receive a $100 gift certificate from the toy giant Toys R Us, redeemable at any of its branches. It was the brainchild of a Dominican businessman named Fernando Mateo; the idea was first suggested to him by his fourteen-year-old son, Freddy, who was so distressed by the number of young people killed by stray bullets in New York that he told his father he'd gladly give up his own Christmas gifts if it would mean fewer guns on the street.

A few days before Christmas, young Freddy Mateo stood proudly beside his father at a podium in the 34th precinct's muster room, bathed in the bright lights of television camera crews, alongside a clutch of high-ranking police officials, including then-commissioner Ray Kelly. Between them and the assembled reporters were three long cafeteria-type tables loaded with guns of all sizes, shapes, colors, and descriptions. They had all been turned in—over 300, with no questions asked—as part of the toys for guns program.

"Aside from the religious and spiritual meaning of Christmas, this is a season to give and receive," the elder Mateo said. "And so, in the spirit of these holidays, my family and I have decided to give gift certificates for guns in order to collect some of the weapons that are taking away countless lives in our streets. The same guns that may be used to assault or mug someone by those who may not be able to afford to buy gifts for their children, could now be turned into gift certificates to purchase toys."

Also on the podium was a city councilman, Guillermo Linares, the first Dominican ever to hold a seat in the city's legislative branch. Linares had come to speak on behalf of the Dominican community.

"While the federal government must tackle the overwhelming problem of illegal guns, this pilot program is a model that shows what the private sector can do to help address this problem in our neighborhoods. I hope this program can be expanded to the entire city," Councilman Linares stated. "In order to reduce the number of illegal weapons in our communities, we must have strong laws and programs that can give an opportunity to those who have guns to turn them in."

More corporate sponsors, such as the Foot Locker chain of sneaker stores, entered the give-away program. Later that season Mateo, with the help of Dr. Benjamin Chavis, executive director of the National Association for the Advancement of Colored People, traveled to Los Angeles (where he received a cool reception) and other cities. But after the cameras had left the 34th precinct stationhouse, the cops who daily did battle with armed citizens expressed their skepticism regarding the program.

"There was a flintlock on that table, for Chrissakes," one uniformed officer said. "So somebody takes grandpa's old gun out of the dresser and brings it in for a certificate. It's not gonna help anything out there. These people don't know how to *live*."

Other officers echoed similar observations, even though the figures tallied for armed assaults during the "toys for guns" period were down 50 percent from previous weeks. Not all of the officers in the 34th, or in the city as a whole, shared such a cynical view of the program, however. Some even said that the mere appearance of such cooperation between the police and the community might have had a positive effect on the community itself. Despite news reports to the contrary, police in the 34th precinct have enjoyed some measure of cooperation from the Dominicans and other minority communities in Washington Heights. A year and a half earlier, however, a number of factors combined to threaten that delicate relationship.

———

Young Dominicans had for years alleged that some police officers in the 34th were stealing drugs and money from street-level drug dealers, and making a pretense at keeping order in the neighborhood by relying on heavy-handed enforcement methods that included acts of brutality. That such witnesses are not the most credible must be acknowledged. The question in such cases is how seriously these witnesses' claims are investigated—if at all—in order to provide independent verification. In the summer of 1992 the community was well aware that the 34th precinct was under investigation by federal authorities, due to allegations that some police officers were taking money from drug dealers in return for "looking the other way" upon favored operations. In a separate development, it was also widely known that Mayor David Dinkins had called for the creation of an all-civilian police review board. Many in the community expressed hopes that the violence against them would come to an end.

Many of the strongest proponents of the review board on the streets of Washington Heights were also complainants in brutality cases that had gone nowhere; they were also not choirboys, by any means. But in appointing the all-civilian board, Dinkins was making the statement that all New Yorkers must enjoy the protection of the law, even those accused of crimes. An independent review body was the only answer.

Both the police department's Internal Affairs Division and the Manhattan district attorney's office, according to a high-

ranking police official, were aware for at least a year of complaints made against Officer Michael O'Keefe. The twenty-
nine-year-old veteran was assigned to the 34th precinct's anti-
crime unit, and had a high arrest profile. But officials
interviewed by the *New York Times* said the complaints against
O'Keefe had never been substantiated. The complaints had,
after all, been made by convicted drug dealers.

O'Keefe's unit, dubbed "Local Motion" after a decal on its
battered unmarked auto, was well known in the neighborhood for drug and gun arrests. The unit was anything but undercover, according to *New York* magazine writer Peter Hellman:

> The Local Motion cops, with their ponytails and scruffy
> clothes, cruising in battered cars, ought to blend right into
> the streets of Washington Heights—as drug customers if not
> as residents. But they might as well be wearing clown suits,
> so quickly are they spotted as they turn the corner into a
> drug block.

On the night of July 3, 1992, O'Keefe was on patrol with
two other "Local Motions," Matteo Brattesani and Thomas
McPartland, at about 9:15 P.M., when he noticed a man later
identified as Jose Luis "Kiko" Garcia standing near the doorway of 505 W. 162nd Street. Garcia, a part-time grocery clerk,
had come to the United States from the Dominican Republic,
and lived in Washington Heights with his mother. People in
the neighborhood would later say that Garcia was the last person they would ever expect to have a gun. Hellman gave this
account of what happened when the cop and the grocery clerk
met:

> [Garcia was] steps in from the northwest corner of 162nd
> Street, pulling the right side of his jacket. He appeared to be
> covering a bulge at the waistband. "It's not only the bulge

or the arm motion you notice" explains O'Keefe. "A gun—
especially a large gun—unbalances the guy just a little bit.
You learn to notice it."

According to accounts by O'Keefe and his partners, including the one by Hellman, the plan was for O'Keefe to bail
out of the car to avoid suspicion, while the others made a U-
turn and then backed him up. Hellman's riveting account continues:

> O'Keefe held his radio with his right hand and put his left
> on the suspect's shoulder. "Policia. No se mueva." Garcia
> lashed back with unexpected strength . . . the two men grap-
> pled and tumbled in the lobby. Try as he might, O'Keefe
> could not reach Kiko's gun. They crashed through a pair of
> interior doors, and Garcia broke free . . . O'Keefe found him-
> self staring into the barrel of Kiko's gun. It had an oversize
> barrel. He grabbed Garcia's wrist and at last drew his own
> revolver. At point blank range he fired one shot into Kiko's
> stomach, whirling him around. But he was still standing
> and holding his gun. About six feet now separated the com-
> batants. "I saw the barrel come around toward me," remem-
> bers O'Keefe. "I fired again." This time Kiko fell. O'Keefe
> knelt to handcuff him . . .

Jose Garcia, the handcuffs still around his wrists, was dead
on arrival at Columbia Presbyterian Medical Center. The cause
of death, according to death certificate number 92-036219, fix-
ing the time of death as 9:58 P.M., was as follows: "Multiple
gunshot wounds of torso with perforation of lung, major
blood vessel and spinal cord."

By O'Keefe's account, the shooting would easily have been
considered justifiable. But there were two other accounts of the
incident, those of two women who lived in the building; one of
the women told reporters she had witnessed the death of Gar-

cia. Their account differed radically from O'Keefe's official story. One of the women was thirty-six-year-old Juana Madera; the other witness, her sister, was Anna Rodriguez. Madera, who did not witness Garcia's death, spoke to reporters, and delivered an account of what Rodriguez saw. She told the tale of an unarmed man being brutalized and shot by police, apparently for no reason. Both women later said that after returning from a shopping trip they watched from a stairwell as the confrontation edged toward them.

"The police officer kicked him onto his stomach and pulled out a pistol," Madera told the *New York Times*. While his face and body were being battered the long length of the hallway, the women said that Garcia—who saw the two women—kept crying out, "Mommy, mommy help me," and "I don't know why he's doing this to me, he's trying to kill me," in Spanish.

There were problems with Madera's credibility as far as the press were concerned, including the fact that she herself was not the key witness. As for Rodriguez, there was the matter of allegations that her son was a neighborhood cocaine dealer. In fact, investigators would later develop information that would help paint Rodriguez in the worst light. They made her out as a woman who was lying—perhaps because she did not know better, or perhaps because, as the mother of a Dominican drug dealer herself whose sense of solidarity was greater than her sense of the truth, she would purposely besmirch the name of a police officer who had nearly paid the ultimate price for protecting the neighborhood.

The sisters' account soon reached the Garcia family. Word that Garcia had been executed, "shot down like a dog," spread through the neighborhood like wildfire. It soon became difficult to separate fact from rumor on that sweltering night—especially the rumors that Garcia and O'Keefe had known each other. Existing tensions had already reached the boiling point, and the anger over Garcia's death made its way through the hilly streets of Washington Heights with potentially deadly consequences. New York's worst nightmare—a reenactment of Los Angeles—was feared to be in its formative stages.

Mayor Dinkins addressed the situation immediately, and said that there would be a full investigation into the circumstances of the incident. The *New York Times* gave this account of Dinkins's words: "There is much anger in the community, understandably, about the death of Jose Garcia. But one does not obtain justice by being unjust to others. You do not build a better city by tearing it down." His tone angered police officers, who felt they were being sold out by city hall. Efforts by Dinkins, Councilman Linares, and even John Cardinal O'Connor to make peace in the overwhelmingly Catholic community were harshly criticized by the police union, as well as politicians who had their eye on Dinkins's job. The critical chorus grew when a top mayoral aide, Fritz Alexander, visited Garcia's grieving family, and Dinkins had the family over to Gracie Mansion, the mayor's official residence. The final straw for the cops was the city's agreement to assist in paying for Garcia's funeral services—a choice that would come back to haunt Dinkins when he would come up for reelection the following November.

But even these appeasements were not enough to stem the flow of violence in Washington Heights. As the local television stations and newspapers served up accounts by witnesses of what occurred in the darkened hallway of 505 West 162nd Street, the neighborhood began to boil. There was rock and bottle throwing, and fires were set. Eventually the violence would claim two lives, and scores of people would be injured.

Once again, the driving issue of the Garcia case became not the questionable death of the suspect, but rather the threat of community violence that followed it. In other words, were it not for the threat of violence, the Garcia case would arguably not have received anything near the publicity it did. But even taking into consideration the prevailing tensions in Washington Heights, there should not have been such a volatile public reaction to the case, given the cut-and-dried nature of O'Keefe's account. O'Keefe's story was substantiated in part by police spokesmen at the time, and a .38 caliber revolver was recovered at the scene of the incident. The police said the suspect had been armed, and an officer's life was placed in severe danger.

O'Keefe waited twelve days—until after the rioting, and after the autopsy report was made available to law enforcement authorities—to make a statement to Dinkins's investigators. To the most objective observers there were questions that begged answers, and still do.

Some of those answers could repose in files held by a Bronx attorney named Santo Alessi, a wiry young private practitioner who once owned property in Washington Heights and still has friends there, including some in the Dominican community. The Italian-American Alessi sees many parallels between the treatment he says Dominicans receive at the hands of the police, and the treatment suffered by his own forebears when they first came to American shores.

"Most of the cops were Irish then," the sneaker-clad Alessi said during an interview he gave from behind a gargantuan hand-carved desk in his storefront office. "The Italians didn't speak the language, some of them were petty criminals. It would be 'guinea this' and 'wop that.' Now it's 'Fuck you, you fucking Dominican.'

Alessi met with Jose Garcia's family, who reached out to him through another member of the Dominican community on the night of the shooting. He made his way to their home on the night after the shooting after first taking care of other business in Washington Heights, the case of a young neighborhood man arrested for allegedly throwing fireworks onto a street. After pressuring the police to free his young client with a desk appearance ticket from the 34th precinct's lock-up, Alessi took a walk on the street where Garcia had spent much of his time, and where his life had ended the day before. People on the block showed him Garcia's building, and he entered the vestibule.

"The first thing I noticed was the blood," Alessi said. "There was too much of it, all over the place, on the walls of the vestibule, into the hallway, all the way to the place where he was shot."

Alessi began asking questions and locating witnesses. He agreed to be retained with no advance fee by the Garcia family. In the meantime the police investigation, which Alessi alleges was "a sham," continued.

The case caused substantial political damage to the Dinkins administration. A media war of words raged on, with many parties, among them Policemen's Benevolent Association (PBA) president Phil Caruso, accusing Dinkins of coddling the family of a drug dealer who *could* have shot a cop. A grand jury was impaneled by Robert Morgenthau, the Manhattan district attorney, while Alessi, preparing to file a notice of claim for wrongful death against the city, collected his own witnesses. In addition to Rodriguez and Madera, he had assembled some young men who witnessed the early part of the incident, and Dr. Michael Baden and Dr. Peter DeForrest as forensic experts.

The district attorney's office, meanwhile, made an unprecedented move. Information concerning the secret grand jury proceedings apparently was somehow leaked to the media. The secrecy of grand jury proceedings is established in New York State by section 215.70 of the criminal procedure law penal code, which says:

> A person is guilty of unlawful grand jury disclosure when,
> being a grand juror, a public prosecutor, a grand jury
> stenographer, a grand jury interpreter, a police officer, or a
> peace officer guarding a witness in a grand jury proceeding,
> or a clerk, attendant, warden or other public servant having
> official duties in or about a grand jury room or proceeding,
> or a public officer or public employee, he intentionally dis-
> closes to another the nature or substance of any grand jury
> testimony, or any decision, result or other matter attending
> a grand jury proceeding which is required by law to be kept
> secret, except in the proper discharge of his official duties or
> upon written order of the court. Nothing contained herein
> shall prohibit a witness from disclosing his own testimony.
> Unlawful grand jury disclosure is a class E felony.

Eliciting comments from a prosecutor's office on a matter
before the grand jury is virtually impossible under almost any
circumstances, and with good reason, given the provisions of
the law cited here. The debate over the grand jury as an effective prosecution tool in police death cases notwithstanding,
one must question why a prosecutor would make public information that could *remotely* be construed as being the fruit of
testimony in the grand jury room, "except in the proper discharge of his official duties."

News that the grand jury in the Garcia case would *not* indict O'Keefe soon appeared in the local newspapers and was
repeated on the radio and TV. Credibility problems with witnesses in the case were publicly discussed (as they could be
without violating the law) because the information was gathered during preparatory interviews prior to testimony.

But Santo Alessi was outraged, and fired off a letter to
Governor Mario Cuomo asking that a special prosecutor be
appointed.

"I respectfully request that you investigate what appears
to be an impropriety with respect to the conduct of Robert

Morgenthau . . . with respect to the 'Intentional' news conference and press release in the grand jury investigation," Alessi
wrote. His letter continued:

> I am of the opinion that there is an appearance of impropri-
> ety when the district attorney's office:
> 1. Allows the grand jury decision to be disclosed
>   through the *New York Post* prior to court filing.
> 2. Discloses the nature of the testimony of 2 expert wit-
>   nesses retained by the Garcia family, whom [sic] ap-
>   peared before the grand jury (which in fact was inac-
>   curately disclosed).
> 3. Discloses the nature of the testimony of the eyewit-
>   nesses whom [sic] testified before the grand jury
>   (once again not quite accurately). Anna Rodriguez
>   never spoke to the media. She had a brief interview
>   with the district attorney's office as a condition of her
>   testifying before the grand jury and then she testified
>   before the grand jury. Disclosing this pre-appearance
>   interview of Anna Rodriguez undermines the secrecy
>   protection of the grand jury proceedings and deters
>   future witnesses from wishing to come forward to
>   testify in future grand jury proceedings.
> 4. Releasing a prejudicial videotape to the media show-
>   ing Jose Rodriguez [author's note—the son of the
>   witness], without his permission, stating he has co-
>   caine in his hands, which actually was laundry deter-
>   gent, even though Jose Rodriguez has never been
>   convicted of a crime.

According to Alessi, the district attorney's office undermined its own grand jury presentment by badgering witnesses
to the shooting while they were on the stand, and questioning
them about their own involvement in the drug trade rather
than focusing on what they saw and how they saw it. The law
enforcement community had become convinced that Rod-

riguez and Madera were lying, because, it was assumed, of a personal hatred for the police that has never been substantiated. The videotape referred to in Alessi's letter was, he maintains, a homemade movie produced by young Rodriguez and his friends after they saw the film *Scarface*, in which Al Pacino plays a Mariel boatlift refugee named Tony Montana who becomes a cocaine kingpin. Rodriguez and his friends posed with large plastic bags, allegedly filled with cocaine, mugging and swaggering for the camera. It was a prank by a bunch of teenagers, Alessi maintained, and its shock value negated the fact that nobody knew whether an actual illegal substance was in the bags. It was nothing more, according to Alessi, than what some Italian kids had once done with an 8 mm movie camera, parodying *The Godfather* by staging a fake mob hit.

The testimony of Dr. Peter DeForrest, a forensics expert retained by the Garcias, was subverted for the district attorney's public relations purposes, Alessi maintained, because Morgenthau's disclosures were "inaccurate and incomplete." DeForrest had testified as to whether the two women could have seen what they claimed to have seen from the staircase, where they hid after the action got too close. A view of an unarmed and falling Garcia hit by one shot, and then the administration of the coup de grace, could have been provided by that vantage point.

The local media had been widely criticized for disseminating Madera's accounts of what happened. But the district attorney's surprising disclosure of the claimed discrepancies was all reporters needed for a new spin on the story. If the press had fanned the flames of the Washington Heights riots by presenting Madera's account, then it had a comparable responsibility to expose the perpetration of what appeared to be a fraud. The district attorney's office felt justified, considering the great tensions that existed in Washington Heights, to release material pertinent to the grand jury's decision in the interests of keeping peace. Once again, "keeping the peace" appears to have been the overwhelming motivation for the public's interest in the case—and the ostensible cover-up.

Both Madera and Rodriguez denied having been interviewed by detectives after the shooting. The police claimed otherwise, and used the alleged interview to bolster their claim that the stories told by both women were "inconsistent."

"How could Juana's testimony be inconsistent if Juana claims that the meeting [the alleged interview] never took place and was a police fabrication?" Alessi said. "Further, on her TV interview in the lobby, her Spanish was translated to English by a third party [which might not have been accurate] and she didn't go into detail because it was only a TV interview."

"They testified that upon entering the lobby, they paused on the stairs to watch the ongoing assault. When the officer got too close for comfort, they then retreated to the second floor landing, which enabled them to see the final episode, which took place in the final-third section of the lobby area," Alessi continued. "Dr. DeForrest stated that from the second-floor landing the range of vision would be 130 inches from the foot of the stairs. And it was at 130 inches from the stairs that the large pool of blood was collected, even more so toward less than 130 inches. At the point of 130 inches one would see a person's feet. As the person moves closer to the stairs, more of his body would be visible. In fact, if the victim was lying on the floor within ten feet of the foot of the stairs, the view would have been unobstructed or the entire body could have been seen. The district attorney's claim that the witnesses could not have had a clear view is simply not accurate."

Another problem arose from the prosecutor's office, which claimed that a bullet mark on a marble pillar of the lobby was consistent with O'Keefe's version of the events. Alessi also sees this as open to question, however.

"Dr. DeForrest stated to the grand jury that it was impossible to determine if the 'mar' in the pillar was from a cop's bullet or from another previous incident. He stated that there was no mar, only a lead smear, which indicates that at some undetermined time a lead bullet struck that point," Alessi said.

DeForrest stated the following, according to court documents, in reference to the question of whether Garcia—felled by the first shot—was shot again after being struck down:

> I found no evidence of an impact mark on the floor, but I could not rule out the possibility that the bullet did hit the floor. The floor was dirty. Areas were covered by candle wax and other foreign matter, which may have compromised the scene examination. Analysis was limited due to time constraints imposed by the grand jury schedule.

Alessi sees further evidence of a fallen Garcia having been shot for the second time while lying helpless on the floor in the fact that there was no exit wound in the dead man's jacket.

"The bullet wound to the abdomen entered through the front of Garcia's jacket, but did not exit out of the jacket's back," Alessi said. "This is not consistent with an upright Garcia, [but] rather is more consistent with someone who fell and had the back of his jacket raised upon his falling back onto the floor, which would explain why the bullet didn't exit the back of the jacket. Dr. Baden revealed that the alleged first shot through the abdomen damaged Garcia's spinal cord and left him paralyzed from the waist down, raising the issue of whether a second shot was necessary. Dr. Baden informs me that it is possible that Garcia was hit in the abdomen with a bullet and then turned his upper body not to get another bullet in the abdomen. This would not be inconsistent with the eyewitness account."

Alessi then addressed the question of why the sequence of

gunshot wounds was not determined by police investigating the case: "The two bullets which entered Jose Garcia's body were made by two different manufacturers. So we know which bullet created which wound. By recording the location of the fired shell or casing in the chambers of the cylinder of the revolver one could have clearly made the sequence determination. The recording procedure of fired shell casings is hardly new, and is practiced in many jurisdictions. It was not done here."

The Garcia case presents a unique example of a district attorney's office not only flawing its own potential case by undermining witnesses, but closing its eyes to the truth. The level of the forensics job done by Baden and DeForrest should have been done by witnesses for the district attorney's office, paid for by taxpayer dollars. If this were any other case involving any other defendant, it would have gone to trial. But prosecutors assailed the testimony presented against O'Keefe with the vigor of defense attorneys protecting the interests of a client, rather than as public officials paid to see the law applied to offenders. The implications of this reversal, which is not uncommon, is frightening, especially in light of the question of Garcia's gun. Alessi contends that the gun was a "drop gun"—planted by the police to justify the shooting.

O'Keefe himself said that Garcia was slippery with sweat, thus hampering his apprehension; yet no fingerprints were found on the gun that allegedly belonged to Garcia. Nor were any fingerprints found on the bullets that were in the gun. Fingerprints are less prevalent on cold, dry days, when perspiration is minimal, but on a soggy summer night in the inner city there should have been a wealth of prints on the gun—including those of O'Keefe, who allegedly wrenched the gun away from the dead Garcia—but none were present.

There are practical considerations to the case separate and apart from the forensic issues. The Local Motions' choice of apprehension technique was at the very least bad police work. If Garcia was armed, then he should have been approached by more than one officer, for the sake of officer and bystander safety if nothing else. O'Keefe's solo attempted arrest was foolhardy and reckless by any standards. The question of why any attempt to search Garcia was made at all is also a valid concern.

It is well established that many guns can be found on the streets of Washington Heights. Police officers in that neighborhood rarely even report the gunshots they hear because they are so commonplace. And yet Officer O'Keefe, out of sight of his back-up, chose to approach this allegedly armed suspect under compromising conditions—on a night when, according to the *New York* magazine article, the Local Motions were not seeking to make an arrest, fearing that their Fourth of July barbecues would be jeopardized by any potential overtime obligations.

Another problem is that Garcia's reaction was not consistent with that of most criminals in similar situations. Garcia allegedly forced the officer into the building—a bad move when he could have tried to flee onto the relative safety of the street. And if Garcia was such a "bad guy," then why was he struggling for so long, sustaining pain and injury, when he could have shot the officer right then and there? Additionally, police have branded Garcia as a "drug dealer," second in our present-day society only to being called a child molester. Yet no drugs were found on Garcia's person, and although cocaine was detected in his system during the autopsy, it was determined to be a "minute amount."

But what of a motive for Garcia's slaying? Motives are not required for criminal prosecution, although establishment of a motive helps. One can only speculate. Alessi shrugs his shoulders.

"These guys work these high-crime areas, they get fed up,

they get disgusted," he said. One gets the feeling he knows more than he is saying.

The most important question in the Garcia case is not immediately one of O'Keefe's guilt or innocence to a charge of murder, which could only be determined by a jury. Rather, it is the question of why no criminal court jury will ever hear the case—indeed, will never learn of the information supplied here—because the district attorney's office engineered its grand jury proceeding in such a way as to preclude the existence of a trial.

Alessi has filed a civil case on behalf of Garcia's family, but it will be many years before they see the fruits of any such action, if indeed it is even successful. Family members say that the money would be a small consolation for their loss, but it is the only avenue they have for redress. Their filed complaint alleges the following:

> The abuse to which plaintiff was subjected was consistent with an institutionalized practice of the New York City Police Department which was known to and approved by the municipality, which practice proximately caused injury to plaintiff by embroidering Officer O'Keefe, who was aware of the City's tolerance of police misconduct, to extra-legally physically and otherwise abuse plaintiff; the City communicated its tolerance of abusive misconduct to Officer O'Keefe, *inter alia*, by failing, at any time, to take any effective action to prevent defendant O'Keefe from continuing to engage in such misconduct as that complained of herein and by letting it be known to police personnel, in general, including defendant O'Keefe, that complaints by citizens of police abuse would be taken lightly.

There were several disturbing postscripts to the Garcia case. One has to do with officers assigned to the 34th precinct anticrime unit—the Local Motions—who had a number of cases thrown out of court because of allegedly improper police actions.

"An investigation of a plainclothes police detail in Washington Heights has led prosecutors to drop charges against two defendants, and they are studying several other arrests made by the officers," wrote William Murphy in *New York Newsday* on December 23, 1993. "The officers were members of the anticrime unit in the 34th precinct known as the 'local motion,' who were involved in the shooting death of drug dealer Jose 'Kiko' Garcia last year, which set off rioting in the neighborhood."

According to Murphy's article, O'Keefe himself was not named in the investigation. But the court documents Murphy cited alleged that the officers "might have bent the truth to make their action legally justifiable."

"According to documents the Manhattan district attorney's office has turned over to defense attorneys in a gun case, the federal investigation centers on whether the officers perjured themselves in other cases," Murphy wrote, offering excerpts from the documents:

> ... the officers gave false testimony at a pre-trial suppression hearing when they testified that they had seen each of the defendants carrying guns, cocaine and currency in the course of a security sweep of the [a]partment in which the defendants were arrested ... the investigation has uncovered evidence which seems to contradict the officers' version of the events ... The district attorney's office has reviewed more than 100 arrests made by the officers in the past two years and four are under investigation.

Murphy paraphrased additional information in the documents as saying that the evidence, if sustained, would show that the officers "did not see the defendants with guns, that some contraband was not found where the officers said they found it, and that instead of checking the apartments for weapons they did a full scale search of the premises."

Today, Michael O'Keefe remains a New York City police officer of good reputation, assigned to the office of the Chief of Detectives, and is a defendant in the litigation brought by Garcia's family. Police from the 34th precinct maintain that his criminal prosecution would have been a frame. Some officers communicated their feelings by committing a crime themselves. A videotape taken by a neighborhood resident showed police officers in uniform, on taxpayer time, spray-painting O'Keefe's name and an expletive off of a mural dedicated to the memory of Garcia.

———

If the attempts by city officials to offer the "helping hand" to Kiko Garcia's family in the wake of his shooting indicated that a "softer, gentler" handling of victims of police violence had finally come to New York, that illusion would be shattered shortly after David Dinkins was ousted from city hall and a new mayor took office.

Even as police departments across the country tried to learn the lessons of the Rodney King incident, a new case appeared that seems to have placed New York closer to the threshold of chaos, and once again has stained the city with the appearance of cover-up and conspiracy. It was to be the first major challenge of its type for Rudolph Giuliani, the new mayor; some black community leaders said that his administration's insensitive handling of the new case meant that open season had been declared on young black men.

THIRTEEN

THE MAYOR, THE MINISTER, AND THE IMAM'S SON

No POLITICAL CAMPAIGN in New York's history was as racially charged as the one between former United States Attorney Rudolph Giuliani and incumbent mayor David Dinkins in 1993. In 1989, the year Dinkins first won election to City Hall, the tensions may have been more publicly pronounced, especially as the city tried to grapple with the tragedies of Bensonhurst and Howard Beach. But if 1989 was the year of blacks mobilizing politically because of injustices visited upon members of their community, in order to install the city's first black mayor, then in 1993 Giuliani figured as the great white hope, riding a tide of fear and anger into City Hall.

It is doubtful that Giuliani has an overtly racist bone in his body. By all appearances he is a devoted father, and truly has a vision for New York—albeit one that might have worked well during the Eisenhower years. Indeed, his view of the world appears to be guileless in its simplicity, uncluttered by the complications of a multicultural city. This can be attributed in part to his years as a federal prosecutor, removed from the city's people and neighborhoods, forced by his profession to look at the world in strict shades of black and white without any room for gray. His attitude toward reporters reflects this mindset. When he is prepared to speak with the press, Giuliani can be friendly and even charming. But he dislikes surprises, and arrogantly dismisses questions on topics he does not wish to discuss. After notifying reporters that he would visit the Butler Houses in the Bronx in February 1994 to meet with residents concerned about crime, he barred reporters from the gathering, later telling them that the residents requested the exclusion. Residents said otherwise.

Shortly after his swearing in in January 1994, Giuliani began part of a campaign to reach out to the people. He chose as his venue the WABC radio show hosted by the notoriously divisive and abrasive Bob Grant, who repeatedly and publicly referred to Dinkins as "the washroom attendant." (The mayor has since begun hosting his own radio show on the same station.) The WABC campaign and Grant's show had negative repercussions in the city's black community; many blacks already thought Giuliani had won his mayoral victory by running an anti-black candidacy. *Daily News* columnist Earl Caldwell took Giuliani to task for the Grant gaffe, stating, "Whether intended or not, by his actions, the mayor is organizing the unorganized."

"You could see that on the night Nation of Islam Minister Louis Farrakhan spoke at the 369th Armory in Harlem," Caldwell went on, noting that at least 10,000 people attended the December event and half that many more had to be turned away at the doors.

> For a long time, wise heads have looked in the neighborhoods at the young men who are known as the disconnected. Those wise heads, whose voices were not heard, warned that a time would come when someone would organize that mass of men, whose numbers can be measured in regiments. You look at the armory last week and you wonder is Farrakhan the one?

The controversial leader of the Nation of Islam had originally planned to appear at New York's Yankee Stadium almost on the eve of election night '93, but put off the date until after David Dinkins's defeat. Instead, in late January 1994 Farrakhan filled the Jacob Javits Convention Center with 25,000 of the faithful and the curious. Farrakhan spoke for two and one-half hours, holding the audience's attention in the cavernous hall throughout. The theme was "Stop The Killing," and he urged black men to take control of their communities themselves to rid them of the scourge of crime and drugs. The Minister's elite, bow-tie clad guard, the Fruit of Islam, were everywhere. It was they who body-searched every person who entered the center, reporters included. The initial media reports of the event were mild compared to the kind of press Farrakhan usually generates. There was even speculation that the minister had toned down his message, a feeling that the mindless violence afflicting mostly black and poor communities was so bad that even a voice like Farrakhan's was moved to condemn it.

There was one particularly disturbing moment during the evening, when Farrakhan mentioned the killing of six people and the wounding of at least fifteen others on a Long Island railroad train. Colin Ferguson, a black Jamaican emigree, had been charged with these crimes. Nassau County, New York officials had claimed the shootings were racially motivated. When Farrakhan referred to the incident, there were scatterings of applause. It was one sign of the fact that some blacks in New York, no matter how despicable they may have found Ferguson's act, found the media furor it had created equally repugnant.

Suddenly, it seemed, America had discovered illegal guns. Suddenly, everyone was talking gun control. Suddenly, the depraved violence so highly publicized when it occurred in upper-class, largely white communities—because it was so *rare* in such places—had taken on a new significance. Suburban whites could and indeed had become victims of a wanton, reckless, random, and cruelly violent act, of the sort that happens all too frequently in the black urban core. The possibility of a backlash against blacks by misguided white citizens was such a grave concern that Rev. Jesse Jackson ventured to Garden City, Long Island, where the shootings had occurred, and told predominantly white congregants at an Episcopal church that violence of *all* kinds must be condemned.

No such backlash materialized, but in January 1994 there were fears in New York City that Rudolph Giuliani would see his victory as a mandate for oppression. Crime had already been painted with a black face throughout the nation for decades. New York, it was feared, with its sizable, impoverished, and disaffected African-American population, would visit its wrath upon blacks at the end of a nightstick. Whites feared that the Snoop Doggy Dogg generation was out to get them. The Snoop Doggy Dogg kids thought the same was true in the reverse; to many of them, the exhortations of Public Enemy to "Fight The Power" were already seen as hopelessly moderate, and therefore passé.

Giuliani earned his crimefighter reputation in the 1980s while heading the U.S. Attorney's office in Manhattan. He garnered nonstop headlines by prosecuting crooked stock traders and celebrities, from Leona Helmsley to Bess Myerson (who was acquitted of the criminal charges Giuliani brought against her). Known to be short-tempered and mercurial, he was seen by some voters in 1989 as too volatile a property, at a time when the city seemed to need the quiet and reserved Dinkins. But 1993 proved a whole new ballgame for Giuliani, who was rested and ready after a stint at a powerful New York law firm that was in essence a paid hiatus. The disposition and reputation that had been a curse in 1989 became a blessing in 1993, a year when whites in the city felt as if they had been displaced.

Giuliani seemed to delight in taking swipes at Dinkins, making liberal use of the Crown Heights fiasco and the death of Kiko Garcia to make his points with the voters. In the end, those voters were only too willing to accommodate him in his quest for the city's top spot.

So disturbing to President Bill Clinton was the threat of the Republican Giuliani assuming the mayoralty of the nation's largest city, and so massive was the debt he owed the city's Democrats, that the chief executive made several stump stops in New York on Dinkins's behalf. At one of these Dinkins drew laughter when he said, "While I am running for mayor of the City of New York my opponent is running for warden."

But it was no laughing matter to the black community when Giuliani took the reins of government, surrounding himself with a cadre of advisors who, for the most part, were white men of privilege. One hopeful note was his appointment of William Bratton, formerly Boston's police chief, as New York's new police commissioner. Giuliani's plans to dump Ray Kelly, now a professor at New York University, were met with a cool reception in some circles. Kelly was highly respected and had struck what seemed to be a near-perfect balance between the people he served and the men and women he commanded. "Nobody realizes how much they lost when they lost Kelly," one veteran cop who was close to the outgoing commissioner said. "He had a plan for this city, a real plan that was going to shake things up and bring about some changes."

But Bratton, who before going to Boston had served as New York's transit police chief, came highly recommended. He had a reputation as an innovator, and black leaders in Boston had little unfavorable to say about him. If anything, the fact that many Bostonians were so sorry to see him go was a good sign for New York.

Merely having credentials, however, is not the same as withstanding the heat of municipal battle, and Bratton was put to the test almost as soon as he was sworn in to the office of top cop. On the afternoon of Sunday, January 9, excerpts of Farrakhan's Javits Center speech were aired on WABC-TV. Two hours after the show ended—whether by consequence or coincidence—the Nation of Islam would once again be making headlines.

On the eighth floor of police headquarters, where all 911 calls are routed, operator number 1817 took a report from an unidentified male caller, who related that there was a robbery in progress at "2033 Fifth Avenue, the Minister Farrakhan mosque." The caller described the armed perpetrator as a black male, and said he was sticking up the mosque and selling crack. Ominously and inexplicably, the caller rang off with a curious statement: "Have a happy new year." The information was routed through the police computer system to the dispatcher handling the 28th precinct, and radio cars responded to what was coded as a priority signal "10-30"—a robbery in progress.

The dispatch system automatically designates certain pre-programmed addresses, and even intersections in their vicinity, as "sensitive locations." Mosque #7 fell into this category, as had all mosques, whether affiliated with the Nation or not, ever since the murder of Police Officer Phillip Cardillo at another such location on April 14, 1972—ironically after responding to a bogus 911 call. He was coming to the assistance of another officer, Vito Navarro, who had been jumped by Muslims. Cardillo's gun was taken from his holster and he was shot several times. A man was arrested for the murder and tried twice, once with a hung jury. He was acquitted a second time. *New York Post* reporter Murray Weiss interviewed Cardillo's relatives in 1994; they believe there had been a police cover-up in order to placate the Muslims. Weiss reported that a meeting took place between Harlem congressman Charles Rangel and Farrakhan after the 1972 incident occurred.

Police regulations require that a patrol supervisor must respond to all sensitive-location incidents, and unless absolutely necessary officers are not to enter such locations until the supervisor arrives. In this case, however, the dispatcher neglected to read out the information. In any event, the responding police officers, who should have known that the mosque required special caution, burst up the stairs and encountered members of the Fruit of Islam, the mosque's security force. The Nation of Islam, like other Muslim sects, does not permit guns in its houses of worship; the presence of weapons in such places is considered a sacrilege.

According to the mosque's attorney, C. Vernon Mason, the Fruit of Islam members told the four officers that there was no crime occurring at the mosque and that there was no need for their services, but that they were welcome to check the premises without their weapons. The likelihood of assent to such an invitation, of course, is ludicrous even to consider. According to Officer Merri Piersall, a police spokeswoman who was interviewed the next day, the officers in any event were denied entry.

"A scuffle ensued on the interior stairs and a police officer was pushed down the stairs. Her police radio was taken and her partner's gun was removed," Piersall said. Police Officer Wendy Jarvis was taken to New York Hospital, where she was admitted to the emergency room. Injuries to the other officers were minor, according to Piersall, including those suffered by two who slipped on ice.

Chief Joseph Leake, a respected African-American supervisor who would take the reins of the Housing Authority Police Department in June 1994, and two other police officers negotiated with the people in the mosque, and the gun and radio were returned, Piersall said. However, some police officers were outraged that any negotiations with the Muslims had taken place at all. On the next day (Monday, January 10), the police and the Muslims went public with their different versions of the incident—and with very different agendas.

Mosque #7, under the leadership of Minister Conrad Mohammed—who had said of the Giuliani victory in a speech at the Javits Center event, "It's ninety-four, time to go to war"—demanded that police apologize for "storming" the mosque. In turn, Bratton called for the Muslims, as they had promised, to give up the man who had assaulted the officers, saying that it would be up to the courts to decide who was right and wrong. A public controversy continued, with some members of the black community questioning why police who worked in the precinct were not aware of the sensitive-location status of the mosque—even if the caveat had not been reiterated by the dispatcher. It should be noted, too, that the "sensitive location" designation is used not for the protection of community member, but rather for the protection of police officers.

On the night of Tuesday, January 11, Commissioner Bratton was distracted from the controversy by another occurrence that would be inextricably linked with the incident at Mosque #7, although he had no way of knowing this at the time. That night Bratton was notified of one of the events every top cop dreads. A New York City police officer had been shot in the East New York section of Brooklyn, during a murky confrontation with a criminal suspect. Bratton's official car, red light flashing and siren warbling, sped to Jamaica Hospital in Queens, where the officer was taken. Mayor Giuliani also responded, as did the police department's new deputy commissioner of public information, former WNBC-TV reporter John Miller, whose in-depth television coverage of mob boss John Gotti had made his name a household word in New York.

Bratton, Giuliani, Miller, and other officials walked into the employee cafeteria on the ground floor of the hospital, and sat behind a makeshift dais that had been set up for the purpose of addressing the media. The mayor and the commissioner had already spoken with the wounded officer, and had been briefed on the circumstances of the shooting. It was the first time Bratton would meet the press as boss of a cop who had been shot in the line of duty.

"This is preliminary information," Bratton began, cautiously. "At 9:10 P.M. on Tuesday, January 11, at 499 Williams Avenue, Police Officer Kevin Sherman was shot one time in the right leg. At the time of the incident Police Officer Sherman and others assigned to the 75th precinct responded to a report of a dispute and a man with a gun. During a basement search there was a confrontation with a male . . . Four police officers fired several rounds and police officer Sherman, twenty-six, was shot." Bratton added that Sherman was single, that his mother had been notified, and that she was at the hospital. He was being treated for the wound and was "stable."

Bratton said the suspect encountered by the police had been taken to Brookdale Hospital with gunshot wounds and had expired. No gun was recovered at the scene, but a careful search of the basement where the shooting occurred was continuing. The implication was that Sherman had been hit by friendly fire—whether from his own gun or another officer's, no one could be sure. Deputy Commissioner Miller said the rounds fired were from .38 caliber weapons, not the 9 millimeter guns that some officers had begun carrying.

Giuliani and Bratton were pressed for questions about the dead man and the circumstances of the shooting, especially considering the fact that he had, as far as anyone knew, been unarmed. Giuliani visibly bristled.

"My concern was for the police officer. He is in a state of shock," Giuliani said tersely.

———

The dead suspect was identified as Shuaib Abdul Latif, and he was only seventeen years old. He had been raised as a

Muslim by his father, Imam Al Amin Abdul Latif, a respected
member of the community who was the president of the Majlis
Ash-Shura, the Islamic Leadership Council of New York. The
elder Latif had met with Vice President Al Gore only a few
months before, on November 11, 1993, when he was invited to
the signing of a religious restoration act by President Bill Clinton. The Majlis Ash-Shura was part of the more traditional
black Muslim movement, and had no overt association with
the less traditional Nation of Islam. The elder Latif's title,
"Imam," meant that he was a prayer leader.

"I am in a state of shock," Latif said when reached by telephone at his home on the night of the shooting. He had gone to
Brookdale Hospital and identified his son, who had been, he
said "a good young man who had some problems. He's been
. . . trying to find himself lately."

Shuaib had been arrested in March 1993 for possession of
crack cocaine with intent to sell, and was placed on probation.
More recently he had transferred from his academic high
school to a trade school. Although listed as a youth booster on
a roster posted in the lobby of the tenement where the Majlis
Ash-Shura kept its leadership headquarters and a mosque, his
father said that he had been disassociated from the mosque's
activities.

Seated at a desk on the mosque's second floor the next
morning, Al Amin Abdul Latif wore a face etched with the
pain of a grieving father. A devout and peaceful, Latif bore the
twin burdens of losing a son first to the evils his faith so ab-
horred, and then to police bullets under questionable circumstances. He had gone to the precinct, he said, after leaving the
hospital.

"They had no information and they gave no information,"
he said. "They said I could wait for the detectives if I wished. I
waited but they did not come. Nobody spoke to me."

Latif was not the first churchman to suffer disappointment

from a child who had chosen a different path, and he would not be the last. But on the morning after his son's death he had little time for philosophizing. The answers to what happened to Shuaib, he said, would be found not in the mosque but on the street where the killing occurred.

Thick white snowflakes had turned to freezing rain on Livonia Avenue, where the train that connects that portion of East New York with the rest of the world stops. Sidewalks were slick with ice and snow, and work crews in front of some buildings busily shoveled it out of the way. Williams Avenue was deserted, except for a half dozen or so black and Latino young men who stood in an apartment building doorway. They postured and posed and tried to appear hostile, before finally agreeing to talk about the death of Shuaib Latif.

"They weren't looking for Shu, they wanted me," said a heavy-set seventeen-year-old with mocha-colored skin and the soft beginnings of a beard. "Why they kept him down there so long and then they bring him up, not even any clothes?"

The reporter shrugged, and allowed the street gang to lead him to the building where the shooting took place, a small, three-story brick apartment house. "We hang in the basement down there, we don't bother nobody. Drink some wine, smoke some weed."

"What about the pipe?"

"No. Uh-uh."

The youths were asked if they carried guns and the question was met with laughter.

The lock on the front door was broken, and entry was easily made. There was one apartment entrance at the far end of the long hallway; against the hallway wall a candle burned for the dead teenager.

"Watch your step going down," one of the younger men said, indicating a missing step. Missing steps on basement stairways in drug prone locations are not unusual. They are sometimes removed intentionally to stymie police officers. The basement, its bright blue walls illuminated by a single bare, incandescent bulb, was under renovation, and construction debris littered the floor. There was little to see, and the young men of the block had seen nothing of the shooting. But they did have other information.

"There was a woman," the one with the beard said. "She come here keep trying to buy, an' Shu said no way, thought she was five-oh [police]."

The youth said he himself was one of several who then assaulted the woman, and that was why the police had come to the block, why he had said he thought they were looking for him. Four police officers had responded to a call involving a man with a gun and a dispute at approximately 9:00 P.M., and ended up searching in this basement. They said it was dark, and if that was the case then visibility would have been nearly impossible, given the fact that there are no windows to let in even the reflection of a street light.

According to the police accounts, officers had entered the basement and Latif was confronted, possibly by Officer Sherman. A struggle ensued during which Latif got hold of the officer's gun. Sherman got the gun back, but Latif evaded custody and hid in the basement area, then was confronted once again. Sherman—who, it is worth noting, is himself African-American—fired one round. Police officers Demos Marinakos and Angel Aroyo each fired once, and Officer Michael Wallen fired twice. The medical examiner's office later reported that Latif was hit by two bullets, possibly three.

———

"I seen him around here," said sixty-three-year-old Calvin Reed, who lived directly across the street from the building where Latif died. Reed's large first-floor window had a bird's-eye view of the street itself. "I said to him, 'why are you hanging around with these street kids? You don't look like them, you don't talk like them. You don't act like them. Save yourself,' I said. He told me thank you."

Reed grew up in the segregated south and has driven cabs most of his life. He said he had voted for Giuliani because he was sick of the kids who were waging war on each other outside his window. "I guess somebody's got to put a stop to it," he added.

He said that he had seen the heavy young man with the beard carrying a gun before—"a big one."

"I went to him and said get that gun the hell off this block," Reed said. "Whatsa matter, you wanna give the cops an excuse to shoot you?"

While Reed spoke, Bratton was talking to reporters at City Hall, a world away from Williams Avenue. He was quoted in the *New York Post* as saying, "I'm feeling quite confident that this shooting was justifiable. Drugs may have been involved in this incident." Bratton reiterated the police account of what happened in the basement; this information had already been related to twenty-eight-year-old Darriel Johnson, Reed's niece, after she joined him in his apartment.

"That's a damned lie," she said.

Johnson lived in the only functioning basement apartment of the building where the shooting had occurred, and had a lease to prove it. She often visited her uncle across the street. Johnson said that she had been home on the night of the shooting and was going to a corner bodega for cigarettes when a neighbor who lived upstairs asked her to pick up some Tylenol. Shuaib Latif was standing in the hallway of the building as she left. She knew him, she said, by sight and name but not well. He knew her well enough, however, to make what would be a last request.

"Get me a fifty-cent water," he said, according to Johnson.

When she returned with the water and the Tylenol, however, there were police in the basement, she said. Johnson was hesitant at first to go down the basement stairs, but a cop waved her on, and she headed to the right of the littered hallway to her tiny apartment.

"There was nine or ten of the cops down there," she said. Before entering her room she looked the long way down the hall, and that was when she said she saw Shuaib come out from behind a refrigerator, his hands raised in front of his chest. "They was shooting everywhere," she said. Frightened, she hurried into her room. But not before she saw Latif lurch forward. "I saw what happened and they killed that boy for no good reason," she finished.

She repeated the story again, this time in the basement itself, demonstrating where she claimed Shuaib had fallen, and where the officers were standing. An artist's conception of Johnson's account infuriated police officers, who complained the next day.

"There was a gunshot wound to the chest, back, and limb, to the left arm, with perforation of the aorta and liver," according to Ellen Borakove, spokeswoman for Dr. Hirsch, the medical examiner. Borakove said two bullets were recovered from inside the body. Either of those wounds would have proved deadly. The aorta, of course, is the major artery leading to the heart. The liver, once contacted by a bullet, releases toxic chemicals into the body. "The [bullet] in the back was the one that just went under the skin. Then the other bullet, that perforated the arm, entered and exited—it could have entered the chest." The medical examiner also found that the chest bullet appeared to have entered from the left side.

"Everything about the body is extremely consistent with what Darriel has told us, because she demonstrated that his arms were facing forward, attempting to stand up, and never made it," said Deborah Galloway, who was retained as an attorney by the Latif family. "He was in a stooped position coming up with his right side next to the refrigerator. If there were two bullets the entry was at the outer left elbow area, above the left elbow, exiting inside, descending into the abdomen. It then lodged in the T-12 vertebrate in the spine."

Darriel Johnson admitted to being an occasional drug user, and knew that Shuaib and his friends sold drugs in the lobby and around the building. But she insisted that her story was true. As she told her tale, Latif's body was being autopsied at Kings County Hospital. There was no way for Johnson to have fabricated her story to reconcile with the account later supplied by Borakove. And yet her story coincided to a great degree with what the lifeless body of Shuaib Latif told the medical examiner, about his position and about what angles he was shot from.

A single bullet entering and then exiting the left arm and then entering the chest was seemingly consistent, as well, with Johnson's claim that Latif had been crouched with his hands raised *in front of his chest* when he was shot. Police discounted Johnson's story, however, because (they claimed) she told them she had seen nothing when they had asked her about the shooting. Johnson recalled her conversation with the police differently, supplying the name of the detective who interviewed her, and said that she had answered a specific question.

"They told me 'did you see the kid with the gun,'" she said. "I told them I didn't see nothing like that."

When authorities realized the community status of the dead youth's father, there were some public concerns about the possible community reaction to the shooting. But no reaction materialized that would have been considered threatening to public peace at the time. The media seemed far more interested in the refusal of Commissioner Bratton to meet with New York's most prominent racial gadfly, Rev. Al Sharpton, and his longtime associate, activist attorney C. Vernon Mason.

The two activists had intended to participate in a scheduled dialogue between the commissioner and the Nation of Islam in regard to the mosque incident. The engagement was canceled after some scheduling glitches—and after Bratton learned the two activists were planning to attend.

"Rev. Sharpton is obviously someone who speaks on behalf of black people and someone we cannot discount," said Mosque #7's Minister Don Mohammed.

Sharpton, an itinerant preacher ordained when he was only five years old, was well known in the New York area for his use of "creative confrontation." His best-known tactics involved leading marches protesting racially motivated crimes. His rhetoric took elected officials, the police, and white society as a whole to task for insults to the black community, real or imagined. In 1992 he placed third out of four candidates in a state-wide Democratic primary to determine who would attempt to unseat Republican U.S. Senator Alphonse D'Amato, a respectable showing. In January 1994 he was still trying to choose between challenging either Governor Mario Cuomo or Senator Daniel Patrick Moynihan in their respective reelection campaigns.

Sharpton has had a long relationship with Farrakhan and the Nation of Islam, and it was only natural that his high profile should be lent to the problem facing the Muslims—namely, that no apology was forthcoming from City Hall or the police commissioner. Also, arrests were pending for the mosque members who might have taken part in the repelling of the officers. But Bratton made it clear he was calling the shots; proof of this was his rejection of Sharpton.

Mayor Giuliani supported Bratton's decision to exclude Sharpton and Mason, in an effort to make good on his promises to restore order in the city. As a result, the most vociferous potential critic of his administration had been profoundly dissed. The move, however, may have backfired. It allowed Sharpton an additional day of publicity; he called a joint news conference with the Nation of Islam on Saturday, January 15, the day Shuaib Latif was to be buried. As Sharpton spoke before the cameras in Manhattan, over 500 mourners packed a Brooklyn mosque on Bedford Avenue. In the minds of many who attended, the mayor's seeming indifference to the killing of Latif, coupled with the Nation of Islam controversy, was ominously significant.

The issue was not that the mayor was wrong in standing firm on the mosque incident. Police officers clearly had been assaulted, and in the face of what happened they had, it would appear, used admirable restraint. But by taking a stand to show that he would not be led around by the nose by Sharpton, Giuliani instead catapulted the volatile reverend into a spotlight that would not otherwise have been his to claim. The misstep further alienated Giuliani from black leaders, including many who were elected officials.

Prior to the service for Shuaib Latif, the men of the mosque had anointed the body with holy oils. In the sanctuary itself the casket lid was raised for the grieving father to say one last good-bye. The lid was sealed, and an extended Muslim service—lengthened by translation for the benefit of visitors—was commenced.

"This is not a day for protest," one cleric said, informing the congregation that there would be a protest on the following Monday. Late because of their press conference with Sharpton, a delegation of members from Mosque #7 arrived, led by Minister Conrad Mohammed.

A statement was issued through the Majlis Ash-Shura stating that the killing of the son of its president was the result of "wanton and reckless police action."

"This is indicative of an attitude toward the youth in the inner cities, and to the African-American youth in particular, who seem targeted," the statement said. "The Majlis Ash-

Shura of New York has decided to conduct an independent and comprehensive inquiry into this matter and other related matters which seem to depict a pattern, and will then respond in a manner which is faithful to Islam." The Majlis Ash-Shura further demanded the immediate suspension of the police officers involved, and an investigation by state and federal authorities.

Imam Latif remained calm but firm in his assessment that the shooting of his son might well have been an accident, and that if this was the case the police department should own up to the fact. A Majlis Ash-Shura leader said that the Muslims would be at City Hall that Monday. It was the same day Sharpton had planned for a march across the Brooklyn Bridge, nearly begging to be arrested because of his public announcement that he would do so without a permit. Wisely, officials did nothing to stop the marchers, who numbered less than 200.

Several hours after Latif was buried at New Jersey's Rose Hill Cemetery, Mayor Rudolph Giuliani appeared at a Bronx housing project where a handyman had been murdered, and was asked by a reporter for comment on the continued questions surrounding the claim by the Latif family that the killing was unjustified.

"I don't want to comment while an investigation is continuing," the mayor said. "A police officer was injured doing his job. We still want to know why there were crack vials found near the deceased."

Nobody asked the mayor whether Shuaib Latif, had he lived, would have been charged with possession of a deadly plastic vial. The unarmed corpse had, however, been charged with attempted murder, explained by a police spokesman as a "technicality."

The family and friends of Imam Al Amin Abdul Latif, also numbering close to 200, gathered at City Hall on the following Monday afternoon, circled the old building and its surrounding park while chanting prayer slogans, and then repaired to a nearby mosque. Leaders of the Nation of Islam Mosque #7 appeared as well. All factions of the New York Muslim community pledged solidarity in their quest to end what they saw as unwarranted assaults on black people by the police. Were it not for the mayor's indifferent handling of questions concerning Shuaib, such an event might never have occurred. But once again, the unwitting Rudolph Giuliani had cemented the black community's opposition to his administration.

Later that day Giuliani's press secretary, Christine Lategano, was asked if the mayor had any response to the angry words that had been spoken at the mosque.

"The mayor has already commented on Reverend Sharpton. He has not been a player in this situation, and the mayor will not meet with—"

Lategano was interrupted and reminded that she was being questioned not about Sharpton, nor the Nation of Islam, but about the unarmed youth who had been shot and killed by a New York City police officer with no clear and plausible explanation. She then responded that no new statements would be forthcoming. But the mayor had made it clear that he would not comment while the case was under investigation.

Rudolph Giuliani had made political hay out of David Dinkins's overtures to the Garcia family. At the dawn of his own administration, the shoe was now on Giuliani's own foot. Remarkably, he appeared not to have any way of even knowing which controversy was which in this situation, and had already fallen into the same trap the media itself had been accused of in the past—concentrating on Al Sharpton while there were real issues to be resolved.

In February 1994, journalist Eric Pooley wrote in *New York* magazine that Giuliani's handling of both the Latif case and the Mosque #7 incident had created a serious gulf between the mayor and mainstream black leaders:

This was Giuliani's big mistake: clinging to the notion that the mosque melee was a simple police matter—as if he could make its political and racial ramifications disappear through force of mayoral will. He chose not to reach out, in the early days of the crisis, to those black leaders who actually wanted to help. Then, when he did start looking for allies, Rudy didn't have a scorecard . . . Obdurate and increasingly peevish as the crisis heated up, the mayor insisted on "one standard for one city." He stuck to the line even when, in an unrelated bit of New York mayhem, the drug-dealing son of a Black Muslim cleric (Shuaib Abdul Latif) was killed by police in Brooklyn. Asked if he understood why blacks were upset, the mayor said, "No, I can't understand."

As of this writing Deborah Galloway was in the early stages of preparing litigation on behalf of the Latif family. The police officers involved in the case continued working uninterrupted, with the exception of Officer Sherman, who missed a long time from work for a disability inflicted by a fellow officer's gun, but for which a dead seventeen-year-old had been charged.

There is a postscript to this story, involving another custody-related death in New York, that must be told, in fairness to Giuliani and Bratton.

On April 29, 1994, police officers in Staten Island, the least celebrated of New York City's five boroughs, were conducting a drug sweep near the Park Hill housing complex, which is almost exclusively black. According to witnesses, a firecracker—possibly an M-80—was dropped from a rooftop and startled the uniformed cops. One of these was Donald Brown, a black officer who had established a good reputation for fighting the area's drug dealers. He and at least two other officers—identified as John Mahoney and Gregg Gerson—sprinted toward the sound. They encountered a twenty-two-year-old Liberian national and reputed small-time drug dealer (based on entries in his criminal court history) named Ernest Sayon, who was in the company of at least one other person.

The police—inexplicably—attempted to arrest Sayon, and a struggle ensued. Eventually, a handcuffed and subdued Sayon was placed into a police van. A short time later, police officers realized that Sayon was subdued to the point of not breathing, and they rushed him to a nearby hospital, where he was pronounced dead. The medical examiner, Dr. Hirsch, eventually ruled the death a homicide, caused by asphyxiation.

Tensions ran high in Staten Island. The night of the actual occurrence, the 120th precinct station house was under literal siege by protesters from the community. The three officers were placed on desk duty pending the outcome of a grand jury report. Police resources, including mounted officers and special task force units, were called into the area to prepare for possible violence. But violence—except for occasional scuffles between demonstrators and officers—did not materialize, although there were protests that continued throughout the week.

On Thursday, May 7, after news of the medical examiner's report became public, a particularly raucous group of about a hundred protesters marched to Staten Island Borough Hall seeking answers. Rudolph Giuliani was there, after having attended the wake of a firefighter who had been killed in the line of duty. He agreed to meet with community representatives and discussed the case, while dubious rabble-rousers remained outside the century-old landmark building under heavy police guard.

Non-office-holding political activists (such as the aforementioned Al Sharpton) serve an important function to a community when it feels that elected officials are paying it no heed. What short-circuits such activism (and any negative repercussions that might follow) is the reaching out of government's hand to the affected populace. And while critics of Giuliani have had good cause to bring him to task for past performance—especially in light of the Latif case—the night of the meeting in Staten Island was something quite the reverse.

The mayor eventually emerged from the meeting and stood before a hundred shouting, heckling demonstrators, trying (with little success) to explain to them that the medical examiner's determination of homicide did not automatically mean criminal culpability. He asked the people to have faith in the system, to wait before jumping to conclusions, and assured them that justice would be done. It was a big step for the hard-as-nails former federal prosecutor. These were not the people who elected him (although predominantly white Staten Island had indeed put him over the top), yet he made it clear that these people—mostly poor and lower-middle-class blacks— were part of his constituency as well.

The Sayon case went to a Staten Island grand jury that was not expected to render its decision until some time in the summer of 1994. Legal experts in New York have expressed doubt as to whether an indictment for criminal action will be issued as a result of the hearings, although anything is possible. What we do know is that, no matter what the grand jurors decide, the reasons behind those decisions will be shrouded in secrecy. If the officers are cleared, then their careers will forever be clouded by Sayon's death, no matter how guiltless they may be.

Commissioner Bratton took a strong stance initially in the case, stating that an investigation would be conducted, although his hands and those of department superiors were tied pending the outcome of the grand jury investigation. Giuliani's top cop has won some previously skeptical new believers with his aggressive handling of police officers charged with beating drug dealers, extorting money, and dealing drugs in Manhattan's 30th precinct. Bratton himself removed the badge of one of the disgraced cops, in front of the news media.

But the real work remains to be done. The response of government to community questions in Staten Island was motivated, informed observers must believe, by a desire to "keep the peace." However, there is a difference between keeping that peace and dispensing justice. In the case of Shuaib Latif, it is doubtful that any of the key facts will ever be revealed for full public scrutiny.

FOURTEEN
PRESSING THE ISSUES

AMERICA'S POLICE OFFICERS are uniformed Alices in a looking-glass world of crime, where the seemingly benign can be malevolent and the apparent threat often turns out to be something far less. To understand how frustrating, confusing, confounding, and downright dangerous police work can be, consider this true story of a civilian living in a borderline urban neighborhood who was the victim of street robbery on his doorstep twice within two weeks.

The first robbery occurred in the evening, as the victim was headed home to his apartment with bags of groceries in his hands. As he stepped up to the apartment house door, a man came up behind him, jammed a gun into his back, and said "Give me the money. That's all I want is the money." The victim complied and the robber—whom he had seen was a black male—fled. The police were called and responded very quickly. A search was done of the immediate area, but the perpetrator could not be found. The man went on with his life, as most crime victims do, and made a mental note to be a little more observant of who was around on his block.

About a week later the man was leaving for work, in the morning, when he was confronted in his apartment house vestibule by a white male waving a large pistol, who demanded his money.

235

"Anybody else in your apartment?" the apparently drug-crazed robber demanded. The man lied and said his three roommates were home. (He only had one.) After taking his cash, wristwatch, and attache case, the robber fled. Once again the police were called and an area search was done, and once again the perpetrator could not be found.

This time the victim was severely shaken and became depressed. He didn't want to leave his apartment, lost interest in his work and hobbies, and had anxiety attacks whenever he walked between the subway and his home. Things got so bad that he finally sought counseling from his city's victim services agency. That decision came after a traumatic moment on a lovely summer morning, as he left his home—with great hesitation—for work.

"There was a woman," he explained to the caseworker. "She was sitting on a stoop not far from mine, and I was watching her carefully. Then I saw her reach with a hand to brush her hair back, but when she did her hair came off. It was a wig, and she was really a man. I blinked my eyes and realized it was a hallucination. The woman was still a woman, and she still had her hair, and she sat there smoking a cigarette."

The counselors explained that he was having a reaction not uncommon for victims of violent crime, especially when certain specifics of his case were considered.

"The first attack was at night," the counselor explained. "The second one was in the morning. One perpetrator was black, one was white. One time you were coming home and one time you were leaving. Everything that happened the second time was the exact reverse of the first time. When you saw the woman brush back her hair, your mind was racing through all the possibilities. She might be a he—and you might then be in danger. But somehow your thoughts got mixed up with the reality. You suffered an illusion of fear." After realizing what had actually happened to him, the man became less nervous, and eventually went on with his life.

But now consider the police officer, working in an environment that is often hostile, where thirteen-year-old children carry guns, and grandmothers allow their apartments to be used by drug rings and act as their lookouts (sometimes this is not voluntary). The man who reaches for a gun, or seems to be, might not be armed with anything more deadly than a pocket comb. The kid who dresses in the uniform of the drug lookout—dark hooded jersey, dark hat, dark pants, the better not to be seen by a passing police officer—might just be dressing the part in order to look *bad*, to keep from becoming a victim himself. The list goes on, with the lines blurring ever more.

If it becomes apparent that a police officer has made a tragic mistake while acting in good faith, then it would be unfair, given the circumstances noted above, to jump on his or her case automatically, without knowing all the facts. But does this mean that the police story should automatically be accepted as gospel as soon as it is proffered? Not necessarily—although the police, who of course understand themselves as the good guys and the "other people" as the bad guys, strenuously disagree. The stories the public will hear first, however, are the ones presented by daily newspapers, television, and radio.

By oversight more than design, sometimes those stories bear an overwhelming pro-police bias. This statement may come as a surprise to those who complain of the "liberal news media," and assume that reporters are only too willing to jump down the throats of police officers and the officials who direct them, eager for a scoop at any cost. But the science of reporting, like the science of policing, is prone to human error, prejudice, and oversight. A brief understanding of how the media works on a day-to-day basis is necessary in order for there to be any understanding of how this happens.

———

Newspaper reporters are usually assigned "beats." That is, each reporter is charged with following a particular issue or related group of issues, to facilitate the development of contacts and sources within the particular field. The bigger the newspaper, the more specialized these beats tend to be. In a big-city daily with a large circulation there is often sufficient staff to make crossovers among beats a rarity: the political reporters cover the community's state and national politicians, the City Hall reporters cover the mayor and the city council, the court reporters cover the courts, the environmental or science reporter covers those issues. This also helps when papers throw together "packages" of related stories from different disciplines in order to help cover one event. A murder might initially be covered by a police reporter; when the case goes to trial, it will be handled by whoever is covering the courthouse. The mayor's response is handled by the City Hall reporter, and the legislation the politicians cook up to see that this crime doesn't ever happen again will be covered by the statehouse political correspondent. The system, then, has obvious benefits. With all of the reporters being experts in their fields, it is reasonable to assume that somehow the full story will come out.

But there is a flaw in the equation. Perhaps you might have noticed that nowhere in that list of newspaper beats was there a slot for someone specializing in "people." The sources sought out for each element of the story are official sources, whose aim is to make certain that their particular agenda is covered. But who has the contacts with the people in the street, particularly in those cases where the community with the most to say is made up of minority groups—who are probably not represented on the paper's editorial board, or in its city room, or in any of its major departments? This problem is being dealt with to some degree by many papers as they try to recruit more minority staffers. But at the largest papers minority candidates are often recruited, with especially desirable assignments as inducements. True police reporters are a special breed of journalist, but for many assigned to the "cop shop," the cops-and-robbers game is only a stepping stone to more desirable assignments; the police beat is regarded as anything but a plum job. It is therefore rarely put forward as a minority-recruitment incentive.

There are exceptions to the seemingly pervasive practice of hiring police reporters who are male and white, and devoid of the sensitivity to this special field of urban affairs reporting. One of the most esteemed police reporters in the United States is a woman named Edna Buchanan, who worked for the *Miami Herald* until her career as a book author recently began to flourish. More often than not, however, police reporters share the attitudes, outlook, and values of the police officers and supervisors they cover.

Journalists are supposed to avoid getting too close to their sources. But getting too close to the source, for police reporters, is often inevitable, and in most cases is vital for an effective job to be done. In many jurisdictions, reporters rely on the police to grant them their credentials, their parking permits, and other courtesies necessary for them to get their job done. A reporter might carefully scrutinize in print various policy issues laid down by top police department brass, but this sort of thing is accepted by most police sources. But out on the street, at the crime scene, in the locker rooms and the muster rooms, a police reporter who is consistently critical of the police—especially in covering controversial cases, and most certainly on something as sensitive as a custody death—can find himself the odd man out, short of sources and therefore short of stories, scooped by the competition, and therefore ineffective. If a story presented by police authorities is plausible, then there is a good chance that it is the only story that will get repeated play in the major media.

There are other conflicts as well. *Washington Post* media critic Howard Kurtz writes in his book *Media Circus*, "Robert Terry, a veteran police reporter for the *Philadelphia Inquirer*, is so close to the cops he has covered for thirty years that he borrowed money from the city's police commissioner and other police officials so he could gamble in Atlantic City."

In one sensitive case involving an off-duty police officer who was suspected in a murder, a newspaper's police reporter bristled at suggestions that the officer—whom she had interviewed on occasions in the past and knew to be a "good cop" —could be considered a serious suspect in the crime. Every benefit of the doubt in her stories on the case was given the officer, in a way that no editor would have tolerated if the suspect was a mere civilian.

There is the occasional investigative piece or series dealing with police corruption, or even brutality issues, that makes it into the papers. But such stories are growing more scarce, if for no other reason than that many newspapers cannot spare to expend a single reporter, much less a team, to do such in-depth digging.

Despite all of these realities affecting media coverage of police work, newspapers, television, and radio are often the subjects of sharp criticism from the police, who feel the media are out to get them, and community leaders and followers who say that the press "covers up" stories involving crooked and brutal cops. Neither camp is correct.

For the most part, the controversial story that could be spun in an antipolice direction can sometimes be delayed—or not printed at all—not because of any blatant pro-police bias, but simply because the sources may be sketchy. People have axes to grind, and often will take them to the nearest newspaper or television station under the mistaken assumption that the grinding shop is located there. The mere fact that someone has an allegation is just not enough—most of the time—to allow the actual running of a story for public consumption.

On the other hand, the idea that media outlets intentionally suppress antipolice stories because they are tools of the power structure also holds little weight with anyone who knows how the media actually operate. The decision to run or kill a story is made not through any desire to cover up questionable police actions, but rather a series of tests that any story must pass before it is deemed suitable for printing. Many of these tests have to do with the credibility of witnesses or other sources. Some news organizations are reluctant to print stories alleging improper conduct by the police on the basis of nothing more than a civilian's complaint. And if the civilian involved is a drug user or dealer or other sort of suspect figure, then the potential for publication decreases even further.

The beating of Rodney King was on videotape for all to see, and the print media had no choice but to pick up on the television story. Had the tape never been made, police could have said that King received his injuries while resisting them (which was the essence of the accused officers' defense, in any regard), or even that he had suffered injuries in a car accident. In *The Ville*, Greg Donaldson's riveting account of "kids and cops" in the Brownsville section of Brooklyn, he notes how police would beat recalcitrant suspects if their cars had been involved in an accident during a chase. The beating injuries were masked by those said to be suffered in the crash.

To return to a case examined earlier, initial coverage of the Kiko Garcia case in New York was essentially well balanced. But the same news media representatives who had no trouble presenting an account that was less than favorable to the police—when a witness was spoon-fed to them—dropped the ball once the district attorney's office was finally able to come up with a plausible enough explanation for questionable police behavior. Who would want to go digging for more information that would have implicated a police officer like Michael O'Keefe, who coaches Pop Warner football with kids in Washington Heights, when a seemingly valid explanation for everything was offered by the district attorney? Some reporters even tried to re-create the scenario the DA's office provided, which made it seem impossible that the witness could have seen what she claimed to have seen. Yet it appears upon reexamination that the district attorney might well have pulled a fast one.

The best coverage in the early stages of the Shuaib Latif story was a package of stories written by Douglas Kennedy in the *New York Post*, a surprising fact when one considers that paper's conservative bent. Kennedy, backed by his editors, provided a first-rate, *first-hand* account of the events surrounding Latif's death as told by Darriel Johnson. The *Post* allowed Kennedy to cover the story for the day, while its City Hall and police desks provided the necessary balance. In fact, subsequent to the appearance of Kennedy's stories, it appeared that the mayor's office softened its rhetoric on the Latif issue. If any police department action is ever taken in regard to the case, Kennedy's perseverance might well have been responsible. In the summer of 1994, the case was still pending. However, a ranking police official conceded that he expected no actions to be taken by the department, even though questions remained unanswered.

The media has been criticized in some circles for inciting the rage that leads to civic violence—in Los Angeles, Miami, and Washington Heights, especially—but the charge is not valid. The violence that occurred in these communities was rooted in preexisting social problems, and the well-reported police actions there served to act only as catalysts. If anything, it is the news media's *failure* to report the day-to-day events in the inner city (where the most striking examples of police violence occur) in an unbiased, accurate, and timely fashion that leads whole populations to feel neglected and distrustful.

Indeed, it is ironic that the greatest media interest in such police violence cases occurs only *after* it becomes clear that a community is already on the edge because of some unpleasant incident. This sort of interest usually entails a spate of uncharacteristic digging for facts, up to and including Freedom of Information requests and other evidence of hard, no-nonsense reporting. It should also be noted that some reporters who cover the police don't spend enough time out in the field to know what police work is truly about. This creates a climate of suspicion in the law enforcement community, which is also counterproductive to anyone really getting the facts about what's going on in our streets.

New York Newsday columnist Ellis Henican has what may be one of the most unique reporter beats in the United States. He covers the city's subway system, a specialty assignment pioneered by fellow reporter Jim Dwyer. In February 1994, Henican wrote a story about a white, suit-and-tie-clad bank employee who tried to get a transit police officer to intervene after a robbery had been committed on a platform, only to be ignored because the officer was writing out a summons to a woman for smoking. When the whistle-blower, identified as Keith May, tried to take down the officer's badge number, he was handcuffed and arrested. The charges were obstructing governmental administration, disorderly conduct, and resisting arrest. The woman who received the summons also sinned in the eyes of the officer—by making a phone call at the behest of May—and she was arrested too. Henican was interviewed on a radio talk show the morning that column appeared, and he received wide publicity.

The contrast is clear. Such arrests, we have seen, are often used to punish those deemed guilty of "contempt of cop." Most never make it into the newspaper. But then again, not all such "offenders" are white, well-spoken, and work in banks. This is not Henican's fault, and he should be applauded for pursuing the story. But the fact that this one incident is "news" when so many other similar incidents have occurred and gone unreported speaks volumes about how our supposedly unified society is really two separate societies. Abuses of power by the police, which are the first steps toward deadlier varieties of abuse, are news when visited upon one segment of society, and not news when visited upon the other.

As mentioned earlier here, part of the problem is that none of us want to think of the police in the role of malefactor. At early ages we are taught to believe that the policeman is our friend. Much of the mythology that results in less than aggressive news coverage of police violence, public acceptance of such violence, and the way the police view themselves is the product of outmoded ideas of what we as a society expect of the police. A combination of police tradition, the gunslinger myth, and wishful thinking has substantially tinted the attitude officers have about their own work. By extension, this affects their behavior and attitudes on the street, and in places where they are not in public view. More conscientious handling of police violence stories by the news media, however, can go a long way toward reshaping these attitudes, and therefore to making our society a safer, more secure place for the public as well as the police officers who serve them.

FIFTEEN

A QUESTION OF CULTURE

MANY OF US WHO GREW up watching westerns learned early on that the good guys wore white hats and the bad guys wore black hats, no matter how politically incorrect such assessments (or the movies themselves) might have been. It was easy to tell good from bad without a score card, from mere appearances. Any of us who might have clung to such beliefs as we grew older might have integrated well into prevailing police culture.

It is easy for police officers to believe that they are the good guys and, especially in a city gone bad at every corner, that they hold a monopoly on the designation. In New York City the police have at times come to near-blows with members of the fire department over whose agency should take the lead at the scene of an emergency. These instances, however, are proof of a hubris epidemic that infects the ranks of our police forces. "We're the good guys and they're the bad guys," is the way most officers view their work. And for anyone who has spent any time on patrol with them, it is easy to figure out why.

"Good guys and bad guys" may work in the movies, but the lines are decidedly more blurred on the streets of a big city. From ill-advised interdiction efforts conceived by people who wouldn't know the street if it rose up off the bedrock and smacked them in the back, to the constant pandering by politicos only too eager to feed the public's fear, our criminal justice system is operated and managed by politicians who serve the whims of a public largely ignorant of the factors that influence criminal behavior.

The widespread—and inaccurate—perception of an ongoing increase in crime has resulted in a fear epidemic that has a major grip on the people of our cities, even though serious crime has decreased nationwide, according to FBI statistics. Of course, crime is always a hot topic of conversation. Our fascination with crime is not sated by the daily casualty counts supplied by the evening news, so popular entertainment forms like television fill that void for us. The people who police us are drawn from our midst, and share our common beliefs and attitudes. When they go to work, they strap those attitudes on as sure as they do their gunbelts.

Ultimately, it is the gun that sets police officers apart from other civilians, that represents the ultimate power our society has invested in the cop. Certainly not all police officers are gun heavy, and to conscientious and mature law enforcement professionals the gun is a tool. But unlike the carpenter's hammer, the gun is a tool to be used only as a last resort.

Only medical workers can be compared to the police when it comes to the possibility that misuse of professional tools might result in catastrophic consequences to the human body. Like police officers, doctors may employ methods in their work—when necessary—that would constitute crimes if done by nonmedical personnel. But doctors (whose use of "force" in all situations are intended to help, not hurt) receive years of training, and most would never suggest that they have perfected medical work; rather, they *practice* it.

Police officers, by contrast, often must meet minimal educational requirements to qualify for their jobs. While psychological screening is employed to varying degrees by different departments, it is not standardized, which leaves many open cracks through which potentially disturbed people can fall—straight into a uniform. And once applicants are appointed to police positions, they are often woefully underpaid, especially in large urban centers..

In one New Jersey town, the starting salary for police officers is in the $40,000 annual range. Yet once these officers take to the streets they have little to worry about in terms of personal safety, are in no way as challenged as their counterparts in that same state's largest cities, and must perform far fewer varied functions (ranging from emergency medical intervention to social work) than a cop in a high-crime area is often called upon to perform on a daily basis.

According to the Department of Justice, the average annual starting salary for a municipal police officer in 1990 was $24,500, with the average chief executive's paycheck little more than twice that. These salaries are reflective of the low expectations municipal authorities have for their law enforcement officers, as evinced by the dismal state of educational requirements. Fully 85 percent of city police departments nationwide require nothing more than a high school diploma for officer candidates. A two-year degree is required by only 5 percent of police departments; 1 percent require no educational documentation at all.

Federal data also indicate that women are severely underrepresented in police work, as are minorities. In 1990, fully 84 percent of municipal police officers were white non-Hispanics, and only 7 percent of municipal officers were female.

Even more dismal are the protections offered the public—not to mention the police themselves—from potentially dangerous officer candidates. Illegal drug use by police officers, of course, is seen as counter to the aims of law enforcement. But despite the ethical question of illicit drug use among officers, there is a more considerable mental health issue that comes into play in this situation, and should weigh heaviest on the

minds of police administrators. Whether civilian or police officer, a person's use of illegal substances often masks underlying
psychological problems and raises issues of proper social adjustment. Yet only 26 percent of local police departments of all
sizes in the United States require mandatory drug testing of applicants. Of those departments serving populations of a million or more, 21 percent do not require applicants to be tested
for drugs. Worse yet, the longer an individual is involved with
a police department, the less likely it is that he or she will be
tested for illicit drug use. Only 4 percent of probationary officers are required to be tested for drug use among police departments of all sizes, and just 2 percent of regular field officers and
those who are candidates for promotion must be tested.

Police unions have long opposed drug testing, as do many
unions representing large groups of municipal employees.
Drug testing in general is a complicated issue that raises many
complex questions. But in defense of drug testing for police officers, what must be stated emphatically is that no other group
is as capable of inflicting death as part of the performance of
their assigned duties, while at the same time having as much
opportunity to cover up such a death.

Finally, James Fyfe, one of the foremost experts in the field
of police use of force, wrote in 1989 that simple incompetence
is often the principal cause of many excessive force incidents:

> Such violence occurs when police lack the eloquence to per-
> suade temporarily disturbed persons to give up their
> weapons, but shoot them instead . . . It occurs when officers
> called to quell noisy but non-violent disputes act in a way
> that provokes disputants to violence . . .

On a chilly Saturday afternoon at a small New York police
station in the midst of a public housing project, it is time to

change shifts; officers just coming on, just going off, or taking an authorized meal break are gathered in a cafeteria, where a football game is on the television. The joking is the kind of good-natured, fraternal humor one might expect to encounter anywhere groups of men gather for relaxation. As this particularly exciting game reaches a climax the wordplay turns into horseplay, which includes wrestling, the throwing of objects, and the repeated slamming of nightsticks against tables. If testosterone carried a smell the air would be reeking with it, and to someone new to these environs the scene might even be frightening—although the same sort of thing could be expected, say, in a high school locker room. A few officers shake their heads and lightly inject some comments, seemingly embarrassed by the foolery. One of these is berated by his louder colleagues, and questions are raised about his masculinity.

It would be wrong to begrudge this sort of release for people working in such a high-tension job. But the behavior is frightening in its potential consequences. All of the men must exhibit this sort of machismo or risk being ostracized, and being ostracized is sometimes tantamount to death in a big-city police department. A few weeks before this scene, a police officer in that same city, attached to one of the specialty emergency rescue units, slapped an oxygen mask on the face of a man who was dying from a gunshot wound inflicted by another officer during a confrontation. The shooting was justified; had he not fired, the officer involved might have been killed or wounded, since the suspect had a loaded firearm. But the officer who did his duty by protecting the suspect's life was given the cold shoulder by other officers later on.

"That guy tried to shoot a cop," he was told. "You didn't even look to see if the *cop* was all right." This was perceived as a grievous slight, despite the fact that the officer involved in the shooting had not shown any sign of injury when the rescue cop arrived.

Ironically, the rescue cop's efforts to comfort the injured suspect were futile, and he knew it. The man had a sucking chest wound, and never made it to the hospital alive. People in this job learn to steel themselves against the emotional effects of bearing witness to such deaths on a regular basis. His fellow officers' criticisms, however, had a dramatic effect on the rescue cop. When he showed up for work the next night his partner nearly had to drag him to their rescue truck after roll call, and they spent the better part of the first half of their shift trying to locate the cops in the precinct where the incident had happened in order to make peace. Finally, to the relief of everyone who knew this amiable and easy-going officer, who was devastated by the treatment he'd received from his compatriots merely for doing what he'd been trained to do, peace was made.

Is it any wonder, then, that when a police officer acts inappropriately, so many of his fellow officers will lie, perjure, invent, obfuscate, or otherwise color the truth for his benefit? The peer pressure is so enormous that one might look at the psychological state of development among police officers as perpetual adolescence. The closing the ranks around a fellow who is the subject of departmental scrutiny, or even of a possible law suit or employment action, is understandable considering the usual municipal attitude toward such occurrences.

Most municipalities fear messy, costly, high-profile lawsuits as much as anything else. If a police officer wanted to make amends for an inappropriate action—to apologize, to admit publicly what really occurred in the interests of truth and justice, even if only to pay heed to nudges from his conscience—the chances are he would lose his job. Better to go along with the department line; after all, the police are the good guys and the perps are the bad guys, and the good guys have to stick together. If something were done or said inadvertently that could in any way aid litigation against the municipality, the fate of the unfortunate officer would very likely be unemployment.

————————

In examining these attitudes, we must consider the partial profile we've pieced together, recognizing the limitations of these public guardians whom we've placed on the streets armed with guns and clubs.

Nationwide, most police officers are overwhelmingly white, male, and undereducated. Some may have undetected drug problems. Almost all of them—especially those who work in our biggest cities—are underpaid. In many cases, those same underpaid and undereducated white male police officers grew up in a thoroughly different world than the one they now work. One must ask why anyone who grew up in a middle-class or lower-middle-class suburb would pursue a career that would place him in constant danger, that asks him to perform tasks requiring a high degree of personal sensitivity, that requires him to exercise sophisticated problem-solving and dispute-resolution techniques, and that demands both a flair for public relations and an understanding of human behavior—all for substandard wages.

The answer in many cases, based on interviews with sociologists, psychologists, and police officers in the field, is that a large number of officers conceive of themselves as urban adventurers, willing to put up with a tough job for minimal compensation for the same reasons other men may have volunteered for military service. Police work is represented in our culture as exciting and action-oriented, displayed in vivid tones on our movie and television screens. Our fictional police heroes are the ones who throw the rules out the window, knowing that the Constitution may be okay for history class, but in the "real world" all court decisions do is keep them from doing their duty. The Dirty Harry-style cop who throws the suspect through the window gets cheered in the theaters. The wet blanket throughout such movies is the superior who keeps reminding the officer of rules and regulations.

The Christopher Commission in Los Angeles noted that officers involved in cases where excessive force was alleged were often those who not only had good records of service, but also had high marks from superiors for "high activity." "High activity" police officers are those who have made a high number of arrests, especially for felony crimes. They are more likely to take risks that endanger themselves, arrestees, and the public at large, and they are often the ones who bristle at the scrutiny they must suffer under superiors. But trained police managers know that high activity can often be an indicator of potential trouble.

This is especially true in today's world of policing, which is changing radically from what it was in the past. The greatest innovation is the advent of community policing and problem-oriented policing programs, which require the police officer on the beat to act more independently of police administrative structures in order to address specific problems, whether working alone or in concert with the community. These new programs rely heavily on proactive, decentralized policing. The cop on the beat, more than anyone else in the department's management structure, is aware of what specific conditions exist that require his or her intervention. The fundamental strategy is *not* to rack up high arrest figures, which for too long have been the barometer by which good police work was judged. Firefighters have long known that the fire that was prevented is the best one to have fought—the one you never *had* to fight. The police are beginning to get the same idea.

New York City has encountered a host of problems implementing its community policing programs, which were first instituted when Commissioner Lee Brown, whose community-based efforts were successful when he worked in Houston, first took office. The biggest problems have been with the officers themselves. Community policing just doesn't fit with the cops-and-robbers role many officers prefer to play. If anything, the success of community policing is measured by a *lack* of arrest activity, since an officer doing good proactive work on the beat should have less opportunity to apprehend bad guys.

Other opposition to community policing has come from those in management—sergeants and, especially, lieutenants —who fail to see the effectiveness of problem-oriented, proactive police work. In fact, community-oriented policing was a failure in Cincinnati specifically because middle-level managers were not properly figured into the policing equation. There was resistance based on a mistaken belief that community policing was just another tactical tool for traditional "crimefighting." In that context, the program didn't have a chance.

The most successful community policing innovations have occurred when a target precinct or district develops and deploys a structured program. After the bugs are worked out, it can then be adopted citywide, as was the case in Houston. But community policing can work in other ways as well. In Baltimore County, there was a lack of support for the community policing program from officers doing traditional, reactive, radio-call follow-up, and Chief Neil Behan recognized that the only way to save the concept was to institute it countywide, after which the program found its feet.

Too many police officers, however, still feel that to do their job well they must break down doors, engage in risky, high-speed pursuits, and participate in dangerous gunplay. Unless educational requirements (at least two years of college) are adopted as a national standard for police officers, then innovative ideas will fall on deaf ears at the most important level—

the street level, since the patrol officer must be the backbone of any community policing program.

For too long patrol work has been the assignment successful cops left behind as they worked their way up the professional ladder. The mark of a successful police officer was the "gold shield"—the perks and pay and prestige that come with being a detective. Of course we need detectives of good quality to solve crimes and make good arrests. But as the cream of any police department gravitates toward its detective bureau, the rest are left foundering on patrol, bitter and resentful, often having to work second jobs to support their families or themselves. The patrol officer is and should be regarded as a unique professional, and should receive the pay and prestige he or she is due. We cannot complain about rising crime if we are not willing to support those we ask to stem it at its source.

———

One program that has been implemented by some police departments is relatively new—too new, in fact, to be accurately assessed. But all indications are that police cadet programs, such as the one currently utilized in New York, are the wave of the future. In the New York program, young men and women who *live in the city* join an elite group of unarmed, gray-uniformed cadets who assist police officers at all levels, from administration to patrol. The cadets serve for two years, during which time they can continue their educations, receiving a stipend and a forgivable loan to be applied toward college tuition. In return they must serve at least two years as police officers after attending the policing academy.

The New York City Housing Authority Police Department has made extensive use of the new cadet program; this department is becoming a success story itself, according to some experts, and cadet utilization can only help further its goals. Fourteen cities, including New York, have separate police departments specifically dedicated to patrolling public housing projects, according to the Department of Housing and Urban Development (HUD). "New York City probably has the most professional [department] and they are the largest," said Earl Simons, a HUD spokesman. Agency officials say they'd like to see more such departments nationwide.

Detective Paul DiIorio pounds a housing beat in Police Service Area number 5 (PSA-5) in upper Manhattan, which oversees twenty-nine developments made up of 300 buildings, whose 50,000 official residents earn an average of $12,500 annually.

DiIorio is the patrol community officer (PCO) for a group of buildings called the Jefferson Houses. When he worked in the nearby Johnson Houses the kids there called him Supercop, because he seemed to be everywhere at once. He was so effective, in fact, that the drug dealers began to make threats on his life.

"I didn't take any of it seriously, really," DiIorio said in a soft voice with a decided New York accent. "But the department did so they transferred me here to Jefferson." The difference between the graffiti-scarred, fetid hallways of Jefferson and the brightly lit public areas of the Johnson Houses is striking. Tenants at Johnson say they miss DiIorio, who hopes to bring similar positive change to his new post.

The Housing Authority police have long considered themselves the stepchildren of New York City law enforcement, but recent innovations by Chief DeForrest Taylor—including bicycle patrols, increased plainclothes narcotics units, anti-graffiti programs, and a new emergency rescue squad—are credited by cops with boosting morale. Officials say it is the old-fashioned beat cops like DiIorio who keep per capita crime levels at a remarkable 50 percent lower rate than that of the city as a whole, even though the projects are traditional breeding grounds for armed criminals and drug dealers. While arrests

remain the measure of how well most cops do their jobs, DiIorio's effectiveness is more difficult to gauge. He contends that
effecting arrests—given the rapid-fire speed with which New
York's criminal justice system revolves—can actually be counterproductive.

One Thursday evening in late 1993 found DiIorio riding to
the roof of a Jefferson building in an elevator that smells of
weeks-old cat litter. With him are two cadets, Xavier Crandell,
twenty-one, and Rhonney King, twenty. The elevator door
opens and DiIorio sees two trespassers on the roof landing. He
pounces on one and the cadets take the other.

"Open your hand," DiIorio orders, and the grizzled man
in his thirties, dressed shabbily but warmly against the winter
weather with the jersey hood that is the uniform of the streets,
drops a narrow glass pipe that bounces but does not break. He
says his name is Rambo, and he has a vial of crack in his
pocket, but after a search he and his companion are sent on
their way with a stern warning.

Theodora Lee, a Jefferson resident who spends three hours
a day, five days a week, sitting in the lobby of her building on
tenant patrol, prefers the low priority given arrests for such
nonserious offenses.

"I think so long as the police make them leave and they do
not come back, it's better to keep the police out here and available instead of locking them up," Lee says.

"This building will be free of crime tonight," DiIorio says
after visiting Theodora Lee. "They'll just go somewhere else."

Short and muscular, DiIorio, thirty-five, the father of two
children, is himself a product of public housing. He grew up in
a project in the Chelsea section of Manhattan, and takes his job
personally.

"We didn't have this when I was growing up in the projects," he says, pointing to building entryway lights blacked
out by the young men who perform lookout duty for drug

dealers. The lookouts wear black jerseys with hoods and black pants to avoid being seen. As part of his community policing efforts, DiIorio will be certain to notify building maintenance of the blacked-out lights so that they will be repaired as quickly as possible.

DiIorio had intended to go into banking, and did work in that field for a while, but then changed his mind and went into policing. "I had a brother-in-law who was a cop," DiIorio, himself the son of a longshoreman, explained. "When he used to visit, my parents would go through all kind of trouble and roll out the red carpet because he was a cop. I told them, 'I'm gonna be a cop so you can see that you don't have to roll out the red carpet.'"

He feels badly for the many families struggling to raise children in such tough environs, but points out that it is the children of many of the people who live here who are the ones dealing the drugs and marking up the buildings.

"How can you do that to someplace you live? How can you do that to your home?" DiIorio asks.

He recalls the time when he stopped to chat with an eight-year-old who was running with a pack of young drug dealers.

"I asked him to empty his pockets and he had eighty dollars," DiIorio said. "He said his mother gave him the money for boots, so I took him up to the apartment to verify the story." DiIorio said the mother had at first said she gave the boy eight dollars, but then her child gave her a high sign and she changed her story.

"What was I going to do?" DiIorio asked. "Charge him with criminal possession of money?"

By knowing the people on his beat, DiIorio has a better idea of who is trouble and who is not. He realizes that this eight-year-old will need to be the subject of special attention if he is to live long enough to register to vote.

DiIorio says that a three-way cooperative effort between

police, tenants, and building management can go a long way toward eliminating crime. Replacement of light fixtures, graffiti cleanup, and repair of broken doors, coupled with tenant patrols, prod violators to do their damage elsewhere.

The community policing approach is one of the tools Inspector Edward Tuller, DiIorio's boss, says has helped decrease the numbers of major felonies in PSA-5 by 12 percent—without a corresponding population decrease—from 1,666 incidents in 1992, to 1,465 in 1993.

Gloria Wright, president of the PSA-5 resident's council, is pleased with the work the police are doing but unimpressed by the statistics.

"If you just got mugged that doesn't mean doodly squat," the feisty organizer says. What concerns Gloria Wright and other leaders among the housing authority's 600,000 tenants is the possibility that the city's new mayor, Rudolph Giuliani, might combine the housing, transit, and city police departments for purposes of financial expediency. "We don't have enough police as it is," Wright said. "If they take our housing police away we're going to be in a helluva fix."

The Housing Authority Police Department also operates its own emergency rescue unit (ERU), their newest tool for fighting crime and upgrading the quality of life in the projects. New York has the first housing police department in the nation to organize such a unit. Since October 1993, the elite rescue team's four trucks have been called out to rescue suicidal jumpers, provide lighting at crime scenes, search roofs and basements, rescue people down shafts, and remove errant large rodents and mammals from the apartments of hysterical occupants. Each truck is equipped with $80,000 worth of special gear paid for with drug forfeiture money, ranging from the so-called "jaws of life" (useful for extracting victims trapped between elevators and shaftways) to locksmith kits.

Officers assigned to ERU have been trained in everything

from rappelling down the sides of buildings to giving emergency first aid. All are emergency medical technicians.

"I tell them that they have to be prepared to give first aid to someone they may have just had to shoot," says Lt. Ralph Pascullo, an energetic supervisor who stresses service-oriented policing to his unit's members. "When we rescue people from stuck elevators we make sure the elevator gets repaired, too," Pascullo said. "We have lots of senior citizens in our buildings. When we drill a lock out of a door to reach someone who's injured, or to get to abandoned children, we do it in a way that makes for easy replacement so the apartment will remain secure."

"They're highly motivated officers who take their mission very seriously," the Housing Police Department's Lt. Thomas Sbordone said of the unit at its inauguration. "The special training of these officers, coupled with their familiarity with the projects, aids their response and effectiveness, and our overall mission."

The innovations of the Housing Police Department, with their palpable results, are the wave of the future in policing. By encouraging young people like cadets Xavier Crandell and Rhonney King to be involved in police work, the agency is making an impact on the prevailing cultural ethos. Besides the fact that both are African-American and city-born and raised, they reflect contemporary urban culture in other ways. Both are the products of one-parent households in high-crime neighborhoods. They both express enthusiasm about police work, and both say that two years on the street and around the stationhouse without a gun will make them less prone to resort to unnecessary force later on, once they are appointed to the police department.

"I've been learning how to use my mouth instead of my hands and talk my way out of something," Crandell said. "It's not what I thought it would be, though. I thought it was all action and running and chasing guys. It's a lot more than that. You've got to use your head."

At a time when so much bad news is coming out of our cities, Crandell and King are emblematic of hope. As they patrol with Paul DiIorio, slogging through slush and snow, their faces eager, a couple of neighborhood kids check out the patches on their arms, pretending to be nonchalant.

"How do you get to do that?" one of them asks the cadet. It is a bright moment in a neighborhood largely bereft of brightness. When you look into the eyes of the cadets, you see a glimmer of light for the future.

However, there are clouds on the horizon, at least in New York City. In June 1994 Mayor Giuliani once again stated intentions to merge the Housing Authority police with the city's police department. The result, according to critics of that plan, will be less effective coverage of the city's housing projects. Giuliani has stated that the merge is necessary due to financial considerations.

Shortly before this book was published, Chief Taylor was ousted from his position, and replaced by an NYPD assistant chief, Joseph Leake, who supports Giuliani's merger idea.

While other cities seek to follow New York's example, that city's own great experiment in policing is on the verge of becoming nothing more than a memory.

"If they lose this department then they will lose the projects," a veteran Housing Authority police detective said. "When they lose the housing projects, they will lose the city."

SIXTEEN

NOWHERE TO TURN

I N MOST OF THE CASES PRE-
sented here, the families of people who have died in police
custody under questionable circumstances have eventually
filed civil lawsuits for damages. The wrongful death actions
filed in state courts and civil rights suits in federal courts recite
a legalese litany of wrongs visited upon men and women by
the people sworn to protect them. Civil suits ostensibly serve
to punish the guilty officers and their municipal employers,
compensate the injured, and deter future misconduct. Too
often, however, they accomplish nothing more than the generation of legal billing by the attorneys involved.

In fiscal year 1991 New York City paid out $10 million in
brutality lawsuits; these figures, which are backed up by the
New York City Corporation Counsel's office, are expected to
continue rising. While increased litigiousness, the rantings of
"self-appointed" civil rights activists, and still other factors
might be cited as causes for this fiscal burden by apologists for
police misconduct, it is ultimately the acts of police officers
themselves that gave rise to the problem. More importantly, it
is the responsibility of our nation's police departments for failing to stem such behavior. Litigants cannot—and should not—
be faulted for suing. Indeed, what other options do they have?
Civil lawsuits have limitations as regards the satisfaction of

261

the injured parties. For one thing, individual officers are in most cases indemnified from liability if the actions they took were in good faith and did not fall outside the guidelines expected of them. Thus it is the municipality that is punished in such suits, not the individual officer.

In the case of Kiko Garcia, one suit was brought against Officer O'Keefe individually and another against the city, on two different causes of action, and it is possible that the upholding of one may well negate the other. The case may not work out this way—but attorneys for both defendants will likely tie up the cases for some time, with one defendant trying to shift responsibility to the other. Often, in these situations, the municipality must protect itself by trying to place the burden of responsibility on the officer. Having officer and employer as *de facto* adversaries in this way is not conducive to the truth emerging from either litigant; it is counterproductive to justice, and further proof that the options available to citizens seeking remedy are few and ineffective. What results, then, is justice for none. Too often the process leaves both the police officer and complainant hung out to dry.

Yet, despite the risk they face in the form of civil litigation, police officers are often vociferously opposed to any sort of outside review; most would claim they are capable of cleaning their own houses, though the record indicates otherwise. Community review boards, staffed in whole or in part by civilians, are a thorn in the side of law enforcement—despite the fact that such boards have been woefully inadequate in the discharge of their duties.

New York's Civilian Complaint Review Board (CCRB) had until 1993 functioned as part of the police department's Civilian Complaint Investigative Bureau (CCIB). Since then, the CCRB has been a fully civilian unit. Other police departments around the country are also experimenting with community review boards, however, and a cursory look at CCRB and the situation in New York could be helpful in determining how successful such boards might be, whether staffed entirely by civilians or not.

The stated goal of New York's CCRB is to conduct "objective, thorough, and timely case investigations," and it has the capacity to review complaints in a variety of languages. By identifying problematic officers, the CCRB is able to keep police supervisors at the precinct level—and sometimes higher—advised of potential trouble sources. Annual reports on civilian complaints are prepared at the precinct level for presentation to CCRB.

After actual inquiries conducted or supervised by CCRB investigators are completed, they are classified into three categories: full investigations, "dependent on the availability and cooperation of the complainant"; conciliation cases, involving nondisciplinary findings; and cases where the complainant withdraws, fails to cooperate, or cannot be found or identified. Those falling into that final category are designated "unsubstantiated"—which should not be confused with "unfounded." As of March 1993, 1,045 of the 1,311 completed CCRB cases were marked as unsubstantiated.

Actions taken against specific officers are difficult to tabulate, since they are regarded as personnel matters and are not usually public record. In 1992 there were 295 disciplinary actions *recommended* by the CCRB, ranging from special instructions to superiors to actual departmental charges against officers. When one compares this number to the number of complaints actually received, however—even allowing for a high number of cases where allegations of improper use of force, or the uttering of ethnic slurs (both of which come under CCRB jurisdiction), may have been false or misleading—the results don't seem to show any significant effectiveness. By comparison, substantiated complaints against taxi drivers in New York are much greater—and often carry harsher penalties. It seems fair to say that whether by accident or design, the CCRB program does not inspire confidence among those people who wish to bring forward allegations of police misconduct.

The investigators employed by the CCIB parent board are, it should be noted, still employees of the police department itself. Also, when a complaint raises other issues, such as police corruption, that complaint is then routed according to that other issue through other channels, and may not show up in the CCRB or CCIB totals.

Based on the above information, it would seem that police officers who feared the creation of the all-civilian board had little to fear from it. Not included in CCRB's annual report (though its findings bear it out) is the fact that ultimately it is the police commissioner who decides what should be done with a complaint that is found to be substantiated. When a complaint is found to be unsubstantiated, the complainant is notified and no further action is taken, with no provision for appeal from such a decision. In essence, this amounts to star chamber justice.

The Medgar Evers Center for Law and Social Justice (CLSJ) conducted its own investigations into complaints involving police violence and compared them with the CCRB figures. The differences, published in 1992, were astounding. CLSJ used less stringent criteria for definition purposes; although this might tend to skew the overall findings, it should be remembered that it is the overall CCRB structure, and not just its own definition process, which is felt to be ineffective. One glaring example of this variance in data is the CCRB claim that the percentage of white officers named in complaints was around the 75 percent mark; the CLSJ study determined this figure as being at least 10 percent greater.

CLSJ has done what is probably the most extensive outside study of CCRB effectiveness. Its dismal report is only further substantiated by CCRB's own figures.

The CCRB data, contained in its annual reports . . . confirm
the fact that there exists a perpetual pattern of police violence against African-American males, followed close behind by African-American females, and that the primary
perpetrators of this violence are white officers. Yet, the
CCRB still has refused to take any significant action to insure discipline of the perpetrators of this violence by sub-
stantiating the complaints received against them. Instead,
the CCRB has largely ignored this pattern of violence and
continued to substantiate only 2 or 3 percent of the complaints . . . despite this fact, the CCRB continues to demonstrate pride in its low substantiation rate. As a result many
victims of police violence, quite correctly, no longer believe
they can obtain favorable results by filing a complaint with
the CCRB.

The CCRB's work, then, no matter how well intentioned,
is flawed. Optimal effectiveness requires vigorous pursuit of
the complaint by the complainant, with the CCRB having no
driving mission of its own to seek the truth—and justice—for
its own sake. Compare this with the New York State Commission on Corrections, established by statute and charged with
performing its fact-finding mission whether or not there is a
cooperating complainant. With its goal clearly defined as investigating only those deaths that occur in what is defined as
an "institutional" (jail or prison) setting, the Commission on
Corrections has the authority to intervene in such cases,
whether the lock-up involved is run by a city, county, or the
state itself. Insiders say it has been effective in identifying cus-
todial deaths within jail confines and seeing to prosecution
when that has been necessary. All that this means is that before
one can have a supervising agency review whether potentially
deadly actions of officials are appropriate, one must be incar-
cerated first.

The baby should not be thrown out with the bath water as

regards CCRB procedures in jurisdictions that use them. Such complaints can often be the first signal that a particular officer may be a problem. But the CCRB still amounts to a police-run agency with no real power that must answer to police officials, and amounts to nothing more than the police policing the police. History has shown this process to have minimal results.

One stumbling block to effective government response to the police brutality problem is the notion that police actively target minorities for acts of brutality. This is an area that should be carefully examined, because it is so easy to fall into the racial pitfalls of our race-conscious society.

While it is true that more police officers in our cities are white, it is also true that more minority civilians come into contact with police officers in the cities than white civilians, for reasons that are not the fault of the police. Sensitivity issues notwithstanding, it is a mistake to view police violence solely through the distorted lens of racial politics. Most studies, including one cited by the Condon Commission in 1987, have shown that the percentage of whites who are the target of *police shooting incidents* versus the percentage of blacks is statistically moot. Little of the relevant data examined since then has changed much in this one specific area.

The Condon Commission's study found that data on both blacks and whites killed in shooting encounters with police were virtually identical for both races. Forty-seven percent of both blacks and whites were attacking a police officer and 44 percent of blacks and 42 percent of whites were fleeing at the time the officer decided to shoot. Fifty-three percent of blacks and 47 percent of whites were armed with guns at the time of the shooting.

The incidents that are cause for the greatest concern, however, have not involved shootings. In the Malice Green case, which did not involve a gun, there were no substantive racial arguments made regarding why Green was beaten to death. While the beating of Rodney King created a maelstrom of racial tension, race was not decided to have been a causative factor. And in the case of Shuaib Latif, the officer who was alleged to have had the greatest opportunity for contact with the deceased, Kevin Sherman, was himself black. But race will continue to play a role, however, for as long as cases involving police violence are used to enhance the agenda of racially divisive provocateurs on all sides.

This is not to say, however, that race does not have some root responsibility for untoward police violence. For one thing, police officers working high-crime (read that nonwhite) neighborhoods are in all likelihood more likely to need to use force initially, thus increasing the possibility that things can get out of hand. The criminal justice system does not escape responsibility here for its disparate treatment of whites and blacks, nor does our economic system, nor our social fabric as a whole.

The matter of race could not be more relevant to the overall pervasive and systemic injustices inherent in the way our nation functions. But in terms of cases such as these, police violence becomes a mere symptom of the underlying problems. By focusing on the racial aspect of the police violence debate, complainants (except in those specific cases where race undeniably played a role) weaken their position. There is a question, then, of how much victims or survivors can benefit if the complaint or suit hinges on the issue of race when it is not readily determinable, or whether civil rights advocacy organizations can generate much more than headlines when focusing on these cases. Conversely, while race may not play the key role in determining why a civilian was killed or injured, it can be instrumental in determining how the subsequent complaint *is dealt with*. The issue of systemic responses and options thus becomes one that is highly race relevant.

———

New York State's Knapp Commission of the 1970s rhetorically asked whether history would repeat itself; the findings of the Mollen Commission hearings of 1993 proved, to some extent, that indeed it had. Sadly, police corruption and police violence pose just as great a threat now as they did a quarter-century ago.

It comes as no surprise that graft and other forms of police corruption go hand in hand with abuse of physical power, since both types of actions are taken by people who have chosen to overstep their legal boundaries. Indeed, police violence itself must be looked upon as a form of corruption. It too requires the cooperation of incorrupt officers (who are then tainted by the cover-up) and superiors (who don't wish to make waves) in order to flourish.

By 1990 New York state's special prosecutor office was eliminated, and with it the opportunity for any wholesale assault on police brutality. *New York Newsday* reported in 1993 that for the two preceding years, only five New York City police officers had been fired for brutality. Only one was fired for corruption. In a special statement on police corruption released in 1993, the New York City Bar Association noted these and other deficiencies:

> All of the factors that necessitate a special prosecutor for corruption also exist in the area of police brutality. Those who try to separate the two miss their key points of commonality. The underlying problem is police illegality whether it manifests itself in assaulting a prisoner, giving perjured testimony, or taking a bribe.

The idea of a watchdog or prosecutory agency at the state level has the potential to be one of the more effective solutions to these problems. The New York State Commission of Investigation, in a 1989 report on the handling of a prisoner death, recommended that the now-defunct special prosecutor's office pursue cases of alleged excessive force, stating that the potential for favoritism that justified a special prosecutor's office also extends to police custody deaths:

> The problem is not solely one of appearance. The same factors that explain and justify the public perception of prosecutorial favoritism to the police may indeed cause a district attorney, even if unconsciously, to act favorably to the police.

According to the New York City Bar Association's 1993 statement, the idea of a statewide prosecutor is one whose time has come, and in its lengthy position paper the association went further in citing the reasons why:

> . . . the [State Investigation] Commission issued a report on the Suffolk County District Attorney's office and police department which found that personnel from both had engaged in serious misconduct without adequate oversight. The Commission reported that in police brutality cases where victims might sue, the only investigation would be conducted by the County Attorney's office with the single purpose of developing evidence to defend against a claim.

The Bar Association statement concluded that:

> It is truly unfortunate that the special prosecutor's office was dissolved. It is quite probable that the office's demise sent precisely the wrong message to law enforcement personnel. The decline in serious internal disciplinary mea-

sures parallels the abandonment of the special prosecutor's office. The Criminal Law Committee of the Association of the Bar of the City of New York strongly advocates the recreation of the office of special prosecutor for criminal justice with state-wide jurisdiction over brutality as well as corruption matters.

The Bar's message—communicated out of a sense of outrage over injustice, rather than the sort of fear that erupted in some jurisdictions in the wake of the Los Angeles riots—continues to go unheeded in New York state. It shall probably continue to go unheeded until the next Rodney King case comes along—and another Rodney King case *will* come along. The death of Shuaib Latif took place in January 1994, during one of the most bitterly cold winters New York City has ever seen. Considering the tensions that exist because of peripheral issues of race, culture, religion, and economics, the city was perhaps lucky that it had not occurred in the middle of a hot summer.

Yet if municipalities as well as states continue to shirk their responsibilities in custody-death and brutality cases, surely there would be someplace else to turn. The federal courts, after all, heard the Rodney King case after justice was not done at the state level. Unfortunately, the facts reveal just how much of a fluke prosecution of the King case was in the federal courts. When it comes to police brutality, Uncle Sam is still not truly paying attention, despite the violence in Los Angeles.

SEVENTEEN

THE COURTS OF LAST RESORT

There is an understandable demand for law and order . . . the preservation of order requires an adequate infusion of law.

—Hon. Jon O. Neuman

AT 2:00 P.M. ON MARCH 20, 1991, the House Subcommittee on Civil and Constitutional Rights of the Committee on the Judiciary convened in room 2141 of the Rayburn House Office Building.

Subcommittee chairman Don Edwards presided, and subcommittee members John Conyers Jr., Craig A. Washington, Michael J. Kopetski, Henry Hyde, Howard Coble, and Bill McCollum prepared to hear testimony on the police brutality problem in the United States.

"Police work is dangerous, difficult, and often unappreciated, but there is no excuse for the type of behavior recorded on videotape in Los Angeles," Edwards said in his opening statement. "Seeing that man being beaten was offensive to all Americans, particularly to the tens of thousands of dedicated law enforcement officers who would never engage in such conduct."

The subcommittee's purpose, Edwards said, was not to focus specifically on the Rodney King incident, but rather on the broader issues. "We want to know how effective the federal government's response has been. We want to look at the question of training and the question of internal discipline," Edwards said. "We want to look at the federal laws and whether they need to be strengthened."

A number of witnesses were heard, among them Wade Henderson, director of the Washington Bureau of the NAACP, who testified about the pervasive nature of police brutality allegations.

> Regrettably . . . examples of chronic police violence we have received reveal an all too familiar pattern of cover-up and denial. These instances are by far the more numerous examples of police abuse that we see within the NAACP . . . When affected communities lack the political will necessary to achieve meaningful reform, a strong federal hand is needed to ensure equal protection of the law. The NAACP believes that when public servants who are hired to protect people instead become their oppressors, it is time for the country as a whole to demand corrective action.

Henderson went on to relate the story behind litigation the NAACP had brought against the city of Reynoldsburg, Ohio: "A special unit within the Reynoldsburg Police Department called itself the SNAT squad, and took it upon itself to harass blacks found passing through town. It was later discovered that SNAT is an acronym for 'Special Nigger Attack Team.'"

According to Henderson's testimony, blacks in Reynoldsburg were followed for no reason until some minor infraction was found. They were then stopped, searched, and subjected to thorough computer checks for any outstanding traffic tickets, or other matters, from any jurisdiction covered by the police computer. On some occasions, Henderson said, it appeared that drugs were planted on suspects during these "manufactured searches."

He then revealed information the NAACP collected from its various branches during an investigation and case compilation project. It should be noted here that the NAACP (contrary to what many of its critics might believe, and often to the consternation of police violence victims) is painstakingly thorough when it looks into an allegation. In Kingston, New York, NAACP officials asked numerous questions in attempting to verify the claims made by Gerald Graham, the man who had allegedly been beaten by police officers who later arrested him for filing a "false" complaint of police brutality. The organization's active members feel that the credibility of the entire NAACP rests on such cautions.

"It has been almost two years since Gregory Habib died during a struggle with the Prince Georges County [Maryland] police," Henderson told the congressmen. "The scuffle between four white police officers and Habib in Langley Park touched off a bitter controversy that exposed long-term and deep-rooted tensions between the police department and the county's growing black community."

According to Henderson, Habib and his brother Martin (who suffered a broken jaw in the incident) were stopped for a traffic violation at about 3:00 P.M. on May 20, 1989. Police claimed that the unarmed Habib brothers approached Corporal Steven Kerpelman in a "menacing fashion" and that Kerpelman was forced to defend himself. Within seconds, according to Henderson, a fight was on and Kerpelman was radioing for help. A few minutes later the incident, which was played out before more than a dozen witnesses, was over. Gregory Habib was dead.

There was scattered violence in Prince Georges County after the medical examiner's report indicated that Habib, a slight man who weighed only 115 pounds, died of "blunt force trauma"—which to many people suggested he had taken a beating. Misdemeanor indictments were returned against Kerpelman by a county grand jury for his action in arresting Martin Habib, but no wrongdoing was found relative to the death of Gregory Habib. State's attorney Alex Williams, the county's first black prosecutor, rejected those findings, contending that the process had been tainted by possible perjury and obstruction of justice among members of the predominantly white police department.

Henderson next spoke of Tampa, Florida, where five men died in police custody within four months in 1987. The incidents followed a severe beating inflicted by police on New York Mets pitcher Dwight Gooden one year earlier. The custody deaths sparked rioting in Tampa and, after the ashes had cooled, a study was conducted that found a lack of discipline at all levels in the Tampa police department. In Tampa's police brutality cases, a shocking lack of accountability for officer conduct was cited.

Tampa and Prince Georges County, however, were cited as *success* stories by Henderson, who told the subcommittee that after attention was focused on the wrongs committed, there were sweeping changes in both police departments. But not all of the stories Henderson told the subcommittee members had such "happy" endings.

On February 27, 1990, Sidney Bowen, the first black mayor of Bolton, North Carolina, was shot by a member of the state highway patrol as he stood in his own front yard. The trooper had stopped the mayor for driving over the center line of the road, and a struggle between the two ensued that eventually brought the two out of their cars in front of Bowen's home. On the day following the shooting, a preliminary state highway patrol investigation found Patrol Officer A.E. Morris to have taken actions both "reasonable and prudent" in shooting Bowen. Subsequent investigations suggested that Morris had been the subject of a history of excessive force accusations. Nonetheless, Morris was allowed to go on working, despite the fact that investigations into the case by both the FBI and a state grand jury were still in progress. That case is still pending.

Henderson then detailed how in December 1990, a Texas grand jury—the fourth to investigate the killing of Houston security guard Byron Gillum by police officer Scott Tschirhart—had disbanded.

On November 15, 1989, Tschirhart pulled Gillum over because he was not wearing a seat belt. The officer had become curious because Gillum allegedly slowed down to 10 MPH when he saw the patrol car. Tschirhart claimed Gillum said, "You're stopping me just to harass me and you should be going after real criminals." The officer noted that Gillum was "highly agitated." Henderson said Tschirhart made Gillum wait for thirteen minutes in his car during a records check, and that when Gillum's record came up clean Tschirhart then told the dispatcher, "Please say you have something on Gillum . . . bad attitude."

Upon returning to Gillum's car, Tschirhart claimed he then spotted a pistol he hadn't noticed earlier, wedged between the car's bucket seats. Tschirhart said he twice ordered Gillum to get out and not touch the weapon but, he alleged, Gillum reached for the gun regardless. Tschirhart then opened fire and continued firing as Gillum lunged through the open passenger window, fleeing for his life, Henderson recounted. Eight bullets from the officer's gun were eventually recovered. Four of them had struck Gillum in the back.

Tschirhart later contended that he had been following procedure, remaining true to his training by shooting to kill in order to defend himself and continuing to fire until the target went down. Tschirhart said he feared Gillum was armed—but an investigation proved he was not. Gillum was the third man—all persons of color—who had been shot and killed by Tschirhart during his police career. A subsequent study found that for the years 1989 through 1990, twenty-six different officers in Houston were each responsible for the death or injury of at least three persons. Three officers were involved in the shooting deaths of at least three people, and one was responsible for four.

Finally, Henderson related how in New York City on December 29, 1987, police responded to a report of a man acting irrationally at the Queens home of his wife, who had an order of protection against him. According to witnesses, the man, named Albert Sanders, complied with police demands to remove his hands from his pockets, withdrawing a wallet and a piece of paper and throwing them onto the hood of a police car. Sanders hurled anti-white epithets at the officers, who kept their distance. A few minutes later, while police waited for an emergency service unit (for restraining devices—Sanders had been adjudged as emotionally disturbed) eleven bullets were fired into him by two officers. A knife recovered at the scene bore no prints. It was not the first time police had encountered Sanders, who was the alleged victim of a police beating in the past. When the case was presented to a grand jury, evidence that the officers—who claimed Sanders had lunged at them with the knife—had in prior situations used racial epithets when dealing with black males was never introduced. The grand jury returned no indictment. District Attorney John Santucci, who had presented a prosecution case that Henderson described as "open-ended" and "unfocused," said that the jury "obviously concluded that the officers acted reasonably in defense of their own lives."

"It has been reported that the Department of Justice has received almost 8,000 complaints of criminal civil rights violations in the past five-year period," Henderson concluded. "Regrettably, this represents but a fraction of the police abuse cases . . . There is a paucity of thorough investigation by the Department of Justice in response to complaints of police abuse, and only a bare minimum number of cases is actually presented to a grand jury."

When John R. Dunne, assistant attorney general of the Justice Department's civil rights division, gave his testimony before the subcommittee, he spoke of the attorney general's commitment to civil rights prosecutions.

"I'm proud of the record of the Civil Rights Division in investigating and prosecuting incidents of police misconduct throughout the nation," Dunne said. But he cautioned that the federal government's role should not be "overstated." He continued, "We are not the front-line troops in combatting instances of police abuse. That role properly lies with the internal affairs bureaus of law enforcement agencies and with state and local prosecutors."

The statute most often employed in criminal cases brought in the federal courts is Section 242 of Title 18 of the United States Code, which carries criminal penalties for anyone acting "under color of law" to deprive a person of their civil rights. In his testimony, Dunne elucidated some of those protections.

"They include . . . the right to be free from unwarranted assaults, the right to be kept free from harm while in official custody, the right to be free from illegal arrest and illegal searches," he explained, adding that race or other such classifications need not exist as an issue.

However, when citizens do find that their civil rights have been infringed on by law officers, they are often forced to pursue justice by means of the federal government. Through phone calls, letters, and other means, the Justice Department in Washington or any of the United States Attorney offices throughout the United States—as well as the FBI—all receive complaints of alleged violations of this federal law. Usually the local FBI field office is called on to investigate. Their report

is submitted both to the U.S. Attorney's office and to FBI headquarters for dissemination to the Civil Rights Division. The
criminal section of the Division reviews the case, and if
deemed warranted, a grand jury investigation takes place.
After the grand jury investigation, the Civil Rights Division, in
consultation with the local U.S. Attorney, makes a decision on
whether an indictment should be sought.

"We request indictments from the grand jury where we believe that we will establish, to a fair-minded jury, the defendant's guilt beyond a reasonable doubt," Dunne told the
committee, before advising them of how difficult such prosecutions can be:

> Almost always, the victims of police abuse have themselves
> committed some kind of law violation which has brought
> them to the attention of the police in the first place. Thus,
> their credibility is not always easy to establish. Community
> feelings that tend to credit, rather than discredit the law en-
> forcement representative also make it difficult to obtain suf-
> ficient corroboration to support a victim's claim to allow
> criminal prosecution.

The record of the Department of Justice, in which Dunne
expressed such pride, showed that in 1991 a total of 9,835 police abuse complaints were received. Of those complaints, only
3,583 were ever investigated, resulting in sixty-two present-
ments to grand juries, resulting in forty-three indictments and
twenty-three "informations," which are accusatory instruments for less serious charges. The 129 resulting defendants
(many cases involved indictments of more than one defendant) included sixty-four police officers, and twenty-six trials
were held. There were thirty-six convictions, thirteen acquittals, and seventy-two guilty pleas entered. In 1990, out of 7,960
complaints received, 3,050 investigations were conducted. Of

those, forty-six were presented to grand juries with thirty indictments and thirty-three informations, with a total of ninety-
seven defendants subjected to action, including thirty-five police officers. There were seventeen convictions and three
acquittals, with fifty-one guilty pleas entered.

Included among the complaints deemed unfounded by
the Justice Department were those involving Operation Rescue demonstrators subjected to the use of nunchukas in Los
Angeles. Another was the case of Kevin Thorpe.

A table containing the figures for the years 1986 through
1991 is provided below. Figures for these five years, as well as
the preceding years through 1981, hovered roughly around
the same levels.

	1991	1990	1989	1988	1987
complaints received	9,835	7,960	8,053	7,603	7,348
complaints investigated	3,583	3,050	3,177	2,892	2,826
cases presented to grand jury	62	46	40	44	57
indictments	43	30	26	35	40
informations	25	33	33	8	18
total number of defendants	129	97	84	71	105
number of police defendants	64	35	21	49	74
trials	26	14	23	30	24
convictions	36	17	23	21	17
acquittals	13	3	10	26	17
guilty pleas	72	51	68	50	36

Rep. John Conyers pressed Dunne on the 1990 findings:
"Now in between 7,000 complaints and the 3,000 investiga-

tions there's 50 percent difference, and then between the investigations and the cases presented to the grand jury we get 46 presented, and 3,004 investigations are question marks. What happened to them?"

Dunne deferred to William Baker, assistant director of the FBI's criminal division.

"Of those complaints received, many of them on their surface have no statutory merit for further investigation," Baker said. "The range of arrests in this country, the number of arrests is enormous, as we all know. And, then, the number of these complaints received is an infinitesimal fraction of that overall number of arrests. So, if you really need to put it into perspective, there are hundreds of thousands of arrests made without that initial complaint . . . But, to focus on your concern, those investigations are initially conducted after we look at the basic complaint, contact the internal affairs department in many cases, and determine whether an investigation is merited. From that, I think it might be time—they range from complaints that the handcuffs were too tight to absolute legitimate violations that demand our backstopping review."

Baker then deferred back to Dunne, who said that when the Department of Justice attempts to evaluate whether there should be a prosecution, the first touchstone is whether there has been adequate state and local response "in terms of penalizing the events which we have thoroughly evaluated with regard to severity . . . in most cases we find that there has been." Dunne continued:

> As a backstop, we try to get the fast balls and the wild pitches, those where, perhaps, to carry the analogy a little further, perhaps the local people drop the ball. There was inadequate prosecution. In addition to that, we're weighing in the fact, is there corroboration; what's the credibility of the various witnesses? All of those factors come into play,

and that's why we have so very few of these actual indictments and prosecutions. They are extremely difficult cases to prove . . . really, they are extremely difficult to prove.

Subcommittee chairman Don Edwards noted that the personnel of the entire Justice Department had increased by 55 percent from 1981 to 1990, but that the level of personnel specifically responsible for civil rights criminal prosecutions remained the same.

"What does that indicate?" Edwards asked. "Does that indicate lack of interest?"

"Oh no. No, not—" Dunne responded.

"Why," Edwards interrupted, "wouldn't the personnel have increased rather than staying almost exactly the same for nearly ten years?"

Dunne replied that since the Justice Department has been working more closely with the locally based U.S. Attorney offices, there had been a more effective use of the personnel in question.

"Well, Mr. Dunne, in Texas, for example, you have four U.S. Attorney's offices; only one has a designated civil rights division," Edwards pressed. "According to the *Dallas Morning News* that division has been reduced from three attorneys five years ago down to one now."

"What division is that?" Dunne asked.

"The patterns seems to run through the department on these civil rights cases," Edwards charged.

"I missed—the personnel in which unit has been reduced from three to one?" Dunne asked.

Edwards repeated the allegation, and said that the one assistant U.S. attorney in Texas charged with seeing to civil rights cases was almost exclusively working on drug cases. Dunne could not account for the facts presented.

"It's something that just won't go away," Edwards said.

"Both the problem of the number of attorneys in 1981 and 1990 and the Texas situation."

Conyers then continued his line of questioning, noting that in a Justice Department report the greatest number of brutality complaints had come from the state of Texas.

"The large majority of those were complaints against correction officers," Dunne said. "They were not against the police."

"I'm as concerned about a person that's subjected to brutality in a prison as a person outside a prison," Conyers said.

"We share that, we share that," Dunne said.

"That's a distinction without a difference," Conyers said.

What Dunne essentially told the committee was that the criteria for determining whether the federal government would take a case had everything to do with what information was provided for them and very little to do with independent investigation. Among the cases brought by the Justice Department in 1989 was the prosecution of five narcotics officers in Puerto Rico who pled guilty to shooting at a young couple while the officers were drunk, two sheriff's deputies in Georgia convicted of allowing a civilian to beat up a person in their presence, and an Ohio police officer who punched a woman in the mouth and filed false charges against her. Few of the major cases handled by Justice in the years prior involved actual deaths, even though complaints were made to the department regarding cases where death had occurred. Further, few of those cases occurred in major cities, where police departments have the resources—and the motivation—to cover the tracks of suspect officers.

The trust that the Justice Department seems to have in the law enforcement agencies subject to its jurisdiction is almost child-like, and not at all conducive to proper and thorough investigation. For example, what if Dr. Jiraki in Detroit had caved in to the pressure he claims he was subjected to, and changed his testimony? Would Justice have stepped in and begun a new investigation from bottom to top? Dunne's testimony makes this seem highly unlikely.

In cases of so-called "sudden death," would investigatory work take into account the findings of forensic experts like Michael Baden—who maintains that the familiar cocaine-overdose cause of death cited by many law enforcement authorities is at odds with the probabilities? In the case of Shuaib Latif, would the Justice Department—considering the witness credibility factor—give proper weight to the words of an admitted drug user like Darriel Johnson, whose version of the events is seemingly corroborated by the victim's wounds?

It should be noted that from 1986 through 1990, only two actions were brought against a total of six defendants in law-enforcement shooting incidents, and that during his testimony Dunne admitted, under questioning by Rep. Hyde, that only approximately 1.5 percent to 2 percent of complaints received by the Department of Justice actually go to prosecution. But, as Dunne pointed out in his testimony, the Justice Department is also severely limited as to what cases can be brought, and of what relief can be sought from the courts once a case comes to trial.

The Justice Department lacks the authority to address systemic patterns or practices of police misconduct. Only individual police officers can be prosecuted, and in many such cases juries are famously reluctant to bring convictions. If an officer was poorly trained, or was acting pursuant to an official policy, it is difficult to obtain a conviction (and some would argue rightly so, since the officer could not be morally held to blame for following a department's procedures even if they were defective). Simply put, the Justice Department has no authority to sue a police department *itself* to correct an underlying policy.

Legally put, this obstacle is rooted in solid ground. The

Third Circuit Court of Appeals held in *U.S. v. City of Philadel-phia* that the United States does not have implied statutory or constitutional authority to sue a local government or its officials in order to enjoin violations of citizens' constitutional rights by police officers. The House subcommittee's official report stated, "This represents a serious and outdated gap in the federal scheme for protecting constitutional rights."

The Attorney General has the authority to address patterns or practices of misconduct under eight civil rights statutes, including those governing voting, housing, employment, education, public accommodations, and access to public facilities. The Justice Department can thus sue a city or county over its voter registration practices or its educational policies. Also, private and public employers, including police departments, can be sued over employment discrimination patterns, and injunctive relief can be sought over jails or prisons that tolerate guards beating inmates. But there can be no actions taken against police officers who beat citizens—citizens convicted of no crime—on the street.

The private citizen who has been injured by police misconduct can, as demonstrated earlier, bring a civil lawsuit in the federal courts, but only monetary damages can be sought. This was established in *Los Angeles v. Lyons*, when the Supreme Court ruled that Lyons, who was choked unconscious, could be awarded money. However, the trial court could not issue an injunction restricting the use of the chokehold (from which fifteen people in that city had already died) unless Lyons could demonstrate that he might be choked again—or was indeed choked again.

To bring the *Lyons* decision up to speed in terms of the King case, if the Department of Justice determined that Rodney King's beating was the result of a pattern of behavior by Los Angeles police officers, the agency would have been powerless to bring a suit seeking a remedy to the condition. King himself filed a civil suit against the city that sought money damages, and money damages were the only relief possible under existing law.

———

In light of these cited inadequacies, the testimony of United States Circuit Court Judge Jon O. Neuman, a former U.S. attorney, contained some of the most valuable information and insight presented before the subcommittee. Neuman has been a federal judge for twenty years, served on the U.S. Court of Appeals for thirteen years, and served in the Connecticut branch of the U.S. District Court for nearly eight years.

Neuman made his appearance on May 5, 1992, just days after an op-ed piece he wrote ran in the *New York Times* advocating a remedy to the *lack* of remedy in police brutality cases. In a reference to the Simi Valley jury that acquitted the officers in the King case, Neuman wrote that there is "an inevitable reluctance on the part of ordinary citizens to brand a law enforcement officer as a criminal."

"In a few cases," Neuman wrote, "jurors will impose that label, but often they will not, even if they think that the officer acted improperly." As for federal lawsuits (civil actions):

> . . . the victim alone must initiate the lawsuit, the defendant is customarily the police officer rather than the city or state that employs the officer—and the officer is usually exonerated, despite his wrong-doing, if the jury finds that he acted in good faith . . . A city now pays when a garbage collector negligently causes a motor vehicle accident; the city should similarly pay when one of its officers commits an act of brutality.

The subcommittee could not have hoped for a more qualified expert. In addition to his legal expertise, Neuman had written on the very subject of strengthening the civil rights laws in regard to brutality cases in a 1978 *Yale Law Review* piece.

> Some jurors will understandably fear that convicting a po-
> lice officer of a criminal civil rights offense, even if war-
> ranted on the facts of the case, will send to all police officers
> not only the intended message that civil rights must be re-
> spected but the unintended message that perhaps the police
> should lessen their law enforcement activity and overlook
> some crimes . . . [or] the police officer who deserves to be
> convicted of a civil rights offense does not deserve the haz-
> ardous punishment of imprisonment with ordinary crimi-
> nals, some of whom the officer might have arrested.

Another problem cited by Neuman in the 1978 piece was the shaky societal status of many brutality victims, who may have lengthy arrest records, might have been in a bona fide confrontation with the officer, and ultimately lose their credibility in front of a jury.

> A civil rights lawsuit pitting the victim against the police of-
> ficer (thus) usually begins with the victim at a considerable
> disadvantage, often because of the circumstances that
> brought him to the attention of the police. An obvious solu-
> tion is to authorize the United States to initiate the lawsuit
> on behalf of the injured person . . . it would remonstrate that
> the federal government was interested in the protection of
> civil rights . . . presented by the office of the local United
> States Attorney, usually an office of talented lawyers who
> are well regarded in the community.

Such a policy, Neuman argued, would also mean a more active role for the Federal Bureau of Investigation.

Neuman also noted that if the government was authorized

to bring action against a police officer's municipal employer, police departments would be forced to amend policies and procedures that lead to brutality cases, and to eliminate in action against the government any defense that the officer acted "in good faith"—a pivotal provision, since the "good faith" defense of an individual officer is usually bulwarked by the procedures and rules of the department or municipality itself.

Neuman's op-ed piece and his law journal article were entered into the Congressional Record, as was a piece of model legislation that he proposed for the legislators, titled "The Civil Rights Protection Act of 1992."

It finally appeared that the traditional courts of last resort for police brutality victims might actually be made accessible enough to them for a difference to be made, through a pronounced federal demand for accountability.

Since World War II, our nation's people have become significantly removed from their government's processes, and their elected representatives therefore removed from them. C-Span and other media have in some ways served to bring the process closer to many of us, but the inner workings of government are still seen as mysterious by many others, who hear of committee meetings and subcommittee hearings and wonder what everyone's meeting about and, more importantly, what happens after the hearings are completed?

In the case of the House Subcommittee on Civil and Constitutional Rights, there were several positive steps taken; some were begun even before the second spate of committee hearings were held in 1992.

On April 16, 1991, Rep. Conyers introduced HR 1821, a bill that would provide the attorney general of the United States to seek injunctive relief against police brutality. Its "short" title was the "Police Misconduct Civil Relief Act of 1991," and it stated:

Whenever the attorney general has reasonable means to believe that any state or political subdivision of a state, official, employee, or agent thereof, or any other person acting
on behalf of a state or political subdivision of a state, is sub-
jecting persons in such state to a deprivation of rights, privileges, or immunities secured or protected by the Constitution of the United States, resulting from misconduct by law
enforcement officers, and that such deprivation is pursuant
to a pattern or practice of such deprivations, the attorney
general, for or in the name of the United States, may in a
civil action obtain such equitable relief as is appropriate to
insure the full enjoyment of such rights, privileges, or immunities.

The provisions of HR 1821 never saw the House floor as
legislation. Instead the provisions above were incorporated
into a more expansive bill drafted July 23, 1991, written by Edwards and the other committee members.

HR 2972—"the Police Accountability Act of 1991"—specifically stated that:

. . . it shall be unlawful for any governmental authority, or
any agent thereof, or any person acting on behalf of a governmental authority, to engage in a pattern or practice of
conduct by law enforcement officers that deprives persons
of rights, privileges or immunities secured or protected by
the Constitution or laws of the United States.

HR 2972 would have amended the Civil Rights Law by
making police brutality a specific offense:

Whoever, being a law enforcement officer and under color
of law, subjects any person to force exceeding that which is
reasonably necessary to carry out a law enforcement duty,
shall be punished . . .

Existing Title 18 fines would be used for punishment, or else imprisonment not to exceed one year for those cases where death or bodily injury did not result from the action. The bill provided that up to life in prison could be sentenced for a death.

The bill also called for the attorney general to collect data regarding complaints about the use of excessive force by law enforcement officers, to be used for research and statistical purposes. The Safe Streets Act of 1968 would also be amended so that funds for such purposes could be made available to participating local governments.

Portions of HR 2972 were incorporated into a new bill, HR 3371, which was incorporated into the Omnibus Crime Control Act of 1991. It defined unlawful conduct, provided for civil action by the attorney general, and also provided for individual litigants in civil suits to seek injunctive relief from pattern or practice violations. The Omnibus Crime Control Act, under the aegis of the House Committee on the Judiciary, passed the House of Representatives in October 1991. But when the bill went to the Senate, it was blocked by debates over other issues contained in the Omnibus package, such as gun control and certain death penalty provisions, having nothing to do with police brutality. As a result, the Omnibus Crime Control Act of 1991, with its police brutality provisions, was doomed.

In 1992, during the 102nd Congress's second session, Rep. Conyers once again introduced legislation, HR 5074, which was based largely on Judge Neuman's recommendations. It provided for governmental employer liability in brutality cases and permitted the attorney general to sue on behalf of individual complainants. The bill did not pass. Neither did HR 5076, another Conyers bill, dubbed the Civil Rights Crimes Act of 1992, which would have amended the Civil Rights Law to allow for tougher penalties in police brutality cases.

In 1993, Rep. Edwards proposed the Police Misconduct Civil Remedy Act of 1992. It provided for governmental unit liability, and eliminated the good faith exception. It too failed to pass.

Despite the conflagration that devastated Los Angeles, despite the obvious signs that every level of the criminal justice and civil court systems have taken on a design and form that is seemingly insurmountable by those who claim they have been wronged by law enforcement officers, the United States Congress has been unable to pass simple legislation that would remedy the situation. The prospects for change appear dimmer still.

EIGHTEEN

WE THE PEOPLE

THE SOCIAL CLIMATE HAS changed in the few years since people first cringed at the videotape of the beating Rodney King received on a Los Angeles street. Death and destruction visited southern California once again in 1994, when an earthquake ravaged highways and homes and claimed almost as many lives as the Rodney King riots. In the wake of that cataclysmic event, it appeared that issues of race and class and abuse of authority were made invisible by the shadows of helping hands extended from one Angeleno to another. As would be expected, the various local police departments performed admirably, providing whatever assistance they could to alleviate the tragedy's immediate effects. A police officer, in fact, was one of the first fatalities.

In other parts of the country, many police departments seemed to have become more aware of the dangers that could come from looking the other way from the problem of police violence. National police organizations continued their efforts to professionalize their member departments, encouraging ranking officials to take steps that might prevent abuse of force, and to take proper disciplinary action against offenders.

Whether this new post-King consciousness has resulted in an overall decline of brutality complaints or incidents nationwide is difficult to gauge. In some cases the King incident might have spurred officials to take even deeper cover when questionable cases arose, out of fear of public criticism or civil disorder. There is still no central, national clearinghouse for reports of such incidents or their dispositions.

The outlook for true reform in the area of abuse of force remains bleak, because those with the greatest power to force change in policy, procedure, and law have chosen to remain silent. The failure of the federal legislation that attempted to address police violence is proof of this.

The Clinton administration, despite its seemingly benign public pronouncements, offers little hope for reform either. One of the most egregious uses of force by law enforcement officers in the past century occurred within the first few months after Bill Clinton took office, when a standoff between federal authorities and heavily armed Branch Davidian church members in Waco, Texas ended with a literal firestorm that claimed the lives of several adults and children. The ill-fated and ill-conceived initial raid on the compound was itself a tragedy, resulting in the deaths of four highly dedicated and motivated Bureau of Alcohol, Tobacco, and Firearms (ATF) agents hand-picked for the assignment from the New Orleans field office. The deaths of the Branch Davidians and their children only compounded the scope of the misadventure, and there has been little accountability demanded by the government or the public to whom it answers for the government's decision to storm the compound, precipitating the inferno.

Attorney General Janet Reno said that she was taking responsibility for the catastrophe, but her mea culpa seems to amount to little more than a pronouncement of regret. There was little organized public criticism of Reno, nor was there much in the way of demand to know who was *truly* responsible for the Waco holocaust—at least not when compared with the furor surrounding another highly publicized case. New York's Hasidic Jewish community has demanded that the Justice Department investigate the death of Yankel Rosenbaum, the Australian rabbinical student who was killed in the early stages of the Crown Heights riots in New York City.

Brooklyn District Attorney Charles Hynes and other officials continually pressured Reno to launch a federal civil rights investigation into Rosenbaum's death, which she finally—grudgingly, it would seem—agreed to early in her stewardship at the Justice Department, in March 1993. Difficult as it is to bring actions in cases where government employees such as police officers are accused of civil rights violations, the prosecution of private citizens for such offenses is even more problematic. Experts at the attorney general's office may have felt—perhaps quite rightly—that such an investigation would result in little of value, and would serve only to be symbolic. Symbolism, however, can often serve an important purpose; if nothing else, a full-scale federal investigation into the Rosenbaum case could ease fears among members of New York's Jewish community that they are not equally protected by this country's laws. The case would never have received federal attention, however, without the intense pressure.

Legal experts interviewed for this book have said it is possible that the inability of the attorney general to seek pattern or practice bans through the courts could be overcome, on a case-by-case basis at least, through inventive use of the Racketeer Influenced Corrupt Organizations Act, known as the RICO law. Putting together a civil RICO case against a police department that evinces a pattern of abuse through commission of specific crimes—such as murder or the intimidation of a witness—would be a difficult and controversial task, but could be seen as one of the weapons in the Justice Department's legal arsenal. That is, it could be if someone there wanted to stem police abuses badly enough. But little that is new should be expected from the Department of Justice in the way of police brutality prosecutions. If there will be no official accountability for the deaths of the children and adults in Waco, then how can the Department of Justice be expected to set the example for local and state law enforcement agencies and officials when an unarmed drug dealer is shot under questionable circumstances?

The public has become ever more preoccupied with the fear of crime, with renewed calls for the death penalty in states that currently prohibit its imposition. How could one expect outcries from the public against police brutality when its existence is denied or excused, or glanced at with a knowing wink that says, "We know you shouldn't have done it, but we're glad to be rid of him anyway?" One octogenarian in New York, upon seeing the Rodney King videotape, surprised her family and friends when she blurted out, "Why didn't they shoot the son of a bitch with the camera?" As Judge Neuman has pointed out, the victims of police brutality are often the people whom the rest of society wishes would go away. The current social climate would seem to tend toward a secret dark desire for summary dispatch of felons with extreme prejudice.

And yet, in most of the cases cited in this book, the dead and injured were not gun-toting felons with innumerable scuff marks from justice's revolving door on their rap sheets, but more often than not merely petty criminals, or even just the troubled, the substance addicted, or the mentally disturbed. This makes America's indifference to this problem that much more tragic.

Until a bomb exploded in New York's World Trade Center, we could only remotely identify with the terror that grips the citizens of Belfast or Israel or Sarajevo, or those unfortunates who died or were maimed in Iraq during the Gulf War. Only when the Long Island Railroad's 5:33 was turned into a death train by a crazed gunman did white suburbanites across the country realize that they could run but not hide from the threat of urban crime and violence. Only then did some measure of gun control legislation pass Congress for the first time in over a quarter century—by a hair's breadth. What was curious about the Long Island tragedy was the fact that public officials who had not supported strengthening the penalties for bias-related crimes were among the first to seek prosecution of Colin Ferguson under those same statutes.

To paraphrase Malcolm X, America's chickens were coming home to roost as the century drew to a close, and not one by one but in droves. Yet the message was still not clear. The death of Shuaib Latif in Brooklyn took a side stage in the media to the posturing and posing of Al Sharpton, whose name was easier for reporters to spell and pronounce than those adopted by the imams of Al Amin Abdul Latif's mosque.

America's focus on violent crime is currently blurred by its fascination with quick fixes; witness the popularity of the latest criminal justice catchphrase, "three strikes and you're out." Legislators pass more laws for more people to break, which will require the building of more jails which are nothing more than universities for crime in their current form. The requisite focus on poverty, unemployment, crumbling school systems, and deficiencies in child care, let alone on police brutality, is anything but popular. New York City has elected a mayor who seems intent on undermining its community policing program, one of the few positive changes in law enforcement to take place there in years. And one of the first salvos against crime fired by Rudolph Giuliani was aimed straight at a helpless underclass, when he pushed for criminalization of the homeless, with an emphasis on locking up squeegee-wielding panhandlers.

Most Americans would rather not hear the cries of police brutality victims, and choose to deny the pervasiveness of such abuse of power unless they can view it on videotape. Apologists argue that the police have a hard enough job as it is without unnecessarily dwelling on their deficiencies. What the apologists have yet to realize is that cops who use deadly force indiscriminately make the job of good cops even harder yet. Such drum beating and mindless simplicity should not be surprising, however, at a time in our history when Rush Limbaugh and Howard Stern make it to the bestseller list, when television news shows are dominated by sensational tabloid stories such as the Bobbitt dismemberment and the exploits of Joey Buttafuoco and Amy Fisher.

If Americans were truly interested in addressing the deadly force issue, then the legislation proposed while the King case and its violent aftermath was still fresh in everyone's minds would have passed in one form or another. But there was no continuing public outcry from our country's dominant white middle class—because beatings like King's don't happen "to people like us."

There is an Italian-American high school student in the Bensonhurst section of Brooklyn who feels differently. In 1993, this young man, the star of his school's football team, got into a fight with another student. A beat cop broke up the fracas, and in the process assaulted the football star.

"You make a complaint about this," the cop said, "And I will arrest you."

The football star told his parents, who took him with them to the Bath Avenue stationhouse, toting along some heavy baggage of righteous indignation. They were told to wait. True to his word, the officer then arrested the youth; after this, their complaints fell on deaf ears. The initial beating was compounded by an abuse of authority that the parents thought could never be used against people like them.

Norman Siegel, director of the New York Civil Liberties Union, agreed to review the case; at the time of this writing, litigation is pending. The youth's name is thus not yet part of the public record. The parents said that they never thought they would seek the help of the NYCLU, which until they needed it was definitely *not* on their list of favorite charities. How many more working-class, nonminority young men will have to be abused by police before their parents are stripped of their smug sense of security, and realize that excessive use of force and abuse of authority is their problem too?

As for the police themselves, it is highly unlikely that the majority of officers in this country who read the horror stories between these pages will react with anything but revulsion— especially to the paucity of accountability demanded by the official response. Good police officers have little to fear from proper administrative handling of excessive force complaints; if a more open attitude is taken, then those who are truly innocent of anything they could be charged with will benefit as well.

A nation of laws cannot and should not elevate anyone above the law—not ourselves, not the president of the country, and not the cop on the beat. Only when we seek justice for justice's sake, rather than weakly permit it to be effected in order to avoid the next riotous outburst, can we truly call our society worthy of being spared the wages of someone's next sins.

Until a system exists that demands accountability at the highest levels for police actions that result in needless death, with an open, public forum as the venue for the fact-finding process, the credibility of our entire system of justice will exist under an ominous shadow of mistrust and doubt.

BIBLIOGRAPHY

Annual Report Fiscal Year 1990 of the Office of the Chief Medical Examiner of the City Of New York, 1991.

Arce, R. "Tompkins Square A Year Later: A Legacy of Lessons For NYPD," *New York Newsday*, August 4, 1987.

Arrarte, A. "Letter From Miami: A City Waiting For An Explosion," *US News & World Report*, November 27, 1989.

"As Hispanic Presence Grows, So Does Black Anger," *New York Times*, June 20, 1993.

"Autopsy Is Put On Trial In Detroit Beating Case," *New York Times*, August 1, 1993.

Baden, M. *Unnatural Death: Confessions Of A Medical Examiner*, Random House, N.Y., 1989.

Booth, W. "Law Officer Is Acquitted In Florida," *Washington Post*, May 29, 1993.

Booth, W. "Miami Community's Progress Suggests Riots' Scars Heal From Within," *Washington Post*, June 5, 1992.

Bouza, A. *How To Stop Crime*, Plenum Press, N.Y., 1993.

"Briseno's Attorney Looks Back At Trial," *National Law Journal*, May 17, 1993.

Caldwell, E. "Rudy Signals New Racial Tension Over Hate Radio WABC," *New York Daily News*, January 28, 1994.

Carte, G. *Police Reform In The United States: The Era Of August Vollmer*, University of California Press, Berkeley, 1975.

Church, G., et al. "A Shocked Nation Wonders What Went Wrong and How To Mend It," *Time*, May 11, 1992.

Civilian Complaint Investigative Bureau, Annual Report, Police Department, City of N.Y., 1992.

Clark, J. "Charges Fly As Chemical and Stun Gun Lead To Flame" (cited in Geller), *Law Enforcement News*, September 30, 1990.

Clines, F. "Candidates Attack The Squeegee Men," *New York Times*, September 26, 1993.

Conot, R. *American Odyssey*, Morrow, N.Y., 1974.

"Cops On Trial," *Time*, November 30, 1992.

Crime In The United States 1991: Uniform Crime Reports, U.S. Department of Justice, Federal Bureau of Investigation, 1992.

Dao, J. "Angered By Police Killing, A Neighborhood Erupts," *New York Times*, July 7, 1992.

Day, S. "Shooting The Fleeing Felon: State Of The Law" (cited in Geller), *Criminal Law Bulletin*, July 1978.

DeSantis, J. "Confederate Insurgency Monument Stirs Controversy Over Race, History," *Chicago Tribune*, April 2, 1993.

DeSantis, J. "Flips, Flops and Cops," *New York Newsday*, July 21, 1993.

DeSantis, J. *For The Color of His Skin: The Murder of Yusuf Hawkins and the Trial of Bensonhurst*, Pharos Books, N.Y., 1991.

DeSantis, J. "Monumental Division in New Orleans," *Washington Post*, March 22, 1993.

DeSantis, J. "Soccer Hooliganism In Jackson Heights," *Queens Tribune*, September 23, 1993.

DeSantis, J. "Tourist Is Treated Badly But What About Others?"*New Orleans Times-Picayune*, December 4, 1992.

DeSantis, J. "Young Agent Died On The Front Lines Of Dangerous Duty He Loved," *Washington Post*, March 5, 1993.

"Detroit's Papers Under Fire At Trial of Officers In Beating," *New York Times*, July 11, 1993.

Donaldson, G. *The Ville: Cops and Kids In Urban America*, Ticknor & Fields, N.Y., 1993.

Drugs, Crime and the Justice System: A National Report From the Bureau of Justice Statistics, U.S. Department of Justice, Office of Justice Programs, Bureau of Justice Statistics, 1992.

Elmsley, C. *Policing and Its Context*, Schocken Books, N.Y., 1984.

"Excerpts: L.A. Police Sentences Explained," *National Law Journal*, August 16, 1993.

Federal Response To Police Misconduct: Text of Hearing before the Subcommittee on Civil and Constitutional Rights of the Committee On The Judiciary House of Representatives, 102nd Congress, Second Session, U.S. Government Printing Office, 1992.

Federal Response To Police Misconduct: Text of Hearing before the Subcommittee on Civil and Constitutional Rights of the Committee On The Judiciary House of Representatives, 102nd Congress, First Session, U.S. Government Printing Office, 1991.

"Fire and Fury," *Newsweek*, May 11, 1992.

Geller, W. and Scott, M. *Deadly Force: What We Know: A Practitioner's Desk Reference On Police-Involved Shootings*, Police Executive Research Forum, Washington, D.C., 1992.

Girgenti, R. *A Report To The Governor On The Disturbances In Crown Heights: A Review of the Investigation into the Death of Yankel Rosenbaum, and the Resulting Prosecution*, State of New York, Division of Criminal Justice Services, Office of Justice Systems Analysis, Albany, N.Y., 1993.

Girgenti, R. *A Report To The Governor On The Disturbances In Crown Heights: An Assessment of the City's Preparedness and Response to Civil Disorder*, State of New York, Division of Criminal Justice Services, Office of Justice Systems Analysis, Albany, N.Y., 1993.

Hackett, G. et al. "All Of Us Are In Trouble: Miami's Riots Die Down But Racial Tensions Linger," *Newsweek*, January 30, 1989.

Hentoff, N. *The First Freedom: A Tumultuous History of Free Speech In America*, Delacorte Press, N.Y., 1980.

Holmes, S. "Miami Melting Pot Proves Explosive," *New York Times*, December 9, 1990.

In The Matter of Kenneth Ramirez: Los Angeles County District Attorney's Final Report, 1981.

Kelling, G., and Bratton, W. *Implementing Community Policing: The Administrative Problem*, National Institute of Justice and the Program In Criminal Justice Policy and Management, John F. Kennedy School of Government, Harvard University, July 1993.

Kennedy, D. *The Strategic Management Of Police Resources*, U.S. Department of Justice, Office of Justice Programs, January 1993.

Killed In The Line of Duty: A Study of Selected Killings of Law Enforcement Officers, Uniform Crime Reports Section, Federal Bureau of Investigation, U. S. Department of Justice, 1992.

Kocieniewski, D. "The Blue Wall: Dowd, Fellow Cops Allowed Shakedowns, Drug Payoffs," *New York Newsday*, September 28, 1993.

Krosch, C. "Task Force Report: Some In-Custody Deaths Cited As Preventable," *Law Enforcement Quarterly*, August 1992.

Kurtz, H. *Media Circus: The Trouble With America's Newspapers*, Times Books, N.Y., 1993.

Lacayo, R. "Lock 'Em Up!" *Time*, February 7, 1994.

LaFave, W. *Arrest: The Decision To Take A Suspect Into Custody, Report Of The American Bar Foundation Survey of the Administration of Criminal Justice In The United States* (cited in Geller), Little, Brown & Co., Boston, 1965.

Lamar, J., et al. "A Brightly Colored Tinderbox," *Time*, January 30, 1989.

Lessenberry, J. "A Detroit Judge As Attention-Getting As His Case," *New York Times*, July 30, 1993.

Levin, D. "Four Detroit Officers Charged In Death: 2 Face

Counts of Murder In Police Beating of Motorist," *New York Times*, November 17, 1992.

McFadden, R. "Commissioner Orders an Overhaul In Fight Against Police Corruption," *New York Times*, November 17, 1992

Meese, E. *Community Policing and the Police Officer*, National Institute of Justice, U.S. Dept. of Justice, Program in Criminal Justice Policy and Management, John F. Kennedy School of Government, Harvard University, Cambridge, Massachusetts, January 1993.

Mendez, G. *Role of Race and Ethnicity in the Incidence of Police Use of Deadly Force*, National Institute for Justice, 1983.

"Miami Officer Is Hospitalized In Suicide Attempt," *New York Times*, Apr. 18, 1990.

Monroe, S. "Complaints About A Crackdown," *Time*, July 16, 1990.

Morales, E. "After Kiko," *Village Voice*, July 21, 1992.

Morgenthau, T. "Beyond Black and White," *Newsweek*, May 18, 1992.

Morgenthau, T. and Katel, P. "Looking For A Place In The Sun: Miami's Many Ethnic Groups Fight For Power," *Newsweek*, December 17, 1990.

Mydans, S. "Time For Punishment In King Case," *New York Times*, September 26, 1993.

Neuman, J. "Suing the Lawbreakers: Proposals To Strengthen the Section 1983 Damage Remedy for Law Enforcers' Misconduct," *Yale Law Journal*, January 1978.

Neuman, J. "How To Protect Other Rodney Kings," *New York Times*, May 1, 1991.

"New Unrest Is Reported In Miami," *New York Times*, June 28, 1991.

Omnibus Crime Control Act of 1991: Report of the Committee on the Judiciary House of Representatives on HR3371 Together

With Additional, Dissenting, and Additional Dissenting Views, U.S. Government Printing Office, 1991.

"Pathologist Says Police Blows Alone Didn't Cause Death In Detroit," *New York Times*, July 25, 1993.

Pooley, E. "Rudy and Race," *New York Magazine*, February 7, 1994.

Raab, S. "Police Corruption Panel Goes Public This Week," *New York Times*, September 26, 1993.

Raab, S. "Ex-Rogue Officer Tells Panel Of Police Graft In New York," *New York Times*, September 28, 1993.

Raab, S. "Detailing Burglars In Blue: Violent Search For Booty,"*New York Times*, September 30, 1993.

Raab, S. "Witnesses Tell Of Cover-Up In Police Graft: Investigators Describe An Unwritten Policy," *New York Times*, September 29, 1993.

Rakoff, J. and Goldstein, H. *RICO: Civil and Criminal Law and Strategy*, Law Journal Seminars Press, N.Y., 1991 (orig. pub. 1989).

Ramsay, A. *Sir Robert Peel*, Books For Libraries Press, Freeport N.Y., 1969.

Repetto, T. *The Blue Parade*, Free Press, N.Y., 1978.

Report of the National Advisory Commission on Civil Disorders (The Kerner Report), 1968.

Report of the Independent Commission on the Los Angeles Police Department, 1991.

Report To The Governor: New York State Commission on Criminal Justice and the Use of Force, 1986.

Ricker, D. "Behind The Silence," *American Bar Association Journal*, July 1991.

Rohrlich, T. "L.A. Police Considering Reviving The Chokehold: Advocates Say Its Use Is Safer Than Baton, Opponents Say It Can Kill And Has" (Cited in Geller), *Los Angeles Times*, September 2, 1991.

Salhols, E. and Washington, F. "Detroit's Brutal Lessons: Why

Its Police Beating Case Isn't Like L.A.'s," *Newsweek*, November 30, 1993.

Schmalz, J. "Miami Officer Is Sentenced To Seven Years For Two Killings," *New York Times*, January 25, 1990.

Sherman, L. et al. *Citizens Killed By Big City Police 1970–1984* (Cited in Geller), Crime Control Institute, Washington, D.C., 1986.

Sherman, L. *The Quality Of Police Education*, Jossey-Bass, San Francisco, 1978.

Shuit, D. "Police Patrols: Too Many Or Not Enough?" *Los Angeles Times*, September 21, 1978.

Skolnick, J. and Fyfe, J. *Above The Law: Police and the Excessive Use of Force*, Free Press, N.Y., 1993.

Sourcebook, 1992, U.S. Department of Justice, Office of Special Programs, Bureau of Justice Statistics, 1992.

Statistical Series, Annual Emergency Room Data, 1991: Data from the Drug Abuse Warning Network (DAWN), Series I, Number 11-A, U.S. Dept. of Health and Human Services, Public Health Service Alcohol, Drug Abuse and Mental Health Administration, 1992.

Statistical Series, Annual Medical Examiner Data, 1991: Data from the Drug Abuse Warning Network (DAWN), Series I, Number 11-B, U.S. Dept. of Health and Human Services, Public Health Service Alcohol, Drug Abuse and Mental Health Administration, 1992.

Steele, P. *Riots*, New Discovery Books, N.Y., 1993.

Stone, I.F. *Clarence Darrow For The Defense: A Biography* Bantam Books, N.Y., 1958.

Swan, A. *The Politics Of Riot Behavior*, University Press of America, Washington, D.C., 1980.

Terry, D. "Death After Police Beating Stirs Fear In Detroit," *New York Times*, November 8, 1992.

Terry, D. "Two Murder Convictions, And A City Heaves A Sigh of Relief," *New York Times*, August 29, 1993.

Terry, D. "Ex-Officers In Detroit Guilty In Beating Death of Motorist," *New York Times*, August 24, 1993.

The Need For A Special Prosecutor for Criminal Justice, Association of the Bar of The City of New York, Committee on Criminal Law, 1993.

The Problem of Police and Racial Violence 1988–1991: Fact Versus Fiction, Report of the Center for Law and Social Justice, Medgar Evers College, City University of New York, October 1992.

"The Fatal Force Case," *Detroit Free Press*, May 29, 1993.

Van Blaricom, D.P. "K-9 Use Of Force: A Biting Example Of Questionable Policy" (cited in Geller), *Law Enforcement News*, July 1992.

Vecsey, G. "Amid Uneasiness, Super Bowl Visitors Stream In," *New York Times*, January 19, 1989.

Walker, S. and Turner, K.B. *A Decade Of Modest Progress: Employment of Black and Hispanic Police Officers, 1983–92*, Department of Criminal Justice, University of Nebraska at Omaha, 1992.

Whitman, D. "The Untold Story of the L.A. Riot," *US News & World Report*, May 31, 1993.

"Wild In The Streets," *Time*, December 17, 1990

Williams, T. *Crackhouse: Notes From The End Of The Line*, Addison-Wesley, Reading, Mass., 1992.

Woodford, F. and Arthur, M. *All Our Yesterdays: A History of Detroit*, Wayne State Univ. Press, Detroit, 1969.

Wright, C. "Report On Tompkins Square: Report On Park Melee Rips Top Cops At Scene, Top Cop Retires, Retraining Is Urged For Crowd Control," *New York Newsday*, August 25, 1988.

Wright, C. "Charges Against Five More Cops," *New York Newsday*, October 27, 1988.

Zimring, F. and Hawkins, G. *Encyclopedia of Crime and Justice* Free Press, N.Y., 1983.

INDEX